Jesters and Devils

Florence – San Giovanni 1514

Maria-Luisa Minio-Paluello

Jesters and Devils

Florence – San Giovanni 1514

Carafulla, chief of a *Fusta piena di matti,*
a Venetian Ship of Fools, on a Midsummer voyage.
Was there method in their folly?
And humours, rumours and emulations
between Florence, Rome and Venice
in the Spring–Summer of 1514

2008

ISBN: 978-1-4092-4414-1

Key Words: Pope Leo X, Savonarola, Soderini, Mèdici family in Florence, restoration of 1514, Mèdici civic festivals, Renaissance Festivals, Fools and jesters, Crusade's dreams, Venice's fleet for hire, *fusta* a Venetian ship. The Holy see in 1514.

The author can be contacted at: isaminio2@googlemail.com

Printed by Lulu.com

Preface

The author was born in Italy from Venetian parents, and educated, if that's what it was, in various cities, a convent school and the University of Venice. The author has a very long name so she, or better I, I am normally known as Isa Minio.

After graduating in Modern Languages at the University of Venice, I taught English at the University of Naples, then Italian at the University of Aberdeen in Scotland. Several years later I went back to Italy where I taught English, and then, attached to the Ministry of Foreign Affairs, I served in the Cultural Office of the Italian Embassy of Mogadishu and then the Embassy in Washington DC. After a relatively early retirement, I lived in London for a time, and now in Scotland again near to my sons and two grandchildren.

This book is the translation of a revised and updated version of my book entitled *La 'Fusta dei Matti' – Firenze giugno 1514*, which was published in Italian, in Florence, in 1990.

The research for this book was done in Florence in the early eighties, published in Italian in 1990. When I was living in London, where the main attractions for me have always been the wonderful libraries – as well, of course, as the excellent classical music – I took the opportunity to go through the book again, revise it and translate it. This is the new edition, in English.

I am grateful of the privilege of having been able to use the British Library, and the Warburg Library, where one can find anything that might be necessary and desirable for research into the Italian Renaissance. The Warburg, in particular, user friendly, quiet, comfortable, has been an island of peace where I spent many contented hours checking, collating and updating this research. So thanks go to that establishment, its comfortable desks, the easy access to books and its competent and courteous staff.

Maria-Luisa Minio-Paluello

Illustrations (pp. 179–92)

Illustrations 1 to 4; Woodcuts from Dürer and derived, illustrating the ship and the traditional fools. From the facsimile edition of *Das Narrenschiff* (publisher Valentin Koerner, 36 Hermann Sielcken Street D-76530 Baden-Baden).*

Illustration n. 5; From Leonardo da Vinci, from some edition of his notebooks.

Illustration 6 some drawings of the evolution of the Jester's bauble or *marotte*. From W. Willeford, *The Fool and His Sceptre* London E. Arnold, 1967.**

Illustration 7); sketches in the margin of an edition of Erasmus da Rotterdam's *Praise of Folly* probably by Hans Holbein (c.1497–1543)

Illustration 8; *Stultitia* (1306) by Giotto (1267–1337), fresco in the Scrovegni chapel, in Padua.

Illustration. 9; *Temptations of St. Anthony* by Agnolo Gaddi (1350–1390) in the Castellani Chapel in Santa Croce in Florence. Fotocopy obtained from: *Agnolo Gaddi* by Bruce Cole NY Clarendon Press, 1977.***

Illustration 10; From Josse Bade *Stultiferarae Naves*, Lion 1502.

Illustration 11; H. Bosch, (1450–1516) drawing of 'a dwarf walking' with a ship of fools on his shoulders. Photocopied from: *The Complete Drawings of Hieronymous Bosch*, Introduction and notes by Charles van Beuningen. Imprint: London, Academy Editions, 1973.**

Illustrations 12 and 13; drawings of the boats by Botticelli (1444/5–1510) for Dante's *Divine Comedy*, *Inferno* VIII, and of devils with barbed hooks for *Inferno* XXIII. Photocopies obtained from: The drawings by Sandro Botticelli for Dante's Divine comedy after the originals in the Berlin museums and the Vatican / Kenneth Clark. Imprint London : Thames and Hudson, 1976.***

There are instances where we have been unable to trace or contact the copyright holder. If notified the publisher will be pleased to rectify any error or omissions at the earliest possible opportunity.

* Permission kindly granted by the publisher.

** Permission applied for from the publisher.

*** Publisher's reply informs that the works are not subject to copyright, or that they do not hold copyright for the illustration.

Contents

Chapter III
The *Fusta piena di Matti* – San Giovanni 1514. .... p.49

SECOND PART

(The historical moment)

Chapter V
Performance and watchers. 137

Epilogue
Symbols and validations. p.153

APPENDICES

The stage
(and the *mise en scène*)

It was the best of days for the Medici in Florence. The best since the death of Lorenzo il Magnifico. It was the 31st August, some say the 1st of September.

In the year 1512, at the beginning of September, the family of the Mèdici, in the persons of the two remaining sons of Lorenzo the Magnificent: Cardinal Giovanni, envoy of pope Julius II, Giuliano, and their nephew, Lorenzo (di Piero), the Magnificent's grandson[1], re-entered Florence, and were restored to the Government (*Signoria*) of the city.

The Medici's approach to the city[2] was aided by the armies of the Holy League of Julius II, and at this point particularly by the Spanish troops led by Viceroy Raymond Cardona

It is the fall of the Republic which had been declared after the death of Lorenzo the Magnificent – *il Magnifico*, now called also '*il Vecchio*' – (1492) and the exile of Piero his heir (1494), caused by Savonarola, with the support of a French invasion.

This Republic of Florence, had had rather a mixed history with a '*Cristo Re* -Christ the King' under Savonarola's absolute theocracy (1494-1498). Having Savonarola been interdicted by Pope Alexander VI and then condemned as a heretic, he was caught *a furor di popolo* from his convent of San Marco, was hanged first, and then and burnt at the stake in the piazza della Signoria in May 1498. A grim sort of reward, or *contrapasso*, for when he used to perform his ritual burning of the 'vanities', at Carnival time, on bonfires called '*capannucci*', where books, musical instruments, art objects, women's rich clothes and ornaments, collected by his gangs of youths during his reign of terror in the city up to 1498.

Thereafter a more 'normal' Republic was established with a '*gonfaloniere a vita*', a permanent head, in Piero Soderini.

The theoretical model of the (short lived) recently fallen Florentine Republic was that of the 'Venetian form', as theorized by the third of the Soderini brothers, Pagolantonio, who was political advisor to Savonarola, and to Piero Soderini after him, one presumes.

Piero Soderini now becomes the exile, eventually taking refuge in Rome, where his brother Francesco is a powerful Cardinal.

In Florence, for the Carnival 1513, a famous *trionfo* is staged by Lorenzo's *Compagnia del Broncone*, accompanied by a poem by Jacopo Nardi, that celebrates 'The Return of the Golden Age' (*Il ritorno del secol d'oro*)[3]. The return of the golden age was a theme well loved by Lorenzo the Magnificent. He represented the theme by using, the 'motto' '*le tems revient*'. The theme is celebrated also in his poem *Selva seconda* as that world (the golden age) which Saturn ruled in the peaceful golden age – it is also the theme of 'the happy islands', the 'Isles of the Blest' (and the land of Cockaine, on another level, of course).

This ideal world of Lorenzo *il Magnifico* 'il *Vecchio*' (who died in 1492) is the world that his nephew by the same name of Lorenzo intends to revive now.

In Rome, for the carnival of the same year, 1513, went a float (*va un carro*) representing the 'Wheel of Fortune' (other theme, and emblem, used by Lorenzo the Magnificent) with the '*Marzocco*', the sitting lion of Florence, on his way up, a Medici represented at the top, and Piero Soderini at the bottom, represented by a figure wearing a hood.

Pope Julius II died during these days of celebration[4], Cardinal Giovanni de' Medici is – unexpectedly – elected pope on March 10th 1513, and takes the name of Leo X. Both Rome and Florence celebrate Medicean apotheoses.[5] Many go to Rome for the celebrations. Giuliano remains in Rome.

In 1514 the young Lorenzo, the only one of the Mèdici family settled in Florence with the task of governing the city – yet still on behalf, or in conjunction with, the older Mèdici, Giovanni now Pope and Giuliano, occupied in Rome – celebrates once again the restoration of the Medici family to the '*Signoria*' (the government) for the feast of Saint John the Baptist, patron Saint of the city Florence.

This official civic festival is engineered to suggest continuity, to suggest a virtual return of Lorenzo the Magnificent 'il *Vecchio*' as a person, with the staging of the '*Trionfo di Camillo*'. This was a pageant composed of seventeen allegorical floats dominating one of the three days of the festival. The allegory this time is historical rather than mythical (as was the Return of the Golden Age). The reference now is to a Roman figure, Camillo, who will stand for a collective Mèdici, with elements, however, pointing to facts of the Magnificent's history .

Lorenzo '*il Vecchio*' as well had represented himself with a Roman figure in the '*Trionfo di Emilio Paolo*' in the Carnival of 1491. The Roman theme also adds to the multiple threads that bind ideally the two ages and the two Lorenzos.

The story of Camillo, central to the celebrations in Florence in 1514, refers to the return of a leader who had been wrongly exiled and unjustly accused of embezzlement (like Lorenzo) and exiled (like Piero his heir) who returns (like this Lorenzo, son of Piero) in triumph, rehabilitated, and recognized as a saviour of the city. Camillo had saved Rome from the Gauls. Florence had undergone a French invasion which had finally exiled the Medici in 1494. French threats loom again, but the Medici are back to guarantee the safety of the once 'ungrateful' homeland and to restore her old splendour.

The seventeen rich floats of the pageant '*Il Trionfo di Camillo*' were accompanied by a poem by Jacopo Nardi, the *Trionfo della fama e della gloria*. Fame and glory for Lorenzo, in Florence. And *for* Florence.

But before the *Trionfo di Camillo* pageant, before the words of the *Trionfo della fama e della gloria*, on the first day of the celebrations for the festival of this San Giovanni, on the evening of June 22nd 1514, a ship on a wagon pulled by two pairs of oxen passes through the city of Florence. The ship is full of fools, and is surrounded by devils.

This ship is a *fusta*[6], a Venetian ship, and a well known character, Antonio di Pierrozzo da Vespignano, a master hood-maker by trade, nicknamed Carafulla, is chosen to be captain, or governor of the ship. This ship of fools is our '*Fusta piena di matti*', it is an episode defined as 'burlesque' (Trexler), intended to 'amuse the people' (Masi).

At the beginning of the four-day festival, opening the games, this *Fusta piena di matti* goes through the streets of the city. Calling and inviting the people to celebrate.

On the evening of the first day, after the religious processions of the Magistrates and the other civic authorities. Surrounded by devils.

Where is she coming from?

What is her meaning, what is her symbolical value? A condemned ship (surrounded by devils), with a load of fools, mysterious beings covered by hoods, and with a maker of hoods as a captain?

What are the origins, the relationships, the values, both symbolical and traditional, in the festival, of the ship, and the fools, in Florence?

Are there traditional, literary, iconographic sources, in Florence, for such a ship?

Furthermore, in the details of the characters, their dress and actions, we find indications which, from the realm of symbols, put her back into a temporal and geographical reality. The *fusta* is a fifteenth century Venetian ship, not a mythical vessel. Antonio di Pierrozzo da Vespignano, and Gio. Tancredi, in their different ways, are people and characters with curious and typical histories of their own, Carafulla being a well known person in Florence, a master craftsman, but also a semi-professional jester. Gio. Tancredi complements and validates his function.

Such is the description of the *Fusta piena di matti* given by Giovanni Cambi in his *Istorie della città di Firenze* :

> 'The year 1514, on the evening of the 22nd day [of June] went the Magistrates, with the Six [della Mercatura] went in procession with the offerings (in the procession of the Offering). And also, while the said procession was going on that street, a *fusta* full of fools, that is jesters or buffoons, also went, with many devils at the foot of the said *fusta*, and they played many pranks and buffooneries, and having put in her a certain character, who was a little silly but smart of tongue and pleasant, and was called with the nickname of Maestro Antonio di Pierrozzo da Vespignano, who was a maker of hoods, and whom they had caught the day before on demand of the 'Masters of the revels', and they had put him in the palace of the Podestà, and then the said day they put him on the *Fusta*, clothed in his black cloak and hood, as he was normally dressed, which was rather worn, because he was poor, and those devils with their hooks tore it off his back. I believe they clothed him anew afterwards..
>
> While they were going on the said procession they came across Gio. Tancredi citizen and craftsman, of the Quart. of S.Croce, who wore/carried the wool and was much more foolish than Maestro Antonio mentioned above, because he was not able to do anything else than carry (wear) wool, and he never even thought he could become *maestro*, and in 50 years never changed his trade; all at once those devils, who were at the foot of the fusta, caught him, the *fusta* sent down a basket, and swiftly pulled him up into the *fusta*, and put him to the oars; and with their clubs made of leather filled with wind hit him several times so as to make him row well, he and the others'. [7]

Bartolomeo Masi also, in his *Diario*, also reports seeing the *fusta*:

> '..that was the XXII day of said [June] a solemn and beautiful procession was made...And afterwards, after dinner, through the whole of Florence went "A *fusta*, well built of wood, [carried] on a wagon pulled by two pairs of oxen, which was made, both in size and in all the details like a

fusta, and they had put in her certain fools (madmen), or we should say half-mad, to entertain the people. And behind the said *fusta* about thirty were dressed as devils, with some hooks and bells in their hands; these caught someone here and there and put them on to the fusta; if he wanted to get out, they made him pay a forfeit. (*taglia*)'[8]

Even though Masi does not remember to mention Gio. Tancredi by name, he remembers the rules of the game better than Cambi: one has to pay a fine to be let free, to escape the ship once one has been caught by the devils...we are reminded of something else here, perhaps the fare the dead souls are required to pay Charon the devil, to be ferried to the other world. Perhaps.

In this that is the principal civic festival of Florence, when Lorenzo celebrates his return and his re-establishing himself as only *Signore* (head of government) of the city with the great theatrical display of the seventeen floats carrying the pageant of the *Trionfo di Camillo*, our ship full of fools plays the introduction in counterpoint. It seems almost the soul of the festa.

It is a herald, a town crier, eccentric, reversed, unconventional, the mock-master of ceremonies.

The *fusta* alludes to the souls of the damned. To the mock-celebration of folly. She parades unreason and *vanitas vanitatum*. It expresses festive gaiety and perhaps horrors to be thereby exorcised. She evokes the ship of the dead, but also the ship of those who sail on voyages of discovery, towards new worlds, and to search for the Happy Isles and the Golden Age.

It is a brief but bewitching episode which has awakened the desire to delve and reconstruct – layer by layer, seeking among sources, and correlated images, through an archaeology of the symbolical themes which give it shape – the fabric of the political and historical appearance in which it is clothed, as well as the taking body in it of the signifying symbolical system of the 'ship of fools'.

In Florence on that 22nd of June in 1514 the ship of fools as a *fusta piena di matti* is a real though flighty focal point, interface between the festive and the tragic, between burlesque and magic, between folly and *sophia*, between civic pomp and the underworld, between local quarrelsome affairs and existential anxiety (*angst*). She is emblem, mirror, hinge, point of intersection and communication between the human and the world beyond (*l'aldilá*), between festive fires and lurid infernal flashes, between ludic *mise-en-scène* and dire plots, between ephemeral gestures, and hidden truths, between the "ship well built of wood and carried on a cart drawn by oxen to entertain the people" and the agile ideal ship which emerges over and over in the metaphors of poets and moralists, in the mythologies of all times and many lands, ship of salvation, boat of the dead, the ship of St Peter, the boat of the ferryman Charon, the symbolic system of the 'ship of fools'.

Many ships project their images to give substance and character to this ship, the *fusta piena di matti* of the St. John the Baptist festival of 1514.

It was essential however, to find specifically Florentine precursors, in order to trace the local genealogy of *this* festive ship of fools.

There are, in fact, correlated fragments from history, literature and art which fall together somewhat like mosaic pieces to indicate a background tradition where the characters and the attributes of the Fool, of the devil, of the boat (or ship) and the water in the realm of festive ritual in Florence can be reconstructed.

Specifically, an oblique recollection of a mock triumph and a Prince of fools is found in a mention by Poggio Bracciolini in a text of the middle of the XV century (in an invective against Lorenzo Valla). He remembers a '*carro dei pazzi*', a 'cart of fools' as usually paraded in the festivals in Florence.[9]

In the middle of the Quattrocento another long and detailed literary construction bears testimony of the existence and circulation of the idea of a *festa* on the water, and a mirror image of a ship-as-state. It is reversed, being a state of outlaws (as is soon revealed), and is related to Charon's boat which ferries the souls of the dead, in *Momus, seu de principe* by he humanist Leon Battista Alberti. In the passage that will be examined here (see 1.2.), there is also clear evidence of the knowledge of the possible subversive nature of the *festa*, its likelihood of transgressing into reality (and affecting politics). This aspect supports the idea that it is not at all unusual to seek, and find, a historical and political interpretation such as will become clear in the case of this *fusta*, in this *festa of 1514*, in the second part of this essay.

Going back in time, a historical event comes to aid, the May Day festival of 1304, on the river Arno, by the bridge *della Carraia* related by Giovanni Villani in his chronicle. This XIV century *festa* is a rich mine of elements, both thanks to the descriptive details of the underworld, the choreography and costumes of devils and of the souls of the damned – which were shirts full of straw, or bladders filled with 'wind'- and for the interpretation of the events of that festa as a point of contact and an actual reversal between natural and supernatural worlds, between staged performance and real happenings, between festive folly and real death. Death by water and fire. Ritual and real.

The interpretation is clearly suggested by the contemporary historian. Villani in fact concludes his record with the words 'so in the festa it occurred that the game, from a jest, became a reality'.

To recognize the idea and the form of the underworld boat with its load of condemned souls and devils as guides (or gaolers) is not a difficult enterprise, nor is it outlandish fantasy, as it is clarified and confirmed by the infernal boats in the drawings by Botticelli for the *Inferno* of Dante's *Divine Comedy*.

The boats drawn by Botticelli, furthermore, operate significantly also on the time scale, because from the distant 1300 of Dante, and therefore near to the 1304 of Villani, they take us to the end of the XV century when Botticelli did the illustrations, a return journey to a date near to where we had started. The Botticelli drawings, although they are not definitely dated, nor were they published then, nevertheless have been used as models by the engraver Baccio Baldini for his illustrations of the very well known edition of the *Divine Comedy* by Cristoforo Landino, which is of 1481.[10]

Here is the ideal model, the *Gestalt*, the system collecting together boat, devils, souls of the damned – although they have ferried also the Master and he who will gain Paradise at the end of his journey. These boats, although not in the 'folly' tradition, they are, however, boats driven by devils, carriers of souls of the dead, therefore definitely belonging to the underworld, but also involved in imaginary journeys. It is in both these functions that the iconographic model poses itself as a sufficiently open source, complex and mobile, enough to operate as a substratum of its transposition into its festive manifestation.

Furthermore, the date *ante* 1481 of the model supports also the decision of taking distance – which one feels one must stress – from the 'gothic' tradition. This is a tradition analogous in its narrative but opposite in meaning – being negative, anti-festive, anti-utopic, and unambiguous – to our subject, the *Fusta,* and it is that of *Das Narrenschiff* by S. Brant, published in Basel in 1494 and illustrated by Dürer in the Latin edition by Locher in 1497 therefore later than Botticelli. (detail and notes, I..4,)

Included into the ship, yet more varied as well as individuated is the character of the Fool. We have fools and devils, reconstructed by collecting information in the rich historical and popular festive tradition, to give it substance and depth. We have been searching for a quasi-mythical being: the philosophical fool, the court fool, the theatrical fool, here acted by a very real person, living in Florence, the eccentric Master craftsman Maestro Antonio *il Carafulla*, also a professional jester. But such is also the whole of the *Fusta,* as a collective character, very much scripted and performed on a stage. We have been also trying to discover what the 'fools' where meant to be in society, what in them, or in society, caused them to be defined as such.

In our discourse, however, we find that the 'mythical' Fool appears in two guises, that of the Fool – in Carafulla, and also Gio.Tancredi – and that of the devils, acting as doubles and opposites. They carry the same distinctive marks and belongings: hood, with the animal attributes of cockscomb and ass's ears, the ever present bells, the clubs, hooks and bauble.

***

This festive performance which betrays signs of a complex tradition which we would like to think as 'archetypal' and metaphorical – ship, fools, *festa* as mirror of life, game playing including hints of subversion, had nevertheless an 'immediate' civic function. This essay is concerned, in its second part, with the historical and political roots of such a performance.

Unpublished letters, studies and chronicles have revealed problems of relationship between Lorenzo in Florence and Leo X in Rome, between the interests of the Florentine State and the Court of Rome, strange diplomatic manoeuvering of the Venetian emissaries, unorthodox leanings of Pope and Cardinals.

Such things were found to occupy and preoccupy minds precisely in the few months previous to the ritual of the festival of S. Giovanni 1514, the grand celebration of the Medicean restoration. It has been possible to follow indications in the description of the *Fusta dei Matti* and interpret a chain of allusions, ironical, impertinent, irreverent even, principally towards Leo X and his 'circle', the Venetian intrigue, dreams of a Crusade (which will not happen), the excessive power of the Cardinals.

The *Fusta dei matti* has, little by little, revealed or rather confirmed humours, rumours and emulations between Florence and Rome, because of power and money, as well as references to Venice. It has detected unofficial rumours and put them on the stage. It has told tales of jealousies, complaints of the great and the powerful that the great and powerful could not openly display in their day of fame and glory. On the other hand they could not, and would not, ignore them or hush them up.

So they made this *Fusta piena di matti* in such a guise that it could speak for them, under the cover of folly, but such as to be deciphered by those who needed to be told.

Thus the apparently traditional, burlesque and silly foolish cortege of ship on the cart, fools and devils assumes in the moment of reality of the 22 June 1514, a full cathartic function, expresses rebellious feelings, reveals what cannot be openly said, satirizes the power above – Leo X and the Papal court – towards whom the (smaller) power that is – Lorenzo and Florence – cannot but be obsequious and compliant..

So here is the (mythical) court fool, in the *fusta piena di matti*. Here is the fool who says the truth, uncomfortable or dangerous as this may be. Here is the wise-fool in all his ambiguity and ambivalence.

Thus the *Fusta piena di matti,* this Ship as Fool, is what carries the spirit of the festival, is what reveals the dark side, what reveals the veiled threats or dangers, in the background of the splendid pomp exhibited by those in power. It is burlesque, but is also the shadow.

At the beginning of a celebration built around a glorious example from the past – Camillo – a shadow goes by, the ship of the shadows. The *Fusta piena di matti* passes through Florence in a turbulence of fools and devils calling the people and opening the way to the three following days of the festival.

1 Giuliano entered the city on August 31st (Roscoe), or September 1st (Landucci), while Cardinal Giovanni at first remained in Prato to try and control the 'fury of the conquerors', and Lorenzo probably arrived later, I cannot find exactly when. However, the 'Mèdici family' was back in power in Florence.

2 On 26th August Ambassadors were sent into Florence to ask the city to join the Holy League, to open to the return of the Mèdici family to the *Signoria*, and to dismiss the *Gonfaloniere* Piero Soderini. On 29th August (ironically the day of the feast of St. John the Baptist's beheading!) the Spanish troops breach the wall of Prato. The whole of the population of the surrounding countryside had taken refuge in the small city with their families and their goods. They were slaughtered in great numbers, (5,000it is said) and Prato thoroughly looted. Prato paid the big price. The 'Sack of Prato' is remembered and commemorated to this day. On August 31st the Ambassadors returned to Florence, and the deal was done. Florence joined the Holy League, Piero Soderini 'went home' for the sake of the people of Florence, and the Palace of the *Signoria* was taken and opened for the Mèdici again.

3 For the *compagnie*, there will be more . See: p.9; II 1., and note 11, full; III.1, n.18 (principal); IV, n.78;

4 Pope Julius II, Giuliano della Rovere, (5th Dec .1443 – 21st Feb. 1513), Pope from 1503 to 1513.

5 Landucci in his *Diario*, (edited by Jodoco del Badia, Firenze, 1889), p. 336, has a very colourful page about Florence receiving the news, first through he does not know what rumours, even before the official news arrives, and the people going crazy through the city, shouting 'Palle, palle, Papa Lione!'(the palle, the balls from the Mèdici coat of arms) and lighting bonfires in the streets and squares, using all the wood they can find, doors, even beams from the roofs, so much so that the city was full of fire and smoke, with great danger, for days. The authorities had to send out banns that on pain of the scaffold they should stop taking down roofs and breaking up shops.

6 *Fusta* is a slim light ship, called also *bireme veneziana (Dizionario della Marina,* Roma 1937): *Fusta* – kind of small slim galley with 18-22 oars on each side... In Venice it was much used from 1498 to 1570.

At the times of the *Governo Veneto* it was kept, at anchor and disarmed, by Saint Mark's Square, in front of the columns, to hold (and train) the prisoners until they were allocated to the Galleys. This latter is the one visible in some of Canaletto's paintings, covered with a striped red and yellow awning. It is also the one spoken about by Elena VANZAN MARCHINI in her *La follia, una nave, una cittá*. In *Storie di pazzi e pazzie a Venezia nel '700* (Mira-VE, Brenctani ed., 1981. It is worthy of notice that archival research has produced notice of *pazzi* , i.e. madmen, fools, on the *fusta* (anchored and disarmed, no longer in active service as from the end of the XVI century) only in the XVII century. In 1514 the *fusta* was still a swift warship. Cfr. also: V.V. A.A. *Venezia e le sue lagune,* Venezia 1847, Vol. I, part. 2, p.219: *legno da corsa* used in war. She was a small galley very fast in running-coursing....

She was also known to be much used by North African corsairs, useful for her speed and low profile. If one reads Ariosto one finds the *Fusta* mentioned as being used in the far North by Hebridean islanders, in Egypt (Alexandria) and in North Africa.

7 *Istorie di Giovanni Cambi fiorentino*, published by Fr. Ildefonso di S. Luigi, Firenze 1786, in: *Delizie degli eruditi toscani,* tomo XXII, vol. III, pp. 43-45. All the original texts in Italian are in the Appendix.

8 *Ricordanze di Bartolomeo Masi calderaio fiorentino,* edited a cura di G.O. CORAZZINI, Firenze, 1906, p 142.

9 Poggio Bracciolini, L.B. Alberti, Giovanni Villani and the drawings by Botticelli as analyzed in Chapter I below.

10 Florence 1481, Nicoló di Lorenzo della Magna.

Prologue

The satirical allusions of the *fusta* must have been discernible to the contemporaries involved in the usual power games. For the general public they were probably just part of a burlesque pageant with traditional symbols and characters, and to be taken for granted – who may ever had asked why there were people masked as devils in a festival? – as well known and respected elements of an ancient tradition. They knew, nevertheless, that this was not the usual popular festival. It was part of the officially organized San Giovanni (1514) of the latest (1512) Mèdici Restoration.

For us, the riddles and charades of the civic *Fusta* on the one hand, and the characters and symbols of the 'ship of fools' on the other, have been an interesting journey[1] a great research game through theatrical puzzles against a backdrop of old traditions and contemporary rumblings of passing thunder. Collecting the hints, spinning of the threads, weaving a tapestry of the festival, and the relief, in it, of the *Fusta piena di matti,* has been for me a historical and a symbolical journey. And, suitably, a feast.

The visual appearance of the *Fusta piena di matti,* the choreography of the event, is found in the reports of historians and diarists. We have three contemporary records of the event, by Giovanni Cambi, Bartolomeo Masi and Marin Sanudo the Younger[2]. The reconstruction of its function during the *festa,* as well as its deeper pervasive meaning, have been made possible by the careful reading of the details of that choreography, the action and details of dress. This is the text.

The indications given by the historians have been examined carefully, with the assistance of the conventional tools of historical research. Diplomatic and personal letters of the Mèdici, mostly unpublished, the letters of Venetian diplomat, friar and now nearly cardinal Piero Querini, contemporary festive literature, contemporary and later further historical and critical material have been searched. These have revealed pre-text, sub-text, threads, strands and yarns to complete a colourful tapestry from that fragment of history.

One can, therefore, reconstruct the civic function of the *Fusta*, a function which plays both a quasi-subversive and a cathartic note. Florence stages a not too understated satire of pope Leo X and the Roman court. Those who are in charge of the restored Medicean rule in Florence feel oppressed by Rome's 'protection', and criticise certain political, (and doctrinal perhaps) positions of the Pope. Unable to proclaim openly a criticism of the bigger power, those of the *Signoria* residing in Florence – most probably through the Compagnie *del Broncone* and *Diamante* – build the *Fusta piena di matti* which, like a collective court Fool, mimes a clever parody of friends, enemies and rivals at the Papal court.

But the *Fusta piena di matti*, truly a 'court fool' in the sense mentioned above, is also a symbolical apparatus, and as such has a life of its own which exceeds the single theatrical performance.

The *Fusta* event, in this festival, beside the social-civic-satirical function, develops a symbolising function of its own, laden with recurring implications.

The renewed display of symbols – ship, fools, devils, cloaks, hoods-cowls-capuches, *cappucci*, clubs-truncheons, hooks, bells – and ritual – the suggested possible death-by-water, a ritual death, the mock punishment of hanging in a basket – made by the Florentine masters of the revels for the S.Giovanni of 1514 is an event of splendid and resounding significance. Even though not necessarily burdened explicitly by all the echoes and resonances which have been evoked in the first part of this essay, the constellation is rich and extensive. It means that a collective heritage has been re-activated and enriched.

This is the true historical fact, the symbolical revival. This is what makes it a piece of history.

In the sense that while the historical documented 'facts' which inspired the occasion, the satirical contents, the topical aspects, are in part of an ephemeral nature, the symbolical system is the durable fact. The *Fusta piena di matti* is the re-activation of a polyvalent, recurring *Gestalt*, a revival of valuable, expressive, significant traditional themes. It is the taking body and surfacing of archetype(s). The ship made of wood on the cart drawn by two pairs of oxen, was there, on 22nd June 1514, it was seen by all, and is remembered now.

The satirical episode of the *fusta* is a historical fact, yes, in the sense that it has occurred, in public, it has been documented in the chronicles, although only a fleeting apparition lasting a few hours.

The historical landscape – from March to June 1514 – that has given it the opportunity of being is, it is true, a background documented by letters and the other usual historical sources. But it is background of moods, opinions, humours and rumours. Goings on in the corridors of power, as it were.

It is a background of projects and facts that could have, but have not, or not all of them, occurred. It is a place of non-events.

On a realistic plane the *fusta* is (was) a warning light, an alarm bell, an admonition referring to unrealized possibilities. It alludes to a Crusade which will not take place. To feared consequences of an alliance with Venice which will fade away. To the possible danger of a new French descent which will be happily resolved shortly in other ways. It alludes to discontent that will be resolved within the family, to banned Florentine *cappucci* and *cappuccetti*, outsiders to be, eventually, safely disregarded.

We are just perceiving trends in the climate of a moment, catching glimpses of a realm of possibilities. Not to be underestimated. Like the threads of a plot. Happily vanished, however

But what gives real life and a body to the *fusta* episode is the symbolical system. It is the collective heritage that gives substance and lasting value to it, over and beyond the ephemeral moment which is the immediate pre-text. The text itself is the weaving of recurring and lasting symbolical themes: the ship, from Isis's ship to the space-ship; the sea of birth and the sea of death; the voyage, from the voyages of discovery to fanciful utopias; the fool as different and the different as fool; cloaks and masks; hoods and hooded creatures, for good or ill; the club and truncheon as phallic weapon; club and bladder full of wind-soul; the mirror of knowledge and self knowledge (the *marotte*).

That is why I say that the symbolical *Fusta* full of fools is the real historical fact. This is the lasting expression, on a background of ephemeral historical moods.

The symbol is a polyvalent mutable phenomenon, made real here. The historical background is many faceted, rich, crowded, yet eventually fading into the ephemeral, slipping into evanescence.

The symbolizing function of the *fusta* has ample implications which are not wholly definable 'objectively'. My reading, therefore, or my vision, is comparatively subjective. A reading resulting possibly, in part, from the intention of the observer [3].

An attempt has been made to reveal and re-design connections, echoes, derivations and renewals of symbols, in the possibly partial consciousness of 'then', with the consciousness and from the position of the observer 'now'.

My reading is proposed here not just as a point of arrival, but in its being woven. In its form, this essay is meant to lead along the road of gradual discovery in several directions, turning back and taking side roads, finding, gradually, open views. The figures, phenomena, symbols, characters are seen taking shape and voice, as they emerge.

As from a journey of discovery I relate what at the end I have collected and deduced, yes, but also the road, the vistas and the resonances, so that the reader may have, if possible, the sense of going along, and the sense of sharing the feeling of excitement at finding the various reasons that lay behind the follies of the game.

This being a reconstruction, both the historical background, and the symbolical event, must live again now. The tapestry that was woven then, is woven, and hopefully seen, again now.

1 I consider myself lucky that at the time I was searching into the Medici letters the Archivio di Stato di Firenze was still under the Uffizi, and the *Filze* and *carte* were not yet available on-line. The pleasure of shuffling those *carte* in their boxes somewhere under the great Gallery is something that I would not have liked to miss.

2 Marin SANUDO, *Diario*, Venezia, 1887, vol. XVIII, 313: '*e il giorno, dopo disnare, sopra un longo carro andò fuora una fusta ornata con tutti soi coriedi'*.... – and the following day, after dinner, on top of a long wagon, a *fusta* was carried out, furnished with all her structures, complete as if really ready to go to sea, and she was manned by amusing men, jesters and buffoons, all in a sailor livery, among whom was also Barlacchii, having collected the few fools found in this city of ours, one of them Carafulla in his hood. And as she went through all the land as if to awaken the people for the festival, it was an amusing pleasantry, where all the population concurred as well as what foreigners there were, as from Rome there were many, among whom seven cardinals, that is Cornaro, Sauli, Bibiena, Ferrara, Cibo, Siena e Ragona, e our *magnifico confaloniere* of the Holy Church [Giuliano], all with their faces covered, but we knew them all.' CAMBI and MASI texts are in the previous chapter, The Stage. See also IV.5.; V.1.; V.2.; and the complete Source texts in the Appendix.

3 For this see III.5., note 67 – Castelli's *Simbolismo involontario*.

First Part

(for a festive tradition –
symbolism and recent manifestations.)

CHAPTER I

Precursors and models in Florence.

I.1. *The cart (wagon, chariot) of fools in the festivals in Florence.* 'Itaque ut florentini solent in festis suis ...'.

In the winter 1451-1452, Poggio Bracciolini, writing his invective against Lorenzo Valla, grants his enemy the glory of a coronation to 'Prince of fools': '*decernemus ei triumphum at lauream coronam, ne amplius addubitari possit Vallam nostrum Stultorum atque insanorum principatum possidere* – we confer him a triumph and a laurel crown, so that there may not be ever a doubt that our Valla possesses the principality over fools and madmen'[1].

The inspiration for this election came to Poggio Bracciolini from the custom he remembers as being in use in Florence, during festivals, of driving through the streets of the city fools and madmen, on a cart, as in triumph, – '*Itaque ut Florentini solent in festis suis aliquando curru triumphali insanos vehere, quod est iucundissimum spectaculum* – in the manner the Florentines are accustomed to, during their festivals, sometimes to carry madmen in a triumphal cart, which is a most pleasant spectacle'. Most pleasant, and exemplary, no doubt.

Bracciolini does not specify whether he refers to Carnivals, May Day celebrations or San Giovanni – the principal seasonal festivals in which a mixture of pomp and revelry exploded in Florence. The model, however, is the ancient one of reversed triumph like that of Sylenus on the ass, of the mock King of Saturnalia, of the mock Bishop of the Medieval *Ludi dei Chierici*, of the *Fêtes des fous*, and the *Fêtes des Innocents*. Festivals which cross the Winter season, from the Winter solstice to the Spring equinox, and within the terms of the Christian calendar go from Christmas to the beginning of Lent, and that have roughly speaking being collected under the term of *Carnevale* [2]. This represents the basic *festa* model.

The model here referred to is that of the circumscribed place of the *festa*, an artificial moment in time, precisely limited, and of space, a *ludic* space, with precise laws and 'rules of the game'.

In the *festa*, the everyday prescriptions, the rules of law and order are, in theory, lifted. In practice, however, in the game of the *festa* those same laws and rules of social life are adopted in a sort of 'reversal' – they are a mirror image – and are recognisable, even in the atmosphere of festive ambivalence and ambiguity. There is 'order in disorder'; it is ritual. The disorder allowed (*semel in anno* – once in the year), yet it is well organised within certain rules, 'the rules of the game', well respected hierarchies, order and rituals of obedience.

The space of the *festa* allows license, where society limits and regulates. But also the game has its laws, and, returning to the cart of madmen driven in triumph, we can see that they are certainly not 'free'. The cart (and the ship, we shall see) encloses and isolates them in space, and they have an allotted time. Within those limits of space and time, they also have a Prince; hierarchy is represented..

Within the principles of the idea of a festival, of the reversal of roles, values and rules, the real example of carrying the fools in triumph, besides it being a paradoxical and tragically risible spectacle (*iucundissimum* as defined by Bracciolini), is in reality a deeply symbolical event.

In fact, leading the fools or madmen – i.e. the examples of the unreason, of disorder, of existential as well as practical incompetence, and perhaps also of illness-contagion, of 'unnatural' psychic instability – to lead them as in triumph through the streets of the city, where society is based (or at least so it is claimed) on reason, on hierarchy of merit, and on the production of what is useful – a society which perhaps also lives in fear of "evil", be it illness, vice or death – is effectively a reversed representation, exemplary and symbolical, of the essential principles on which that society, or civilization, claims to be founded. The fool is the living, reversed, symbol of (absent) reason [3].

The election of a king, a bishop, or a prince of fools is a mirror image of the hierarchy and order normally in place as we know it. The reversal consists of negative values, naturally, the most foolish of the fools is the prince of fools (or madmen, if such they are) as we shall see well exemplified in I.2. following.

This mirror-image aspect installs, *per absurdum*, our order into their disorder. Hierarchy is of 'order', it follows rules, but it confirms disorder, un-rule, by the election of an extreme representative of un-reason to the top of this hierarchy.

So there was a custom in Florence of parading fools in triumph for the festivals, and also of electing a Prince of fools. Now, in 1514, we have a ship, on a cart, full of fools, with a Mock-King, the Prince of Fools, Carafulla. In a *festa*.

I.2. *A literary example.* *Subversion and restoration of order by means of a* festa. *A ship-as-state through the looking glass (of water).*

An exemplary *festa* – exemplary because through the disorder of the *festa*, in fact an organized and circumscribed disorder, a given order is (in reality) overthrown – is found, in a context built upon multiple mirroring reversals, in *Momus, seu de principe* by the humanist Leon Battista Alberti.[4] In this literary testimony Alberti demonstrates how a *festa* can lend itself to be a mirror reflecting, and changing, if needed, everyday reality.

The *festa*, with its license and the' rules of the game' within it, reveals what a charge of instability is often present in the balance of social and political life, and how the *festa* can bring about, even in its suspended time and circumscribed space, a real reversal, a real retribution.

The episode is in the fourth book of *Momus*, and it is a vision, as seen through the eyes of the unusual travellers Charon and Gelasto, of social and political order, in a borderline land-and-sea nocturnal world. There is a *festa* which will be the breaking point and the resolution of a given order, so that a new and 'rightful' order will be established.

The principal metaphor of this passage is one of a ship-as-state (i.e. some organized hierarchical society) [5] in the sea-or-water, where water, we are told, is disorder. There is the sea, that is the water as disorder or un-reason – Gelasto declares to be frightened by it because 'in the sea one cannot discern any path' – outside of the dry land where reason presumably rules.. Then there is also some water circumscribed by the land, a pool, that is used for the *festa* and functions as a mirror or a double [6] to the order (that in this case is doubly unstable) which is reflected into it. In the mirror of the pool society finds the breaking point, a reversal of reality by way of the playtime reversal.

We are in a twilight world of land and sea, repeatedly reversing, seen through the eyes of Charon, the ferryman from the underworld, the world of the dead, now travelling as a 'tourist' in this world, the world of the living, having engaged the philosopher Gelasto as his guide.

Gelasto was a dead soul, a philosopher, as such also poor, so poor that he had arrived to the river and the ferry for the underworld without even the money to pay his fare. Charon offers him a way to pay in kind: he had always wanted to visit the world of the living, and offers Gelasto useful employment as a guide for a 'tour' on land, so as to earn his fare to the underworld.

On dry land Gelasto feels safe, but the sea troubles him: "I realize I could not be a guide on this vast expanse of water, where there is no visible pathway".[7] The philosopher (who follows reason) is confused and fearful on facing the unknown, the unlimited, a place without rules; he stops for lack of roads and recognizable signs. It is unchartered territory. Not to be trusted.

Charon aptly remarks that the sea can be comprehended better as relative to the world of death: "But why do you appear to fear this sea, you who have seen the Acheron (you who are already dead). I don't deny that this seems bigger, but it is certainly not deeper or more troubled" [8] and in fact he, Charon, is at ease on it. It is not strange for the boatman to feel at ease on the water, but the fear of water by someone who relies on reason, the philosopher, is a fundamental concept. It is also right of Charon to suggest that the philosopher should know better, not because of his experience of life (or his philosophy, reason) but because he has experienced death.

This metaphor of the water and the journey into the unknown, thus openly related to death is also fundamental – and the fact that the 'fools' are ready to launch into it is also part of the symbolism of the ship of fools.

As a matter of fact Charon then takes the part of guide, briefly, on the water, reversing the roles, setting his boat in the sea – on land he was carrying the boat on his head, overturned, bottom up (see one drawing for a ship of fools by Bosch, fig 11)

Multiple reversals and mirrors are altogether intentional, and declared, on the part of the author. Alberti, in the first book, in the middle of his considerations about the incredible variety of tendencies and customs of the gods, which had struck him with a wonder even greater than the one he had for the folly of humans, presents the unbridled and perfidious god Momus. The author declares he has 'chosen to tell his story in order to teach how to lead a life according to reason'[9]. One cannot but understand that the teaching will be by way of opposites. In fact the author declares that by telling the exploits of this god Momus 'bizarre, extraordinarily hot headed, a hostile nosy parker, a bothersome scourge, one who enjoyed, unique among all, to hate and be hated' he intends to write a book full of 'jokes and pleasantries' [10] which shall be of instruction, by the title of *Momus seu de principe.*[11]

In the Fourth book, with Charon the tourist, the traveller, with his precious boat that he never abandons and carries on his head when over land, with his guide Gelasto (the walking dead), other points of interest are a ship-as-state, a pool of in-land water in which a festival is performed, and a successful plot taking place during, and thanks to, the festival. The plot succeeds to depose a tyrant by means of a game and its rules, and reverses an established (but not stable) order. The chief is in fact executed (or assassinated) in the game. He was a chief, yes, but the context was of outlaws – unruly like in a *festa* themselves – so the point of departure is a reversal of normal order already, to be reversed yet again. The execution will be by drowning – a ritual death by water – result of a game.

This right and true ritual-plot in a literary testimony is fundamental. We recognize that it bears witness of the consciousness, and almost a codification, of the subversive possibilities in a *festa*, a consciousness that applies also, obviously, to the socio-political reality in which Alberti moved (in Florence in the XV century).

It was known, in Florence, that festivals were potentially dangerous times – the palace of Government was left empty and unguarded, The *Signoria*, the authorities, Magistrates etc. were all in less secure than normal locations, in a church (as in the occasion of the 1472 Pazzi conspiracy when Giuliano, Lorenzo's brother was killed, and Lorenzo himself barely escaped), in public squares or streets. Just recently, Piero Soderini was advised not to go to the San Giovanni of 1512, as he could have been in danger of his life. There was legislation in place to safeguard the city from disorders, from infiltration of foreigners, or exiles, and so forth [12] (see also V.2 , and note 30)

The idea of the ship-as-state, (an idea of Aristotelian origin and revived by Dante) is important here as it appears in the context of a *festa*, and as such part of the game of reversal. The ship carries the concept of ship-as-state, yet it is a state of outlaws, therefore a state, or society, outside of society, a state outside the law. To be outside, out also of the land-as-order, the pirates' ship is not a metaphor, but their only reality. This puts them in a situation where instead of being in a ship representing the order of the state, they are in a ship that is in flight from that order. They are in conflict with the basis of order that is society, as well as of safety, that is the land, the '*terra ferma*'. This will make them, the crew, the pirates, unable to govern themselves, once on land; it will lead them to allow their established order to be overturned.

The pirates' ship is seen by Charon and Gelasto as it appears in the distance, as they themselves are approaching land. They see it in the distance and that's when they expound the concept of ship-as-state. Charon exclaims "say, what is that strange object which runs towards us on the sea? Is it perhaps something which, so they say, brings so many tragedies to the notice of the underworld and is buffeted by the waves?[13].... is it not a state in navigation?"[14] ['at sea' as well one may say]. Gelasto asks him how did he get the "felicitous idea of calling a ship a state?There is no more appropriate image..." and he proceeds to explain how a ship, with her hierarchical organization, is exceptionally well suited to represent the organization of a state, the leader, the subjects, the 'real kings' and the tyrants, unanimity and dissent.[15]

As the ship approaches, however, our travellers realize that this is a ship of outlaws, a pirates' ship, they decide, wisely, that they will be better off out of the way, and split up to hide in separate places. This separation will enable them to observe the ensuing episode, the festival-conspiracy, from two different points of observation, and to see both the game as it unfolds, and the subversive project carried out within the game.

Gelasto sees the landing of the pirates. He sees them as they find some baths with a pool (water contained within the land, a container of water) and organise their party-*festa* in/on the water.

The pool is not only an area of water for play. We read in it, on the one hand, a reversed idea of sea, water as disorder, yes, but limited in space by the land, contained, like the *festa*, as the *festa* is disorder, yes (misrule), but limited in time, contained by the rules of civilized civic life which allow the (limited) misrule of the *festa*. On the other hand we also read in it the concept – reversed – of the ship, a container which normally *excludes* the water and thereby protects and supports life, while this pool *contains* the water, and is no protection from it. For the chief of the pirates the water will be indeed cause of death, by drowning.

The pirates decide to have a revel, a *festa*, they elect a mock-chief, a mock-king. He was in fact, the chief of the pirates, and he had elected himself. A mock election, and therefore not even within the rules of the game. Soon, in fact, they reveal the feeble character of their unstable order: the first mock-king is made to abdicate in favour of another who is found to be more suitable in this choice by negatives, because he was 'the most disreputable among those vile seamen and had proclaimed himself mock-king; he was a sutler – *vivandiere* – which is congruous with the gastronomic basis, clearly carnivalesque and Rabelaisian, of the model[16]. The action develops as a game, a joke, they all approve, they laugh at the jokes, and first of all the chief of the pirates [17].

The latter, however, as his very own caper, breaks again the rules of the game: he refuses to bow and utter the oath of allegiance to the '*re della crapula* – the king of the revel'; he has to be put to trial, and is condemned, according to the rules of the game, to a ducking. He submits to the rule, or mis-rule, and accepts to be immersed into the water. But then he is kept under long enough to be drowned. Here is the ritual death by water.

The outlaw is subjected to the justice of the reversed world of the *festa*, a sea- master meets his destiny in a pool of water, a miniature sea, a bucket-ship – a rebel against society and civil laws finds his death because 'condemned as a rebel with a unanimous sentence' by this gang of pirates, he submits to the law because he accepts the rules of the game[18].

So far the episode validates the model of the ritual *festa* as known by the author. Although this episode is not, of course, a historical document, but an exemplary and didactic invention, it nevertheless demonstrates that Alberti not only knew the model of the *festa* and its rituals, but was also clearly conscious of the subversive potential of the *festa*, its cathartic spirit, which in this case fully coincide.

At the conclusion of their party-revels, the group 'of the royals' (some of them were prisoners with their Prince) proclaiming to have liberated everyone by means of the assassination of the tyrant their jailer, depart and take to the sea again. But completely changed. This is one side of the story.

Gelasto, who had seen the *festa* from his own separate hiding place, goes looking for Charon, who had remained in hiding in a swamp, to keep watch on his boat. They meet and exchange their news. Charon is able to fill in the story with his view from another side: he had assisted, unseen, to the planning of the deed, which was indeed a proper conspiracy. He had eavesdropped on a group of conspirators who had in fact actually discussed and organized the assassination of the chief of the pirates with the pretext, and by means of, the very *festa* (or game) itself.[19]

Here is a clear documentation of the consciousness of the political use of the *festa* by way of its ever present subversive potential.

Furthermore I like to read, and point out, the 'leap', through the looking-glass (interface) of a *festa*, and the mirror of the water. The leap from a worldly-social, to a supernatural, environment,[20] in the real death, result of a game, and *vice versa* to a liberation, in this world. There are multiple leaps from life to death (of the tyrant), from death (the civil death of the prisoners) to life (their regained freedom), and from an artificial order (the illegal chief) to a natural order (the freedom of the Prince, extended to all) by means of the ritual game.

In the enclosed water of the pool, the circumscribed time of the *festa*, the irrational is limited and presumably controlled in the apparent absurdity of the game. Unreason in its only apparent innocence, generates an event that touches something essential, i.e. the point where life and death, reason and unreason meet and flip over. A sacrifice reverses the old, and establishes a new, order. The game overturns reality.

The ship resumes her voyage on the sea of time, towards 'where they had come from'. As far as we saw, they had come from the sea, out of this chartered world.

Charon, a shadow king, or a king of the shadows, guardian of the law in the world of the dead, has seen all. He too resumes his journey, in the boat of the dead, in the sea of eternity 'where there is no recognizable path'.

And so, through the looking-glass, through the mirror of the water, the ship of the living (the exultant crew), and the ship of the dead, resume, each, their own journey. Shadows wandering in the night.

Momus was written between 1443 and 1450 [21]. It is interesting to notice that this fictional elaboration of the model *festa*, with the blundering ship and its incompetent crew, is vaguely contemporary with the evidence given by Poggio Bracciolini of a 'cart, chariot, wagon of fools' as a usual spectacle during the *feste* in Florence written in 1451.

It is also most interesting to notice how the Florentine humanist's (Alberti, 1404-1472) jocularly didactic work *Momus* ran out of print, apparently, in these years of restored Medicean *Signoria* in Florence, and the Medicean Pope in Rome. It happened to have to be reprinted twice in 1520, in Rome.

While Poggio Bracciolini's evidence (prince of fools, and the fools led in the cart) is considered evidence of a real customary occurrence vaguely in the past, the fictional elaboration by Alberti comes as evidence of an unmistakable consciousness of the symbolical values of the 'structures' or systems – sea voyage, hierarchies, rules of un-rule – of the *festa,* and of its potential for subversion and political use, in times not far removed, both before and after 1514, the year of the *Fusta piena di matti* now in our sights.

Alberti's is a literary construction, it is a tale told by one of the greatest names, humanist, mathematician, architect of the XV century.

It is a tale, but it demonstrates knowledge of the customs, the rituals and the explosive potential of the festival. He also knows of the dangers of 'going too far', of the possibilities of subversion, but also of justice, in the *festa.* And of how subversion and justice may even coincide. Therefore there may even be 'just' conspiracies.

And how chaos and transgression can be a means to order. Or how realistic catharsis can be.

So the moment of chaos, the moment of the irrational, or even just laughter, may carry a deeper reason, and deserves careful notice.

I.3. *A historical source. A XIV century* festa. *Boats, devils and death by water.*

A source of information, further back in time, yet so rich and real, coming to fruition in our discourse also in view of the preparation drawn from Bracciolini and Alberti, comes in the form of a historical event of 1304, related by Giovanni Villani in his *Chronicle*.

This is a *festa* vastly relevant to the subject of this essay, in its spirit and detail, as well as in the imploding result in which the festa resolves. The fiction of the performance turns into the facts that were intended only as a theatrical invention, in a veritable capturing of the spectators and plunging them into the action now real. In this case the elements of the *festa* 'precipitate' – like a chemical process – an occurrence which transforms into real life – or rather death – what was intended to be only a theatrical performance, a game, albeit in ritual mode. Reality and imagination filtering through into each other.

The episode, which is part of history, belongs to 1304, is told by Giovanni Villani in his *Chronicles,* and is also put into verse in a poem by Antonio Pucci, the *Centiloquio*.[22]

This is how it went. The *Brigata di S.Frediano*, (the "Company for the Revels" of S.Frediano, a quarter of Florence, '*oltrarno*'), as it was customary for the main seasonal festivals, had organised a great spectacle for the first of May (*Calendimaggio*), and all the citizens were invited. Banns and proclamations went out, heralds called the population to the river where the spectacle was to be staged. The programme was going to be about 'News from the other world'.

'They were going to have a taste of the other world' writes Villani.

A spectacular and realistic scene of hell was staged on the river Arno, on rafts and barges by the Carraia bridge: there were hell fires, smoking cauldrons and devils like cooks holding forks and hooks tormenting the souls of the damned.

The souls of the damned are quintessential festival stuff:

'The souls under such torments Were shirts filled with straw And bulls' bladders full of wind.'	*'L'anime ch'eran poste a tal tormento Eran camicie di paglia ripiene E vesciche di bue piene di vento.'*

This is how Pucci describes the devils:

'Made up as horned devils	*Contraffatti diavoli e cornuti*
Brandishing pitchforks	*che forcon da letame avieno in mano*
All blackened and long fanged' [23]	'*di piú ragion tutti neri e sannuti'*

There were spectators on the *Carraia* bridge, and in the river *Arno* the show was staged on barges and rafts. The stage setting sounds impressive, and above all it is made up of the recurring elements of the carnival-festival: the fires, the cauldrons, the devils, the souls of the dead. Particularly interesting the theme, it must be noted, of 'soul' as 'wind' – contained in the bladders here, as it will be found in the fool's hand atop his bauble, and in the hands of the devils around the *fusta* of 1514, in the shape of 'clubs made of leather, full of wind.'

The festive performance which promised to show news from the other world was very successful in attracting spectators who came in great numbers. They filled the Carraia bridge, like the gallery of a theatre. The bridge, being made of wood, gave way and collapsed under weight of the crowd spilling the spectators over into the water and the fires. Many fell to their death, *spectators suddenly turned into actors.* It is the prerogative of the *festa* to be a collective activity, with uncertain divisions between the performers and the festive crowd, so this was also true to form.

The people who had come to see 'news from the other world', who had the promise, from the banns, that 'of the other life would have had a taste', who thought that they would only take a look and see hell and devils from a distance, suddenly, because of the bridge falling down, fall into that same underworld represented in (and by) the water, with devils, fires and dead souls. A great number died, and became dead souls themselves. By water and by fire, that crowd goes to the other world, for real.

And so goes the comment of the historian: 'In this way the game from being a joke did actually happen for real – *il da beffe torna dadovero* – and according to the banns many, by becoming dead souls themselves, went and learnt news of the other world'.

The poet, going straight to the will of God, makes the point thus:

'It shows that God wanted that in the end
A lot of people should go to the other life,
And get to know the news for real.'

'*Mostra che Iddio volesse, che nel fondo*
Andasse molta gente all'altra vita,
Che le novelle sepper tutte a tondo'.

In this *festa* the revel-performance gives evidence of a double reversal; in the first the supernatural (hell, devils, dead souls) are brought into the social world by way of a theatrical *mise-en-scène*, as a game, while in the second the social world, the people themselves are taken into the supernatural by death, for real. A perfect flip from topside to under world. A perfect leap, through the looking glass of the water.

In the first phase, it is a game with implications of cathartic magic. In the second phase, the real deaths, of a ritual appearance but of a real nature, are the result – casual, yet necessary. Fatally the game turns to reality: mimetic-cathartic magic altogether too successful.

***

This interface between game and reality is deeply relevant to the reading that is being done of the symbolical value of the *festa*, the fool, the ship, the souls and the devils.

In particular, this episode allows a sharp focussing of the connection, festive and symbolical, between water, ship, souls of the dead – the damned and the fools.

The dates also, allow important adjustments (*puntualizzazioni*): a *festa* like the one described by Villani at the beginning of the XIV century confirms a certain antiquity (these rituals are certainly much older, but our Florentine evidence starts at 1304) and a factual expression of the traditions of which so far we had seen only oblique indications. A brief indication from Poggio Bracciolini, and a detailed but fictional one from L.B. Alberti.

Furthermore, Dante's *Inferno* being of not many years earlier, is another casual necessity. Illustrated nearly two hundred years later by Botticelli, it is Dante's *Inferno*, its devils, their boats, its damned and his seekers that are the fundamental elements of the netherworld which we find transposed into the games of the '*festa*'.

Dante's boats, in Botticelli's drawings (ca. 1481), take us back up to the end of XVth century. In them we recognize the most recent iconographic source for the *Fusta dei Matti*.

We shall return to this, in the next section.

The fools on the cart (or wagon), and in the ship, are twilight beings, otherworldly in a social sense. Behind the fools are 'souls of the damned', a fact indicated, for instance, in the iconography of the fool who carries a bladder full of "wind", one of the versions of his bauble, which is soul – such were the souls on the river Arno described by Villani – bladders full of wind – and they are carried in mock triumph like those who, at the end of the *festa,* are to be sacrificed, be it ritually (the Carnival effigy) or really. In fact, those being taken to the scaffold or to the stake, especially when heretics, were taken to the execution as in a mock-triumph in the hangman's cart [24].

As the straw effigy (or *papier mâché* figure), representing the king Carnival is eventually burnt or ducked to death after having been *fêted* during the days of the revels, so the fools led in triumph for a day in the city, ridiculous and tragical example, are destined, at the end of the revels, to be caged, or banned, or imprisoned [25], in any case made to disappear. Like those fools we shall see in the *Narrenschiff,* the *Stultifera navis,* (form that the *currus triumphalis* mentioned by Bracciolini could at times have taken), they are symbolically destined to wander, 'errant' outwith the confines of the land, by water, and, in the mind of the censor, towards certain ruin and shipwreck, therefore to the 'other world'. Theirs is a journey without sense or reason (and without Grace), towards a sort of bankrupt counter-utopia [26] on their search for change and forbidden dangerous knowledge. Towards death by water. This they are condemned to. But they may be seen as those searching for the Golden Age, for the Happy Isles of legend [27], for new ways, new sea routes, and new continents.

The spectators who have undergone death by water in the river Arno, and that the stage set receives directly into hell, become souls of the damned; they could be an example of those who break a taboo [28] '*Noli plus sapere quam opporteat* – do not wish to know more than is suitable.'

Knowledge of the supernatural is the dominion of dogma and in the hands of the Church, not for human curiosity. So those spectators become an example of, and for, those who search for the 'forbidden' knowledge, and meet with the adequate punishment.

A similar threat is aimed at the 'fools'.

I.4. *The Florentine iconographic example.*

While for the figure of the fool and its attributes, in the two aspects of fool as well as devil, there is relatively plentiful iconographic material in which one can read and decode the single attributes as they evolve and become clear (animal attributes – ass' ears and cockscomb, club, bells, hood, cloak), for the ship there is one: the ship, or boat, that ferries the souls over the rivers of the underworld.

The boat that ferries the souls of the damned, those excluded from this world, but also from paradise, to the region of their punishment – this boat exists in the designs by Botticelli for Dante's *Divine Comedy*. Charon's boat and that of the devil *Flegiàs* are central to the illustrations for the of Dante's *Inferno* (Canto VIII) .

The boats designed by Botticelli (figures 12 and 13) meant, like Dante's ones, obviously, for the damned, this time are ferrying those who are only passing. The living poet is one, and the other is his guide Virgil the Roman poet. Flegiás's boat, normally for the regular damned, to the devils' disappointment, carries Dante who will land on the bank – '*più non ci avrai che per passar del loto* – you shall have us only for the crossing of the swamp'. And Dante will pursue his journey towards the earthly paradise, and beyond, to the higher paradise. He is not adrift, he has a purpose and will fulfil that purpose, even though using a devil's boat.

Botticelli subscribes to ambivalence, it seems. And to the non-conclusive boat, as in Flegiás' one which will be examined in this respect at III.5.

Because of the sympathy I feel for the fool I will put forward the observation that, while on the one hand we shall see the devil as the double for the fool, we could also consider the possibility of another double for him beside the devils: a positive aspect as well, someone who will be saved, someone that is not punished on account of his search for knowledge, or for the Golden Age, someone that might indeed find the Happy Islands. Dante's Earthly Paradise is not a fools' paradise, he has chosen his journey, and succeeds in his quest.[29]

The drawings can be dated to before 1481, the year when Cristoforo Landino's edition of the *Divine Comedy* was published, with the engravings by Baccio Baldini based on those drawings by Botticelli.[30] The date is important as we shall have to consider other boats and ships with fools and devils in years not very distant in time, and that we shall also examine, in order to make use of coincidences, and differences. Those illustrations, however, appear in editions dated from 1494 onwards, therefore Botticelli pre-dates them.

The boat or ship, so central to the '*festa*' that the expression *currus navalis* (a ship on a cart) is considered to be one of the possible origins of the term *Carnevale,* is also recognized as bearing funerary connotations (as well as sexual ones) [31].

It is not surprising, in the microcosmic mirror image of the '*festa*', to recognize such symbolical value to the ship. The ship is a vehicle-and-container, egg, ark, boat, casket, sarcophagus, ferry for the dead souls [32]. The ship is apt to represent a mimetic-magic metaphor for the journey of life, for the cycle from the origin to the end, and to new beginnings, on the sea of time. Through death, and beyond death.

We have found Charon's boat associated to a '*festa*'. Here he is only a witness of the symbols and a spectator of the rituals, and an interpreter, in the passage from Alberti's *Momus*. We have seen deaths by water becoming the flip side of festive theatricals, revels on barges on the water becoming a very real journey to the netherworld.

Fools, devils, souls of the damned (of the dead) are figures which intertwine, separate, play doubles, and are met, over and over again, in the historical, narrative and iconographic examples that are emerging in the landscape we are travelling through: the festive mode – not exclusively festive, however, because they touch matters of historical reality, of consciousness, of power and of knowledge. Ambivalence and ambiguity are always lurking and are to be taken into account.

Such is the nature of symbols.

1 Poggio BRACCIOLINI *Oratio prima in L. Vallam,* in *Opera omnia*, Torino, 1964 (anastatic reprint of the Basel 1538 edition), vol.I, p.205. The *Oratio prima* was composed between December 1451 and February 1452, when it was published, as established by Ari Wesseling in his edition of Lorenzo VALLA, *Antidotum primum, his first apology against Poggio Bracciolini*. Critical edition with introduction and notes by Ari WESSELING, Amsterdam, 1978, p.30.

2 For the most ancient *feste* one can see the many pertinent passages in J.G. FRAZER, *The Golden Bough,* London 1967, pp. 763-768 *passim.* We shall also later see the *Lupercalia,* and Ovid's *Fasti* on it. See III.4.ii and note 48.

For the Middle Ages, there is a wealth of information and documents in DE BARTHOLOMAEIS, *Le origini della poesia drammatica italiana*, Bologna 1492, and bibliography. Particularly see Ch. II, the '*Schola Cantorum*' of Rome and the '*Ludi Romani tra il VII e il XII secolo*' and , ch.II,VI: '*Le libertá di dicembre*' pp. 189-215. As rich is Paolo TOSCHI, *Le origini del teatro italiano*, Torino, Einaudi, 1955. Of great interest, and a good read, is C. GAIGNEBET – M.C. FLORENTIN, *Le Carneval. Essai de mythologie populaire*, Paris 1974, collection 'Le regard de l'histoire' Paris, Peyot, 1974. For the North European tradition, reference is made to Jöel LEFEBVRE, *Les fols et la folie*, Paris, Librairie Klincksieck, 1968.

3 See III.1., note 3, p.75, *De dignitate hominis.*

4 Italian edition used is the one with translation, critical text, introduction and notes by G. MARTINI, Bologna, Zanichelli, 1942. All the English versions are mine. See also the edition of *Momus* with English translation by Sarah Knight, Latin text edited by Virginia Brown and Sarah Knight, I Tatti Renaissance Library, 8, Harvard University Press, 2003.

5 The ship, beside being the precise metaphor for state (organized hierarchical society) as from Aristoteles and Dante (*Convivio* IV, iv, 5-7) carries also the connotations of the ship of the dead (shadowed by Charon), of the ship of life which protects and supports life in the voyage over the sea of time, a ship which can protect and support when well governed, while it can lead to perdition and ruin if ill-guided and rebellious, like the pirates' ship here, or indeed the Ship of Fools.

6 Water is matter without form, time without limits, origin of everything yet also unknown future and unmarked destinations, outwith the chartered territory, toward worlds beyond. Enclosed water is somehow regulated, given shape, yet it is only mirror to what is reflected in it; it reflects, and so it is capable of many images, ambiguous, capable of taking other forms, symbol of life like the baptismal font, yet also of ritual death by water.

7 L.B. ALBERTI, *Momus, seu de Principe*, cit. pp. 286-287

8 *Ibidem*, p. 287

9 *Ibidem*, p. 195

10 *Ibidem*, p. 194

11 Even in the title, and considering the statement of intention as declared, the opposites are clear.

12 On this matter see also V.2. and the reference to the Statutes in note 30.

13 DANTE, *Purgatorio*, IV, 77: '*Nave senza nocchiero in gran tempesta*'; *Convivio, IV, iv, 5-7*

14 L.B. ALBERTI, *Momus, seu de Principe*, cit. p. 286 in fact the model from Aristotle and Dante

15 *Ibidem.*

16 Useful studies on the Carnival can be Piero CAMPORESI, *Il paese della fame*, Bologna, 1978; M. BAKHTIN, *Rabelais and his World*, MIT, Cambridge, Massachusetts, 1963. As for the food theme, even Aretino, when he remembers the *fusta,* or a *fusta*, in the *Ragionamento delle Corti*, adds a cauldron of *maccheroni*. And see III.2., note 22

17 L.B. ALBERTI, *Momus, seu de Principe*, cit. p. 288. Emphasis on the chiefs, more or less low, and hierarchies and order, reversed, is not 'a joke'.

18 See J.G. FRAZER, *The Golden Bough*, London, 1967, pp. 405-406, *passim*.

19 L.B. ALBERTI, *Momus, seu de Principe*, cit. p. 288.

20 A similar 'leap', not due to a human-political conspiracy within the festa, but seemingly due to the very nature, deemed transgessive, of the *festa*, (if not even by "God's will") will be recognized in the historical episode reported by Giovanni VILLANI and discussed below at I.3.(pp.21-24)

21 L.B. ALBERTI, *Momus, seu de Principe*, cit. p.VII.

22 Giovanni VILLANI, *Croniche*, Trieste I857, vol.I, cap. LIII, pp. 200-201; Antonio PUCCI, *Centiloquio*, ed. Firenze 1773, in Delizie degli eruditi toscani, vol. 4, pp. 195-198, lines not numbered.

23 We find recognizable masks in the devils in the *Tentazioni di Sant'Antonio* by Agnolo GADDI (Santa Croce), as well as tridents and hooks in BOTTICELLI's drawings.

24 Evidence of ancient human sacrifice remained in the usage of "celebrating" those condemned to the death penalty as if they were 'mock kings' before being hanged or burned at the stake. Giordano Bruno, the mathematician, philosopher, cosmologist, condemned as heretic by the Roman Church, as late as 1600, was burned at the stake, in Rome in Campo dei Fiori, as a Carnival king on 17 February 1600, Ash Wednesday, as it is still done with the Carnival effigy – to cleanse man from sin – as an example. As for human sacrifice in Roman times, see J.G. FRAZER, *The Golden Bough* cit., pp763-768. Later – see III.1., note 11, pp.75-76, note 33, p. 79; (IV.6.i) the fate of the 'heretic' fra Dolcino will also come into consideration.

25 In Florence the 'mad', unless their families took charge, were kept in prison in the Stinche in a special section called *la pazzeria* (*Statuto delle Stinche*, A.S.F., Stinche 1) . Only in the XVIII the institution of proper asylums began.

26 There are indications that, as well as being sent out of the walls of the cities, they might have been embarked on ships to be later abandoned on some deserted shore. M. FOUCAULT, *Storia della follia nell'etá classica,* trad it. Milano 1963, p. 31. He has found only one document from the XVI century indicating that the fools were given in charge to sailors on the barges of the Rhine. It seems, however, that when not imprisoned, they were excluded from the cities. See Salvatore BATTAGLIA, *Mitografia del personaggio*, Milano, Rizzoli, 1968, p. 144. Also Jöel LEFEBVRE, *Les fols et la folie*, cit., p.85: '*il n'y aura pas de débarquement sur aucune île nouvelle...c'est une anti-utopie*'.

There is a painting by Pietro ANNIGONI, it is a negative *Stultifera navis*: it is a boat becalmed, on a murky sea, under a dismal sky; the fools can be seen from a breach on the side, and the ship is piled up with a mess of masts, sails, ropes; the prow is already dipping into the water, yet the feeling of the picture is one of immobility in a sort of paralysis of 'death in life' in a salty remote desert.

27 There was a successful *Navigatio Sancti Brenctani* (VI-VII century) which was one of the best known legends of the Middle Ages, it had more than one hundred Latin versions, and many in vernacular. Brendan was a real VI century Irish Bishop who is reported to have travelled with some of his monks in a leather coracle over the North Atlantic Ocean, to have found found the island of the dead, and also one island with angels, and came back to Ireland after seven years of travel. See also II.2, note19, p. 45; note 23, p.46.

28 *Non plus sapere quam opporteat*: Paul – of course. *Epistle to the Romans*, 12.

29 And indeed, how many who were considered 'fools', or mad, or heretical, and condemned in one age, had to be recognized later as having opened new vistas, having contributed to knowledge? Many. Very many.

30 Giorgio VASARI, *Le vite dei maggiori*..., Vol.V, p.396 and note 2, and Vol. IX, p. 27

31 See for example, Annabella ROSSI and Roberto de SIMONE, *Carnevale si chiama Vincenzo Roma,* 1977, p. 64 and note 17. Also O. PIANIGIANI, *Vocabolario etimologico della lingua italiana:* Carnevale. In Germany during festivals one also finds '*des chars, (parfois en forme de navire)*', see Jöel LEFEBVRE, *Les fols et la folie* cit., p.87.. Also Karl LEHMAN *The Ship Fountain from the Victory of Samothrace to the Galera*, in P. WILLIAMS LEHMAN and K. LEHMAN, *Samothracian Reflections*, Princeton U.P., 1973, p. 213 and note 62.

32 See G. DURAND, *Le strutture antropologiche dell' immaginario*, Italian translation, Bari, Dedalo, 1972, p.251 – the etymology suggested for the word Arca-ark is from the linguistic and psychic family of *arceo* – I contain – and *arcanum* – secret – is an interesting one. As for egg – vase – boat – ship – see pp. 253-255. *Les structures anthropologiques de l'imaginaire,* Paris, Dunod, 1992, p. 286.

CHAPTER II

The battering and survival of the *festa*.

II.1. *The 'spoil sports' (* **I guastafeste** *). The* **festa** *exiled, on land and sea.*

Between *Quattrocento* and *Cinquecento* another tradition came to light, and was widely popular in the North of Europe and in part of France : the tradition of the *Narrenschiff* (soon translated and imitated, in Latin, translated into English by Alexander Barclay, probably from a Latin version, published in 1509). It is a verse narrative, in German, intended to oppose the festive spirit, with a moralistic and punitive purpose. The fiction, however, makes use of the traditional festive characters, the fools and the ship of fools, the '*conscience narragonique*', which is scorned and censured [1].

It seems important to bring this anti- festive tradition to evidence in order to distinguish it from festive tradition, and particularly from the *Fusta dei Matti*. They may be connected as far as the tradition is concerned, but are in opposite fields, and I don't see that any question of derivation can be entertained – as it has been suggested to me on two occasions by professionals playing it vaguely by ear. Distant sources are common no doubt – fools and the cart and ship of fools can be seen as archetypes, therefore emerging in different places without having to derive from one another – but the treatment and the spirit in this case are distinctly divergent. Brant the moralist is the 'odd one out'. The Florentine festive tradition is sufficiently early and rich to sustain our festive *Fusta piena di matti* as stemming out of autonomous traditional local sources.

The didactic satirical poem *Das Narrenschiff* by Sebastian Brant was published, in German, in Basel on the main day of the Carnival, that is on Shrove Tuesday, of 1494 .[2] The day of publication is meant to be a counter blow to Carnival 'folly' which raged in the Northern cities, where it was said to have spread from Italy[3], and which, in those years, was the butt of raging Northern censors.[4]

On the day of the climax of the festivities, Shrove Tuesday, 222 salvos in Alsatian dialect boom from a sort of pulpit [5]. The 222 stanzas of the poem – each an example, each intended to fustigate the folly of each of the orders of society (on the pattern of the Medieval *Dance of Death*), each order guilty, according to the censor, for the chaos he sees in his inventory of the world – thunder from a sort of pulpit [6] meant to strike fear into the hearts of revellers. The factors of the disruption of order, the factors on which correction strikes are 'the individual', the *festa*, imagination, knowledge, the spirit of 'anarchy'. On a ship of fools (by no means a new idea) they are all exposed: the individuals with their fancies, their dreams, their search for knowledge – the illustrations will show fools with their baubles – the baubles being bladders filled with wind-soul, mirrors, miniature portraits of the bearers, all symbols of self knowledge, as I argue elsewhere in this essay and is also unusually accepted by specialists (cfr. Jöel Lefebvre, *Les Fols et la Folie*, often quoted) – 111 fools led by fools to a fools' paradise, chastised and excluded, sent to get lost at sea, to death by water, on Carnival Tuesday 1494. The result was a magnificent edition by Johann Bergmann von Olpe, a university friend of Brant's in Basel, with woodcuts most probably by the young Dürer[7], both beautiful and useful.

In Florence

In Florence as well, on a Carnival (Shrove) Tuesday, only a few years later, there was a violent attack against the festive spirit, and Carnival was chased away. It was Savonarola time. Up to 1498 the Dominican friar Savonarola, who had taken charge of Florence in a sort of dictatorial republic, had celebrated with grim fanaticism a reversal of Carnival. He organized the '*capannucc*'', ritualistic fires, in the squares of the city, where the 'Vanities' of festivity were set on fire. The Vanities were ornaments, books, musical instruments, clothes, all collected, or rather looted, by his bands of youths (the *fanciullini*, hymn-singing authorized young hooligans) from the houses of Florence, damning to hell the 'follies' which used to be enjoyed by the people at Carnival time, in a veritable ritual cleansing by fire and in the very same squares of Florence. He, the friar would-be prophet, will be burnt, after hanging, as a heretic, in the same main square too, the Piazza della Signoria, later in 1498. Retribution over retribution.

On the occasion of the Carnival of 1498 (1497 – Florentine old reckoning) we find a *Carnasciale* – the personification of Carnival, that is of the follies of the world, of festive disorder, of instinctual life allowed to be satisfied (once a year), of excess, and so on. *Carnasciale* (a mock-king) is deposed and driven out of the city[8]. We meet him – or rather someone who makes fun of him, a *piagnone*, meets him and tells the story. He has met *Carnasciale* who is leaving, out of the walls of the city, accompanied by his ass [9] who carries his worldly possessions, with his bundle on his shoulder, rather in a bad shape, wearing a tattered cloak. The *Piagnone*, a follower of Savonarola now in power (the *piagnoni* will later be absorbed or recycled into the category, or faction, of the *Cappucci, or popolani*) taunts and teases him.

'*Chi t'ha tanto schernito, Che 'l mantel t'habbi stracciato?* – Who has mistreated you, so badly as to tear up your cloak?' [10] The *piagnone* presents him as an example of what happens to a madman who has no faith, to an unbeliever, to someone with 'his brains in his feet – *Ch'ha 'l cervel nelle scarpette*', someone, indeed, 'who has gambled off his capital, *che si è giocato il capitale*' [11]. He asks *Carnasciale* 'Are you fleeing from the Officer/bailiff?'. The 'Officer' would have orders to put him into the debtors' prison, or 'as mad': *furiosus vel prodigus*, was the legal definition of madness. This unbeliever, *Carnasciale,* replies that the Florentines have condemned him to fire, so he is going because '*Pazo è chi non li crede* – Mad is he who does not believe them'.

The Florentines had expelled the Medici (1494) and the *festa*, now they have Savonarola and a declared republic, which claims to be based on 'high religious and moral values'. He called it a republic, but a byword was *Cristo Re*, Christ the King, the friar being his representative in Florence, with absolute power, obviously. The *piagnone* however, as a good Florentine, boasts of it in commercial terms: '*Con Viva Cristo! hanno fatto tale acquisto* -With the *Viva Cristo!* they got a good bargain'.

The Florentines, good and wise merchants as they are, have sold Carnasciale down the river, he has no value now.

So *Carnasciale* takes the road.

'I have felt so undervalued now
facing a certain major King;
whereby full of sorrow
I am going to Rome where I am believed'

'Disprezar ognor m' ho visto
Per un certo Re maggiore;
Onde mosso da dolore
Vonne a Roma che mi crede,'

II.2. *Triumphal return.*

Carnasciale's instinct was right, as was to be expected from a representative of instinctual life. The right road to survival was the road to Rome. The Medici were all in exile in Rome.

It is from Rome that, with the Medici. the festivals returns. The Medici will return with great official glory in 1512, restored to power in Florence, backed by the Pope, Julius II at first, and Leo X, the Medici pope, soon after. So the carnivals will return, and the dreams of a Golden Age – the higher mode of the lands of Cockaine and the Happy Isles – not Brant's bankrupt fools' paradise. '*Le tems revient'*, Lorenzo the Magnigficent's *motto*, is revived, the times of the Golden Age are back again.

The *Carnasciale* of the poem of 1498, this '*pazo che non crede* – madman and infidel', the essence of the *festa* whom we have just seen as poor and fleeing the fire, in his exile had followed the road of the Mèdici (Piero, Giuliano and Giovanni, the Cardinal, Lorenzo's sons) and, although this may not be the sense of the poem, he will be back. It will take him some years, but he will be back.

As the Mèdici return, in 1512, *Carnasciale* will also return, promoted to public office himself, in the government's employ, when the Mèdici themselves will form the *Compagnie* of the *Diamante* (Giuliano), and of the *Broncone* (young Lorenzo his nephew), to organize the revels and the celebrations, as well as to *govern the city.* [12]

I do like to stress that this king of the *festa*, this mock-king, had been described as poor, prodigal and mad, clearly a fool, and a fool wearing a tattered cloak which had been torn while on his back. He comes and goes to and from Rome, like the Mèdici, like the *festa*, and, most notably for the purposes of this study, like *Carafulla*, who will be found at the head of the *Fusta piena di matti*.

With *Carafulla* then, also a ship comes to Florence, a festive ship of fools, our *Fusta*. From Rome it comes, where Leo X is at the head of the Ship of Salvation, where his treasury coins were called *navicelle,* where there is talk of a Venetian fleet. So here is the *Fusta piena di matti,* the small agile Venetian ship, full of fools.

This ship comes to land successfully as a splendid and resonant apparition, led through the streets of Renaissance Florence as a herald of the celebration of the feast of Saint John the Baptist patron of the city, in full swing of Papal patronage, heralding three feast days with processions and pageants of classical inspiration celebrating the rightful restoration of the Mèdici. Pageants on the new Golden Age (*Il trionfo dell'età dell' oro*) had been paraded on the previous carnival, and the ideal return of Lorenzo *il Magnifico* is implicit also in the *Trionfo di Camillo* now, and in the new world of young Lorenzo, his grandson and name bearer.

The *Narrenschiff*, by the law professor from Basel, later mayor of Strasbourg, Sebastian Brant, 'son of a craftsman, become an intellectual, a civil servant and official censor'[13], had been a ship launched as a grim prophecy of damnation, a sad moralistic satire 'with no humour or poetry'[14], in an attempt at crushing the follies [15] of the world, and in particular the 'folly' of the festive spirit.. Now the *Fusta dei matti* comes to Florence, a fully festive ship indeed, to announce and open the celebrations. She is the herald of a new dreams of a better world – the Golden Age.

It is a ship of fools indeed , the *Fusta piena di matti,* which acts as the herald of the official festival in Florence, the festival of the restoration of the Medici, and of the restoration of the *festa*.

This ship is governed by *Carafulla*, 'utterly mad', yet chosen as an example to all the Florentines by Leo X himself, for his unselfish interest for the good and well being of the city of Florence his homeland. Leo X's praise for *Carafulla* is reported by Nardi and will be examined later[16].

A ship of life, on the sea of the world is by no means a new idea, it is found in myth, in literature, (think of the Argonauts, of the Ark, of the Odyssey, the barge of Isis, and many more) as well as in popular tradition. One finds it in popular festivals in the form of a cart or a ship with fools and devils [17] . It is not only a means of isolation[18], a ship that separated the fools from the wholesome and proper, but it is also a ship that has a life of its own, intent on her own journey, as all life is a journey, a quest, a search, for a lost paradise, perhaps, for a better world [19]

So, a ship like the one of the Teutonic moralist, Luther's precursor[20] also in his nationalistic zeal and malevolence towards the Latin, Italian and Roman world, he for whom '*en 1494 la Renaissance Italienne n' existe pas*'[21] arrives and makes a splendid and resonant appearance, on a cart, in a Renaissance, Catholic, civic Italian festival, in a Florence fully under papal protection, the day before a processional pageant of classical inspiration, the *Trionfo di Camillo* [22].

There is no evidence that Brant's *Narrenshiff* and its numerous translations had yet crossed the Alps to the southern regions.[23] Yet a ship in the foreground now in a context which is the opposite in sense, meaning and direction, bears witness to the symbolical power and richness of the theme of the ship, the fools in it, and the journey. If adventure was seen as deviation and condemned, now 'deviation' is seen as adventure, and far from being excluded, the fools in the *fusta* are at the head of the celebrations for the order restored, and announce the new dreams of the Golden Age.

II. 3. *Cart and ship. By land and by sea.*

It seems artificial now to keep distinguishing between cart and ship. They really are analogous. (v. illustrations, fig. 1, 2,)

Yet we may add a number of reflections on the confluence of the two. Both are in a *festa* which has a focal point in a processional character, which has movement and flow, both in its 'serious' and in its burlesque aspect. The vehicles are cart and ship, the ship being, on land, upon the cart. The *currus navalis* we have seen as a possible source for the word 'carnival'. The ship is dominant, owing to its being deeply symbolical, and being connotated by the ship of the dead [24]. The cart serves a practical purpose in the circumstances – and carries some of the symbolical features of journey and containment as well. The point is that both cart and ship are means of conveyance and containment, they indicate the journey and lend themselves well to show and display their contents, they lend themselves to contain and display a microcosm, and display as well as contain the 'micro-chaos' of the *festa*. Although, eventually, the ship is the one that can go to 'the other world'.

The microcosm and micro-chaos of the *festa* [25] represents the underside, the humus and loam and devil- infested underside of the *hortus conclusus*, the Earthly Paradise, the Happy Island, the promise of which is indeed pursued by ship, but nevertheless is land and of the land. On the other hand the central theme of the *festa* in its historical evolution is the disorder, unreason, to be displayed in order to be understood . But it is to be contained, in order to be exorcised. It includes fools, devils, folly, rebirth after all – an ambivalent mixture, to be sure. It is a theme tht has travelled in time, over lands and through different cultures, collecting ritual elements, mythical, literary, and iconographic connotations from both terrestrial and seafaring cultures. The world of imagination has contributed to its apparel, and appearance (See Chapter I, n. 28, DURAND)

The analogy of ship and cart – conveyance and containers of life, of Everyman, of the fools, of the devils, of the dead, '*on a souvent remarqué les liens entre les thèmes d'Adam, or chacun, de la Mort e de la Folie* – it has been often remarked how there are connections between the themes of Adam, Everyman, Death and Folly, [26] are amply documented in the iconography. Perhaps with a symbolical prevalence of the ship as mentioned before. The cart however is necessary for the practical purpose of conveyance on land, for the procession, for the civic festivals, for the parallel with the condemned to the scaffold or stake (the heretics as we shall see later), to carry the fools, or the dead, or indeed the ship itself, as in the traditions of old. ..

In the "Northern" tradition of the Ship of Fools, a tradition based (rooted) on Carnival and folk customs, used and transformed in literature in *Das Narrenshiff*, the cart and ship are equivalent. The frontispiece of the first edition of *Das Narrenshiff* is a woodcut bearing both cart and ship in the same page, the top half is the cart, the bottom one the ship, (fig 1).

In art, Hyeronimus Bosch has both a ship of fools, and a similar cluster of fools on top of his cart of hay, the *Haywain* [27]. In Bosch, one sees the same group of fools and follies, the same microcosm of 'deviants' (and waylaid), as well as a 'principal' fool, slightly separate, perhaps wiser than the foolish fools intent on feasting, but also more devil-like – he is on the mast, the tree, like the serpent. The group appears both in *The Ship of Fools* now at the Louvre, and on top of the *Haywain*, as well as in *The Concert in the Egg*, and in the *Oyster's Valve.* [28] Furthermore, the same ship can be found as Noah's Ark balanced on the world, and as the "*Ship of Dreams*" heavy on the head of the walking, travelling 'dwarf' (fig 11,). Other ships of a similar shape are to be found in the '*Temptations of S. Anthony*' (Bosch's naturally), and in '*The Garden of Delights* [29]

About a century later from our *fusta*, in another country, the timeless theme is recalled by Don Quixote who will have the opportunity of combining again cart and ship of the dead: [30]

'You carter, coachman or devil' cried he, 'or whatever you may be, let me know immediately whence you come, whither you go, and what strange figures are those who load that carriage, which by the freight rather seems to be Charon's boat, than any terrestrial vehicle.' "Sir," answered the devil [31] very civilly, stopping his cart, "we are strolling players that belong to Angulo's company…."

They were actors, still in their costumes, travelling from village to village.

1 Jöel LEFEBVRE, *Les fols et la folie* cit., p.109: '*La fête et le mythe sont pour Brant deux manifestations de la folie, de la conscience narragonique* – the *fête* and myth are for Brant two manifestations of the conscience of fools and folly' symbols and context of the road to damnation. *Narragonia*, the utopian land of fools is the 'Land of Cockaine'.

2 The satirical poem in German was greeted by its translator into Latin, Jacob LOCHER, as a descendant of the great satires of classical literature. In Brant he saw the heir to Aristophanes, Horace, Persius and Juvenal, he says that Brant is greater than Homer, and has the same national importance as Dante and Petrarch have in Italy, having written in their vernacular language admirable poetry and inventions. Jöel LEFEBVRE, *Les fols et la folie* cit., p. 77 and notes 1 and 2. As for the (well known) publication date, success, editions, translations and everything else concerning the placing of *Das Narrenschiff* into the literary and festive background, reference is to be made to the excellent and well documented study by LEFEBVRE quoted above, and in particular we wish to refer to the chapter *La Nef des fols oú la nostalgie de l'ordo*, pp.77 and following.

3 Jöel LEFEBVRE quotes a debate (a dialogue) on the *furore* which overcomes the Germans during the days of Carnival in which an Italian, Catone, discusses with Podalirius, a German; while the Italian is horrified of the 'barbarous Carnivalesque customs' he sees in Germany, Podalirius defends them as ancient and necessary, and, on the other hand, he says, the Italians do the same (pp.75-67 and Annexe I)

4 'censeur rigide..., tel Brant, predicateurs, tel Geiler De Keyserberg, moralistes, tel Sebastian Frank' the carnival lasted several weeks and such *censeurs* have left evocations 'horrifiées de la fureur de vivre et la frenesie...' and at the end of the century is censured, regulated, and becomes one of the more pressing problems of the time, problem not only for the authorities and the police, but of a great ethical and religious interest – Jöel LEFEBVRE cit., pp. 64-65.

5 *Idem,* p. 145

6 *Idem,* p.133

7 Dürer was in Basel for a short time in 1494. Most of the woodcuts are recognized as being his.

8 *Canzona di un piagnone pel bruciamento delle vanitá nel Carnevale del 1498*, edited by Isidoro DEL LUNGO, Firenze 1864 (but see at p. 18: '*Mille quattro nove e sette[1497],* (the old reckoning) */ a venti di febbraio, / Carnasciale alzó lo staio; / perse il regno a dí venzette*', from a rare contemporary print. With the added description of the Bruciamento by Girolamo BENIVIENI. Another copy can be found among the *Stampe popolari* in the Florence National Library, Pal. E. 6, 6, 151, n.)

9 This Carnasciale is not on a donkey, yet he is accompanied by the necessary beast. We may remind ourselves of the ass' s ears on the fool's hood, of the '*feste asinarie*', and most importantly of the psychopomp ass as in Piero CAMPORESI, *Il paese della fame*, Bologna, il Mulino, 1978, pp. 26-28. See also C. GAIGNEBET, *Le carnaval*, Paris, Peyot, 1974.

10 The tattered (as well as black and poor) cloak, is a fundamental aspect of the fool, the heretic, and , in this essay, of Carafulla. See Chapter III, notes 11, 32. The full discussion of the 'Company of the Tattered Cloak' is in Chapter IV, (IV.6.i). See also Chapter V, note 20.

11 In jurisprudence prodigality was equal to madness. See Marcantonio SAVELLI, Venezia 1748, p. 338 par. 3, and p. 339, par. 8. In the XII tables, the first and basic tenets of Roman Law, table V, establishes the treatment of '*Furiosus vel prodigus*' as if they were the same (i.e. to be kept under tutelage). See also Piero CAMPORESI, *Il paese della fame*, cit. p. 64 and pp.93-95.

12 See the *Capitoli della Compagnia del Broncone* (edited by G. PALAGI, Firenze 1972), first chapter: '*I nobili et gravi sopradecti giovani* – of the Florentine families allied with the Medici – *A hanno due intenti principali; uno essere uniti e concordi tra loro quanto è possibile, l'altro dilectare la cittá generosamente...et questo pensano sia la loro conservazione* – the noble and serious young men

mentioned above have two principal purposes, one is to be united and in agreement among themselves as much as possible, the other is to entertain the city generously, and this they think is their own preservation', p.10. See also Bartolomeo CERRETANI, in the *Sommario e estratto della sua storia,* at Chapter III, note 18, of the present study.

See also my article *Un' occasione in cui la storia detta il canto alla festa*, in *Il teatro dei Medici*, monographic number of 'Quaderni di teatro', year II, n.7, (March 1980), pp.114-134.

13 Brant will also hold the office of Censor of Publications in the city of Strasbourg which is the first city in Germany to have such an office. See Jöel LEFEBVRE cit., p. 147.

14 Jöel LEFEBVRE cit., p.133.

15 It may be interesting to note here that Brant too reveals a kind of 'folly' widely investigated in contemporary literature, i.e. melancholy. It does not seem Brant was acquainted with them. See Jöel LEFEBVRE cit., p. 147. As for melancholy as illness see also Vanna GENTILI, *La recita della follia,* Torino, P.B.E., 1978, p.9, note 10.

16 See below, Chapter III, at III.3.

17 See R. KLEIN, *Un aspect de l'hermeneutique à l'age de l'humanisme classique. Le theme du fou et 'l'hironie humaniste*. In: *Umanesimo ed ermeneutica*, Padova, Cedam, 1963, p. 17: '*Qu'il s'agisse de nefs ou barques, de traineaux, comme Bosch d'un char de foin, c'est l'idée de vehicule qui importe avant tout, nous sommes embarquès'*... See also Jöel LEFEBVRE cit., p. 87 for the Germanic tradition. As for Florence see: Poggio BRACCIOLINI, *Oratio prima in Vallam* , cit., and Chapter I of the present essay.

18 This is the thesis of M. FOUCAULT, in his *Histoire de la folie à*... [p.31 trad it...]

19 The search for a new world, for a happy world beyond the seas, undertaken by those who are presumably affected by '*conscience narragonique*' is nothing else than the quest for that world that *'Saturno reggeva nel tempo aureo'*, that Golden Age which was supposed to be reborn in Florence with the present Medicean-Laurentian restoration (see Jacopo NARDI, *Trionfo dell'etá dell'oro*; VASARI describes the sumptuous pageants in detail in the Life of Pontormo, without forgetting to mention the pathetic and emblematic episode of the death – by suffocation from the gold paint – of the *putto dorato,* the twelve year old son of a poor baker who, for a little money, had impersonated the reborn golden age, painted gold all over, and dying for it. The same conscience dictated the vision in the anonymous *Capitolo qual narra di un mondo nuovo trovato nel mar Oceano* (early XVI century, quoted by Piero CAMPORESI in *La maschera di Bertoldo*, Torino, Einaudi, 1976, p. 311), and specifically for Florence the vision of Saturn's world in the *Selva seconda* by Lorenzo il Magnifico (*Scritti d'amore*, Milano, Rizzoli, 1958, p. 306)

In the anonymous *Capitolo* we find dreams of a land where 'there are no peasants or workers, everybody is rich, everybody has all he wants' – *Non ci lá contadini nè villani / Ognun è ricco, ognun ha ció che vole* – (vv. 73-74) and 'fields and villages are not measured as there is enough for everybody everywhere' – *non sono partiti campi nè contrade / che la roba per tutto ne avanza* – (vv. 88-89) and also 'the sun and moon never set, it is never night, and the days are always clear, nor there is any quarrel or any argument either@' - *Mai non tramonta lá nè sol nè luna, / Mai non c'è notte, e sempre chiaro el giorno, / Nè vi son lite o quistion alcuna'* (vv. 94-96)

And in the *Selva seconda*: 'The liberal land gave life to all without anybody having to wound her with plough or spade' – *La terra liberal dava vita / comunemente in quel bel tempo a tutti / Non da vomero o marra ancor ferita produceva*.... (stanza 85). And 'Human life was long and happy; the truth was the same in reality and appearance: desire was restrained and contented, nor was there conception of 'mine' and 'yours' – *Era il viver umano più lungo e lieto: / era e pareva un medesimo il vero: / frenato e contento era ogni disìo / nè conosceva il mondo 'tuo' e 'mio'* (stanza 84) and flowers and fruit 'were never destroyed either by sun or frost' – *non mai dal sol, non mai dal gel distrutti* – (stanza 85).

The dreams are the same. When on the learned level it is literature, and it is accepted as work of the imagination. On the popular level it is play and remains in the realm of 'folly'. Yet we are all entitled to long for our Lost – or imagined – Paradise, and to cherish the hope of finding it again one day.

In the everyday world, in a practical sense, we should not forget that such drive, such desire, such quest had just recently (1492) led to the discovery of the New World of the Americas.

Saint Brendan too, an Irish Bishop, who had founded several monasteries is reported having sailed on a seven year voyage with a company of monks in search of the Islands of the Blessed. See the X century *Navigatio Sancti Brenctani*. Elaborations of the legend suggest that they may have crossed to America.....and inspired Columbus. It is one of the best known of Saints' legends of the Middle Ages, it is found in more than 100 Latin MS, and translations in the vernacular. See also note 23 below.

20 Jöel LEFEBVRE cit., p 76 '*Vingt cinq ans avant la Reforme, la Nef est deja le signe des temps*'

21 Jöel LEFEBVRE cit., p.137: '*Le chapître 92 de la Nef s'oppose à la convinction d'un Celeste, pour qui le sèjour d'ètudes en Italie reste indispensable, et d'un Locher, qui continue d'envier la Grece et Rome favorisées par les Muses' and 'Cette fierté nationale, que Luther fara sienne et élè vera au rang de doctrine... contribuait à isoler les pays allemandes des grand courants de la pensée européenne'.*

22 The *Fusta piena di i Matti* also carries a message, a special message over and beyond the didactic function of fools in festivals where they are exposed to ridicule because of their diversity, and clubbed by devils to give pleasure to the people. The point of this, and of the *Trionfo di Camillo,* will be made fully later: see Chapter V, at V.1.

23 See Jöel LEFEBVRE cit., pp. 161-163. It is in fact only towards the end of the XVI century that poems on the model of *Das Narrenschiff,* albeit burlesque in character, are to be found: see G.C. CROCE, *La barca de' rovinati che parte per Trebisonda. Dove si invitano tutti i falliti, consumati e male andati, e tutti quelli che non possono comparire al mondo per i debiti* (poverty and debt, to be noticed) and in *La compagnia de' Macinati i quali sono imbarcati a Patrasso per andare a Trebisonda. Dove si sente il grandissimo numero de' falliti e consumati.....* Titles quoted by Piero CAMPORESI, *Il paese della fame* cit., pp. 93-94.

24 With regard to a boat, or boats, of the dead, on which the souls find conveyance to the other world, as we find an interesting ritual enactment in the South of Italy, near Naples, in the cult of the *Madonna dell'Arco* ('*Arco*' probably from *Arca* = Ark) celebrated annually on Easter Monday (obviously connected with the descent to the underworld and the resurrection of Christ), when people go in procession to the Sanctuary (most likely the place of an ancient Mithraic temple) to take votive boats to the Virgin. The principal protagonists are the *fuienti*, men dressed in white, who climb to the Sanctuary carrying boats on their shoulders, and clearly represent the souls of the dead – people are also known to drive up in cars with boats tied on their roofs. {See Annabella ROSSI e Roberto DE SIMONE, *Carnevale si chiamava Vincenzo,* Roma, 1977)

The search for the Happy Islands is a version of the search for the lost Paradise, which after all is Paradise, the promised prize for a rightful life; it is rather obvious that the journey of the soul should be a sea voyage. This is documented both in Northern mythologies, as in the Mediterranean ones.

See the introduction to the *Navigatio Sancti Brenctani*, edited by M. A. GRIGNANI, Milano, Bompiani, 1975, in particular pp.15 and 16, and p.20. See also n.18 above.

25 'The identity of the world and of chaos', that which Gilles DELEUZE calls the *caosmo*, quoted from P. CAMPORESI, *Il paese della fame*, cit., p.110.

26 R. KLEIN, *Le theme du fou et l'ironie Humaniste*, cit., p.17.

27 Jöel LEFEBVRE, *Les fols et la folie, cit., p.87* indicates that '*des chars (parfois en forme de navire) promenés à l'occasion du Carneval, à travers les rues de certaines villes d'Allemagne*'. In his note 45, however he stresses the ship as a literary theme. Bosch *Haywain*.

28 BOSCH , Hyeronimus...

29 Hyeronimus BOSCH,

30 Miguel de CERVANTES, *Don Quixote* – (1604 – 1615) Translated by P.A. Motteux. Wordsworth Classics, 1993. Part Two, Chapter xi, p. 430.

31 The devil is an actor. They have not changed their costumes, as they will perform again in the next town.

CHAPTER III

The *Fusta piena di Matti* – San Giovanni 1514.

III. 1. '...e io son la follia che vo cercando il mar ch'è periglioso'. *'...and I am Folly who goes exploring the sea that is perilous'* (Chiaro Davanzati – XIII century).

Both a ship with fools – like the one launched as a polemic against the '*festa*' on Carnival day 1494, with an underlying but obvious, and fundamental, fate of shipwreck and death by water – and a 'fool with no faith', the *Carnasciale* Prince of Fools chased from Florence because he 'had been condemned to the fire' on Carnival day 1498 (1497 in Florentine old reckoning)[1] both meet again in Florence, in triumph, in one of those festive occasions which Savonarola and Brant had so fervently condemned.

Here are the Fools, be they silly or mad, at the centre of things. A group of jesters, headed by Carafulla, in the *Fusta*, a Midsummer ship for San Giovanni, acting as collective herald for the feast of the Patron Saint of the city, San Giovanni, are led through the streets of Florence,[2] in a ship, on a cart – pulled by oxen.

Here are these figures of the *indignitas hominis*, the representatives of un-reason, in a world which not only held the *dignitas hominis* at the centre of its philosophical speculation [3], but also a world which was to be shortly proven of a different shape from that of the flat sheet of known drawn maps. It will be round, and soon to be displaced from the centre of the universe, a world rich in new vistas, yet also new uncertainties. The excellence and dignity of reason must have been seen as a most precious anchor for society, even more so when becoming more elusive.

Reason was, with ever greater urgency, to provide a stabilizing function for man, now that he finds under his feet a world that is not flat, as known in the maps and books but round now, all to be re-designed and calculated, and to be soon robbed of its fixed position at the centre of the universe – a fixed position: basis of all truths and conceptions of reality...or basic error and therefore deception from time immemorial, of the senses and the intellect? Soon the earth was to be seen adrift in a new universe, new and unknown 'where there is no visible or recognizable path' [4].

So here are the Fools, symbols of un-reason, symbolically adrift in an unknown and perilous sea, in this more similar to *Chacun,* or Everyman, than one would like to admit, prey to doubt and to Evil. Or perhaps to hope? Here they are showing, and showing off, the example of their madness, their silliness, their irresponsible behaviour (or is it perhaps freedom?), their impotence, even (or is it acceptance, perhaps, of their marginal status?),[5] making of themselves *iucundissimum spectaculum* in the '*Fusta piena di matti*' for the Feast of Saint John the Baptist of 1514. Here are the Fools, visible essence of the '*festa*', in Florence.

It is to be remembered that this was an old tradition. Poggio Bracciolini mentions the old custom of parading fools in a cart as in triumph in festivals in Florence as a matter of fact. Chiaro Davanzati, much earlier, actually takes on the person to Folly, as he travels on perilous seas.

And the fact that news of this *Fusta piena di matti* of 1514 has reached us means only that it was, on that occasion, an event to be reported officially and in detail. It was organized by the official Masters of the Revels (probably the *Compagnia del Broncone*), most likely with a particular agenda of their own. But it does not mean it was the only one of the kind during festivals and carnivals. We have reconstructed the tradition from various indications in Chapter One.

This *Fusta piena di matti* of 1514, like many of the celebrations of these years after the Mèdici restoration of 1512, finds a careful chronicler, it is described in all its details which are both interesting and amusing.

Giovanni Cambi records in his *Istorie* [6] that:

'The year 1514, on the evening of the 22nd day [of June] the Magistrates, with the Six [7] [della Mercatura] went on the procession with the Offerings[8]. And also, while the said procession was going on that said street, a *fusta* full of fools, that is jesters and buffoons, also went, with many devils at the foot of the said *fusta*, and they played many pranks and buffooneries, and having put in the *fusta* a certain character, who was a little silly but smart of tongue and amusing, and was known by the nickname [9] of Maestro Antonio di Pierrozzo da Vespignano, who was a maker of hoods[10], and whom they had caught the day before on demand of the organizers *(I festaioli*, the masters of the revels), and had put him in the palace of the *Podestà*, and then on the said day they put him on the *Fusta,* dressed in his black cloak and hood, as he was normally clothed, which was rather worn, because he was poor, and those devils with their hooks tore it off his back.[11] I believe they clothed him anew afterwards.

While they were going on the said procession they came across Gio. Tancredi, citizen and craftsman, of the Quart. of S. Croce, who wore and/or carried the wool and was much more foolish than Maestro Antonio mentioned above, because he was not able to do anything else than carry and wear wool, and he never thought he could become 'maestro', and in 50 years never changed his trade; all at once those devils, who were at the foot of the *fusta*, caught him, the *fusta* sent down a basket, and suddenly pulled him up into the *fusta,* and put him to rowing; and with a club (cudgel, bludgeon) made of leather (cowhide) filled with wind hit him several times so as to make him row well, him and the others'.

Bartolomeo Masi too saw this *fusta*, a ship well built of wood and carried on a wagon pulled by two pairs of oxen.

'...that was the xxii day of said [June] a solemn and beautiful procession was made...And afterwards, after dinner, through the whole of Florence went a *fusta,* well built of wood [and carried] on a wagon pulled by two pairs of oxen. It was well constructed, both in size and with all the complements like a *fusta.*' [12] .

In another brief description, an anonymous poem printed in Guasti in his *Le feste di S. Giovanni Batista* we read of the small 'castle':

'the leader (*il Duca*) is in the first 'tabernacle' of the handsome ship, which is full of fools who mock and tease one another giving abundant proof of their foolishness[13].

Bartolomeo Masi continues:

'... and they had put in her certain fools or madmen, or we should say half-mad, to entertain the crowd. And behind the said fusta about thirty [men] were dressed as devils, with certain hooks and bells in their hands[14]; these devils caught someone here and there and put him on to the fusta; if he wanted to get out, they made him pay a fine-forfeit'.

It was a game, yes, but it was regulated and compulsory; if the weaker were to escape from the stronger, they had to pay a forfeit.

Although this is a case of a San Giovanni rather than a Carnival [15], the essential meaning of the theme, i.e. its symbolism, does not change, nor does the value of its connotation.

S. Giovanni is a cardinal feast in the yearly cycle, the Summer Solstice, or Midsummer. It is the Summer turn-of-the-year. The feast of San Giovanni Battista is a Solstice feast, it is the opposite and complementary Solstice to the one when Christmas and the Winter festivals, including the carnival, are celebrated.

The Summer Solstice is the 'other door of the sky', the one where the sun begins its descent, as at the Winter Solstice it had started its rising. The correspondence and coincidence of these opposites is recognized also by Christian hagiography and its calendar(ial) distribution [16] which puts St John the Baptist, Christ's 'feral' twin, at Midsummer for that very reason..

The expressive-emblematic element of both festivals, Midwinter and Midsummer, however, is the devil – centre and essence of the negative supernatural.

The evidence we have of this feast of San Giovanni of 1514, as recorded by contemporary historians refers to a civic pageant, fully 'organized' and 'late', or 'early modern' if we want. In these early years of the XVI century, as already remarked, the pageants had a 'propaganda' value. As indeed those of Lorenzo had, at least the ones that have been recorded. The subjects used for the processional pageants were mythological, allegorical or historical, openly proposing a thesis (and apotheosis) on a learned level. Folk/popular themes inhabited the margins, involved the public generically, occasionally inspired some nostalgic edition of collected *Canti Carnascialeschi* and left only sporadic evidence. It is a fortunate case that, inspired by historical/political contemporary topics[17] the masters of the revels, the *Compagnia del Broncone* most likely, found it convenient to dream up a revival of the *currus stultorum atque insanorum* (of I. 1.) combined with the *currus navalis* of the ancient Carnival tradition, of which, therefore, these records (Cambi, Masi, Sanudo), confirm the existence, and perhaps give us the form.

It is thanks to the fact that the *Fusta piena di matti* has been staged on the streets of Florence at a time when celebratory festivals required the greatest resonance, and when recording them was expected both in order to publicize them and in order to make sure they would be remembered, that we have full records of the event. It would not have necessarily happened for the regular yearly celebration of popular festivals of which we have to glean information here and there. On this occasion we have a full description and therefore a detailed recollection of the themes and the shows that Poggio in 1451 remembered fleetingly as of the 'old times'. The political content, the details of which will be discussed later, has been carried by the traditional container, normal in the festivals, but this time used very ably as a disguise.

The feast of St. John the Baptist, or Midsummer, is a traditional high point in the yearly festivals, in many traditions, but in Florence the San Giovanni had become specifically civic. It was, and still is, the feast of the patron saint of the city. The principal families, who were also in government, were involved in the organization of the festivities, and their involvement had also political value and aims. The institution of the '*compagnie*' according to the emblems adopted, both Medicean, of the *Diamante* (the Diamond ring) and of the *Broncone* (the log or branch soon identified as of laurel sprouting green leaves to signify a Laurentian return) was, in 1512, one of the first acts of Government at the restoration of the Mèdici rule in the city. The younger members of the governing and allied families were intended to belong to them, and, so occupied, had two specific aims: one, of keeping friendship and solidarity among themselves; the other, to keep the city entertained, and this was thought to be for their own 'conservation'. The intention was that these *compagnie* would have an opportunity to preserve family alliance and run the city. In fact it was recorded that 'no magistrates were appointed that did not belong to one of these groups'.[18]

It is not clear what happened of Giuliano's *Compagnia del Diamante*, since Giuliano was very occupied in Rome, at least since the election of Leo X in1513. And it feels safe to assume, also in view of the polemical undercurrent in the satirical *fusta*, and of the *Canzona di Firenzuola* of 1515 [19], that it was the *Compagnia del Broncone* (perhaps in part absorbinhg the *Diamante*) the one that remained active in the festivals.

This is why now, in 1514, a San Giovanni could not but be recorded. And it was, fully, at home and abroad.

III.2. *Fools, by land and sea.*

The Carnivalesque cart (which may well have often been a ship – we know that *currus navalis* has been suggested as a possible etymology for the term Carnival) of which we have only an indirect mention by Poggio Bracciolini, and without a proper description, is seen as through a fog, while it was probably a common object in the processions. On the other hand we have four descriptions (as far as I know) of this single elaborate and colourful *Fusta piena di Matti*, whose golden shell has sailed into history, perhaps just when it had ceased being one of the usual elements taken for granted in the everyday-life festivals.

This officially staged show remains. In it, however, are embodied both the ritual model, and the single attributes, of the underlying tradition.

The model is the one indicated by Poggio, of leading the fools in mock triumph, with a prince of fools, though the streets of Florence, only a memory already in the middle of the XV century, as we have mentioned in Chapter One, at I.1.

The model surfaces here in the 1514 *festa* enriched with all the details of the occasion. The details recall those found in the 1304 *festa* (the case related by Villani and Pucci). And the satirical slant finds a premonition in the fictional/didactic episode in *Momus* (mid XV century and many reprints) where the suggestion of a political agenda in the 'game' is unmistakable. This will become a reality in the *Fusta* as the analysis proceeds.

In Alberti we find echoes, and a fictional elaboration, of the '*festa*' as a mirror of society, in its virtual political application (both as *exemplum,* and as realistic conspiracy). We discern 'instructions' both relevant to the principles which refer to order, hierarchies, obedience, and relevant to the consciousness of the precarious standing of the same principles, of their unstable equilibrium, of the possibilities of a sudden and fatal overturning ever present and menacing. Furthermore, everything in the *Momus* episode is elaborated on the *fulcrum* of the the chief. At the centre of a '*festa*' which moves according to ritual rules, there is the head, the (mock) king. He is the centre of the events and the meanings of the game.

In the *Carraia* episode of 1304 (I.3.), on the other hand, we have seen a factual event, which mirrors and precipitates the '*festa*' into reality: there are real deaths and a real journey to the underworld from what was meant to be only a festive fiction. There was not a political agenda here. Not a hint of political subversion. Yet a revolution takes place nevertheless – between the natural and the supernatural planes.

In that '*festa*' turned into real life, the significant occurrence is not of a socio-political character but of a religious-philosophical one. The scene that is being staged deals in the supernatural, and a presumed, or invented, knowledge of the supernatural, while the subsequent occurrence, which is a historical fact, seems to achieve, pragmatically, a knowledge of that same supernatural. Those deaths, the ritual yet real deaths of those who wanted to look and know of 'news of the other world', are a metaphor of 'the fall' (the tasting of forbidden knowledge), if one looks at the episode from a theological perspective, or simply a very real evidence of the dangers of wanting to know too much, a metaphor of the *journey of no return* of knowledge.[20]

The '*festa*', however, and in particular this one of 1514, with the *Fusta piena di matti*' in progress, adorned as it is with all the traditional symbols of popular/mythical imagination, as well as with real persons who are living symbols, occurs in a moment of which it is part, and which at the same time it creates. The event is in balance half-way between fictional elaboration and historical fact. It takes part in both. It is of the imagination and of reality at the same time.

The tradition of the '*festa*', balanced as it is between the imaginary and the real worlds, is by necessity an ambivalent and elusive tradition, a tradition which although functioning through ritual patterns, subsumes the transformations of reality, and changes according to the historical moment. This is precisely the case for this festival of 1514, under examination now.

The recognizable ritual traditional characters, the elected mock-king and the the devils, mandatory in a *festa,* do not have a place either in the text or the iconography of *Das Narrenschiff.* In the latter, however, the themes of 'the Fall', and of the danger accompanying the search for knowledge – the *nosce-te-ipsum* characters seen as mindless fools – are well in evidence.

In any case the basic festive element **not** present in Brant is the essential ritual presence of a chief, king, governor or master. While he is outstanding in the *Fusta piena di matti*. He is Antonio di Pierrozzo da Vespignano called *il Carafulla*, 'duca' of the ship, governor of the company, prince of fools, king of the '*festa*', dutifully and ritually elected as we shall see in his *Rituale di elezione* at III.3. following. Similarly essential is the underworld as represented in the *Fusta* with devils surrounding it, wielding hooks and clubs made of cowhide filled with wind-soul. [21]

That water and the ship or ships which transport, holding them in, the fools on their voyage in which not everyone sees sense, should be common elements (to *Das Narrenschiff* and the *Fusta*) is not to be wondered at, considering the statute of archetype which both the water (as flowing time, and world unknown) and the ship (journey of life, temporary refuge) enjoy.

Both the water, the sea as unchartered territory, the boat of the dead and the cart/ship of fools (those outside normal life) are symbols that recur, as has been seen, in the Florentine tradition, both literary and festive. Echoes are possible, but there is no need to look elsewhere for models.

The games, fictional or historical, and the deaths, take place in the water, and so do the punishments, in the cauldrons managed by the devils as recorded by Villani, and in the pool that is a mirror of the bigger unchartered and unregulated water, as well as a reversed ship, in Alberti's *Momus*.

The ship, precarious container, reversible and reversed, unstable/unsafe shell, but to be cherished and protected as the wise devil Charon teaches – he does not leave it out of his sight, neither in the world of the dead nor in that of the living, on sea, land or marshes – has now been accepted and recognized as a presence belonging in the tradition of thought, and play, (both intellectual and festive) of Florence.

That this ship is, in 1514, a *fusta*, a Venetian ship, is a fact that belongs to the topical allusions it is meant to carry. These will be examined in the second part of this study.

III.3. *The mad Captain.* *The* 'Stultorum atque insanorum principatum' *of Carafulla.*

Maestro Antonio di Pierrozzo da Vespignano, who made hoods, was well known in Florence. Nardi writes that he was 'called Carafulla and commonly reputed in Florence as a buffoon or a fool (madman)[22]. The rather laconic reference by Nardi, the fairly extended and detailed – for a 'common man' - reference by Benedetto Varchi, and the reports in Aretino indicate that Carafulla is a character with all the due insignia typical of a fool and a jester. The essential fool-jester is revealed, to begin with, by the nickname he is known by, Carafulla. Such a name contains the word Fool (follis) and Buffoon (buffa). Both (the breath, the puff, wind) are integral part of the carnivalesque theme which refers to the idea of the souls of the dead, and thus to the supernatural. The figure of the Fool, both in his way of being (a state on psychic instability), visionary, unreal, errant, a wanderer, changeable and undefined, half hidden in his fool's hood, and by means of his constant and characteristic attribute, the fool's bauble, a bladder full of wind, i.e, containing 'soul', which at some point became the fool's own miniaturized face (*marotte*) – thus making him an empty head full of wind – is also to be connected to the devil. This connection to be developed in the section III.4.i and III.4.ii of this chapter.

The appellation of Carafulla, for Maestro Antonio di Pierrozzo da Vespignano, known as buffoon or fool, deserves a little attention. Experienced as he was in handling extravagant etymologies he may well have invented it himself. Or it may have been applied to him meaning fool's face – *cara* being face in Spanish – and *fulla* from *follis/buffa* a puff of wind [23] (follis, fool, buffa, buffone, from which also fool and buffoon). Later we will see him also actually described as 'an empty head, full of whims and fanciful notions'.[24]

Of the fool, Carafulla also wore the uniform, the hood [25] (fool's hoods), and the peculiarity of his trade being a maker of hoods (*Maestro Antonio che faceva cappucci* – a maker of hoods) seems an extraordinary coincidence .[26] (see also IV.6.i. and IV.6.ii)

That Carafulla was a well known character in Florence seems clear. It is important, however, to notice that also the Roman court had heard of him in a very public way, quite recently. He was in Rome, together with many Florentines (from whom he will be distinguished, we shall soon see) who, on the occasion of the rising to the papacy of Giovanni de' Medici, now Leo X, had hastened to Rome, for the festivities celebrating the election, but were also lingering there presumably in the hope of obtaining favours and honours. Leo X seems to have known Carafulla well, and he makes of him an example of probity and unselfishness in a mention which must have been public enough to be reported by the official historian Nardi. This is what Nardi records:

> *'Che fra tanta moltitudine di parenti e di amici e d'ogni sorte di Fiorentini che l'andavano a visitare e fargli riverenze e baciargli i piedi, disse adunque papa Leone che fra tante centinaia di cittadini, non ne aveva trovato se non uno savio (e quegli era stato Piero Soderini) e uno notabilmente matto (e questi era stato un maestro Antonio cappucciaio chiamato il Carafulla) i quali soli, lasciando da parte i propri interessi, gli avevano raccomandato instantemente la città di Fiorenza sua patria*
>
> 'among such a multitude of relatives, friends and all sorts of Florentines who went to visit him, and bow to him and kiss his slipper, Papa Leone said then, that among so many hundreds of citizens, he had not found but a wise one (and that was Piero Soderini), and a notably mad one (and this was a Maestro Antonio maker of hoods called the Carafulla...) who were the only ones who, leaving their own interests aside, had recommended to him immediately the city of Florence his homeland.'[27]

That was Maestro Antonio (di Pierrozzo da Vespignano, when he was recorded with a full name and city of birth for the official business of his election), notably mad, who is now elected for the 'reversed day' of the 'reversed world' of the *festa* – as the youngest of the clerics became the bishop of fools, or the village fool was made mock king in the Medieval Winter festivals. Now, with his poor man's (and madman's, as we shall see) black cloak, with the hood which half hides him but also distinguishes and signifies him, he is at the head of the *Fusta,* he is the chosen jester for this official *festa* of celebration, for which, we shall see, the *Fusta piena di matti* that Carafulla leads is itself the herald and collective jester.

Election ritual

Carafulla had performed a nocturnal ritual of election (and, symbolically, of initiation), as detailed in Cambi: 'they had taken him the day before, on petition of the masters of the revels, and put him in the Palace of the '*Podestà*', and then, on the said day into the said *fusta*...', He spent the night in the Palace and the morning after was put into the *fusta.*[28]. This symbolically can be considered a ritual of initiation, yet it followed, shortened, the procedure of the real politically-administrative election and the subsequent festivities for the end of the magistrates' term of office.

The *Palazzo del Podestà* was the seat of the '*Capitano del Popolo*', from 1250, and then (from 1261) of the "*Podestà*", who was '*il magistato forestiero*', the magistrate from outside, a foreigner who would have the task of keeping a reasonable equilibrium among the parties in the city. Counting on the neutrality of a foreigner, the city had established among its institutions a sort of *arbiter*, a referee, a 'someone' outwith and, hopefully, above the political conflict or rivalries.

Being Carafulla an outsider, both in his geographical origin – he was *da Vespignano* [29] – and in his function of jester, he was eminently suitable to that office. The coincidence is well suited, although in the festive 'reversal', to someone who can be a parallel '*arbiter'* (whether the actual office is functioning or superseded at the time), to the outsider Maestro Antonio da Vespignano.

Carafulla, then, is kept in the Palace of the *Podestà* for a symbolical stretch of time, which happens to be the night (a suitable time of darkness for initiation), and exits in the morning as Prince of the festa, chief, captain, master of the *fusta*.

Another relevant parallel is that a *festa* also was the custom in Florence on the occasion of the election of the Magistrates forming the *Signoria* – during the *comune*, when the members of government take office, as reported by Goro Dati 'on the morning when they take office (the Eight Priors, and the *gonfalonieri di giustizia*, the Keepers of the Seals of the Law, the Magistrates of Justice, and so on) the whole city celebrates, the shops close, and the citizens go to the city square (*piazza della Signoria*) to receive and celebrate those that leave office'.[30]

Carafulla then is received on exiting the Palace of the Podestà as normally those who had finished their turn of office, 'those who come out' used to be received . The Magistrates elected to govern the city were renewed every two months, and while in office they performed their civic duty full time, they lived in the government palace, 'where they sleep and take their meals '*...questi due mesi stanno in Palagio fermi e ivi mangiano e dormono'* [31] and are entertained by an official 'Gentleman herald', (see V.1. and notes)

As the new magistrates take up office, in the morning, the ones who have completed their tour of duty come out and are feasted by the citizens they have served. '*...si fa festa in tutta la cittá con le botteghe serrate e tutto il popolo va alla piazza per far compagnia a quelli che escono'*. Carafulla then, for the purposes of the festival, is both the elected and the one that comes out. He comes out of the Palace of power (his term of office telescoped into one night of initiation) and enters the festive day. In both functions he is at the center of the festivities, rigorously ambivalent in the sum of his functions, and in being the celebrated and the celebrant at the same time. The qualification of being , or rather passing for, "*un pocho isciemo*", 'a bit of a fool', is what he needs to gain his place as mock-king, Governor of the *fusta*..

Later Gio. Tancredi will come along (more in IV.5.). to be taken into the game, as he is '*più sciocco assai*', much more foolish, so as to make the relevance of the qualification even more recognizable

This ritual not only does it adhere to the Florentine traditional civic ceremonial of election time (or the memory of it), but is also faithful to the tradition in use in the Medieval Carnival rituals. We find, for example that in Padua, for the ritual *Rapresentatio Herodis in nocte Epiphania* (which opened the Carnival season) a mock-king Herod was elected the night before the festive performance that was to take place the following day in the cathedral, where mock-king Herod accompanied by his ministers, acts out a ritual of 'beating the Bishop, the canons and the scholars with an air-filled bladder'[32].

In the *festa* those who are normally in authority are to be ritually, but really, mocked and illtreated, castigated, scoffed, insulted – for the day, or season, of the reversal of roles.

Thus Carafulla, the professional fool impersonating a chief for the time of the *festa*, is being attacked by the devils who tear his cloak off his back with their hooks. [33]

Leaving for later the catching of Gio.Tancredi, apparently extemporaneous, but not really, we must proceed to the other basic element of the festive tradition, the devils.

III.4.i. *The Devils (and the Fool).*

'Coi raffi e con gli unciun gente cattiva
che parean tutti diavoli dell'inferno'

"With stick and hooks wicked (ugly) people
who all seemed devils from hell.

'Contraffatti diavoli e sannuti
che forcon di letame avean in mano
di piú ragion tutti neri e sannuti.
(A. PUCCI Centiloquio)

Got up as devils with long fangs
carrying pitchforks in their hands
in various shapes, all sooty and long fanged'.

These are devils in Florence in the *festa* on the Arno in 1304 presented in the first chapter at I..3.

Devils do not have a part in the 'Northern' iconography of *Das Narrenschiff*, and it seems clear to me that the devils in Florence fulfil the function of representing the evil and vices which in the Northern tradition are incarnated in the fools. Hood, coxcomb, ass's ears, vacuous masks grinning or grimacing (fig. 1), they are evil' and 'error', (erring-errant and wandering indeed) vagabond personifications of instincts and vices. Costumes and attributes are both of the devil and of the fool.

There will be later a more complex yet analogous 'moral-satirical' iconography in Bosch. With amazing and moving imagination he takes apart, and recreates, a range of deformities to cover the range of the evil-disorder-sin in a cosmic chaos of precise details reconstructed as examples of the hell of folly, or simply of the unknown, of un-reason and un-rule (with its own reason and rules, however), deformed, different, unfinished, ambiguous.

The indication is that the devil, who hits the fool with his club [34], is indeed a double of the fool. He castigates the condemned, or the elected. On the other hand, the devil is condemned too, in the first place, but for the *festa*, as in his hell, he is the jailer as well as the outcast.

The fool takes to the road, or to the sea, on a search for something (the self, self-knowledge, reality, the golden age) which escapes him. The image (of himself) which he carries, his bauble, is both a fixed answer and a certainty (his sardonic truth) – what he carries can be his own grimacing face, a mirror, a bladder full of wind or soul, on top of a stick, like the world that sits on top of the sceptre – yet it is also a jest, a joke, a fiction. It is his truth as well as *vanitas vanitatum*, which is also a philosopical truth . The fool goes, errant, exile, on an apparently senseless yet persistent search.

For the feast of the patron saint of Florence, *San Giovanni*, on the other hand, there are very realistic conventional devils, with hooks [35] (the reversal of the Bishop's pastoral staff, the crosier) and phallic clubs made of leather (descending from the leather straps of the Roman *Saturnalia*, and the early fools' baubles), and bells. They probably wear masks with horns and beards. They are regular Mediterranean devils direct descendants of the pagan god Pan [36] condemned to the underworld by Christian theology in order to deny and repress instinctual nature. In practice, however, that same theology allows temporary expressions of the same instinctual nature, as in these devils, for didactical purposes, exorcism and catharsis. That is the function of the early Carnivals. Furthermore, it is the same theology that makes of them an instrument of its own power both symbolically, on setting them upon the fools (and making them the gaolers of the damned), or simply using them as decorative and exemplary 'effect' during a procession on a Saint's day, in a *festa* of Midsummer, dedicated to San Giovanni [37] as in the case of the *Fusta piena di matti* under examination now .

As for the devil/fool as doubles, an indication of the transition from 'fool' to 'devil' in one of the many translations of *Das Narrenschiff* (in Latin and the vernacular) can be found in a woodcut (see fig. 10) for *La grand nef des folles* (1502), the translation by Josse Bade, wherein there is a representation of the Fall, with Adam, Eve, the tree and the serpent, in a garden of Eden *(hortus conclusus)* transformed into into a boat, with fools turning into devils at the oars. 'This ship in opposition to the ship of the Church, or of Wholeness, is suggested by an idea previous to Brant's (which comes from an anonymous sermon of circa 1460)' [38] In the more Latin Catholic area, and with a closer biblical-theological connection, the nordic fool turns into a Catholic devil.

The French ship of the J. Bade edition is a veritable point of transition in the representation of Evil: here there are creatures that 'were' fools, wearing a hood and bells, but they already seem to have captured the other fools (those who have lost the grace) and they ferry them over the water. The boatload consists of Adam and Eve and the *Tree of Knowledge* still carrying the serpent (with the face of a woman) [39]. This is the *hortus conclusus* turned into a **boat**. The faces of the two beings at the oars, instead of a grinning or bewildered mask normally given to the fools, carry a countenance of threat and intention – the two seem to consult with each other) as if they had a plan, a route to follow. From their hoods we see very definite horns breaking through over the ass's ears and bells, they do not carry the bauble, the *marotte* of self knowledge, they do not wear a cloak, their legs and arms are hairy, and their hands are turning into talons. They are in the process of turning into devils. All these details can be examined in the illustrations, fig. 10.

Furthermore, these transitional beings, between fool and devil, **man the oars**. They are not drifting helplessly. Those fools metamorphosing into devils are obeying to a sense of direction, not their own, we know the story. They are in service, and certainly not drifting. They have their orders.

It is a change from the senseless and directionless drift of the fools as portrayed by Brant and, for him, by Dürer. Those are adrift – illustrations show a rudderless ship, the sail a sort of flagging rag, or just a sagging standard with no control or propulsion power (fig.3 and 4), and none of their cargo is intent on anything but their toys, games and pipes. The fools seem to have no care or intent (outside themselves). But in the theology perhaps more dogmatic and prescriptive of the Frenchman, and because he addresses a culture less influenced by the rumbles and winds of Reformation, there emerges a positive, intentional and driven Evil which thinks and drives the boat with its human load in a calculated and determined direction. They are taking others to the gates of hell, and that's that.

No doubt, no hope, no pursuit/quest for the Happy Isles, the Islands of the Blest, or the Golden Age.

It is true that also the ship of fools is a negative example to a society meant to be on an orderly, guided (by the Church), sublimated perhaps, journey towards salvation of which the fools are ignorant or uncaring. Brant's ship, in the mind of its author is destined to shipwreck in the sea of the world he knows. That's what he teaches. But his crowd of fools sailing into the unknown, singing, playing[40], and by no means forgetting to hold on to their symbol of self-knowledge, the *marotte,* the ever present and defining 'bauble' (see for instance fig.4, where the pipe-player holds up a very obvious one for all of them), who knows, they may find themselves in a better story after all.

Those fools in fact will meet up again – and we will meet them – still laughing and singing, and indeed preaching, in the world of Erasmus of Rotterdam [41] who, with his *Praise of Folly,* not only will he take Folly onto *terra firma*, the solid land (of reason) of which maps are drawn, with discernible roads (that Gelasto knew), but he will also take Her to climb safely up the steps of the pulpit from where she can preach and explain a few truths. **She**, Folly, is the daughter of Pluto, the god of (underground) riches. She is 'one – indeed the only one – whose divine powers can gladden the hearts of gods and men'. Her opening words announce this as she steps forward 'to address this crowded assembly'.

What was seen, from Brant's perspective, as a sinful lack of restraint and, in Josse Bade as a lack of obedience to the prescriptions of the law , and by both of them seen as sinful rejection of the dogmas and the power of the Father who orders, preaches and promises "certainties", can on the other hand be seen as a – dangerous, if we want – choice of freedom, a choice of doubt, a choice of breaking the schemes and dogmas, which may result in a choice of clarity and honesty. This choice allows the fools the opportunity of a joyous rebellion which can even bring them to find wonders unknown – or indeed real wisdom, as the joyous (even triumphal) vitality of Erasmus's Folly demonstrates [42].

This choice can reach the wisdom of new interpretations of reality, beyond the one upheld by preachers and merchants, grammarians and pedants. Doubt and ambivalence are part of life in and of the world, but they are also part of life's riches, in its many aspects and meanings.

For the moralist who depends on the Medieval sermon and its fixed prohibitions for his certainties, doubt is negative (as is mobility, as is hope in the unknown which makes one set sail on dangerous seas). Doubt here equals *dementia*, un-reason, and is not allowed: either one follows fixed "certainties" as dictated, or one will be lost, cast adrift, out of the limits of the terra firma (flat, of course), as in Brant[43].

Coming towards the South and nearer to the Holy See, catholic dogma (that is starting to be questioned in the North) is more strongly defined and accepted – the archetipe for the transgressor shifts accordingly from the figure of the aimless (apparently) fool, to the definite devil – so that doubt is not a simple lack, not simple un-reason, but is positive and decisive evil, it is the enemy, it is the Devil. So the devil takes over from the simple fool – the fools then are captives driven by devils. They are not even adrift but are being taken to hell. Not even by mistake will they find the Happy Isles [44].

While the devils of Josse Bade, in the woodcut, were creatures in transition, and were rowing, doing some work, in Florence the devils are driving the fools collected in the *Fusta piena di matti*, and keeping them at the oar. The devils are on stable and safe ground, the fools are on board, and are held to the oars – without a possibility of escape – not even aimlessly adrift – by devils with hooks and clubs by means of which they control and drive the fools. The ship is not rudderless and aimless: it is surrounded, held, driven by a precise and well defined power of positive Evil in the person of devils, who, as good servants of power, are not doing the work themselves, but as proper gaolers, overseers, beat with their clubs the slaves at the oars.

And be it clear that while the fools are prisoners, very much 'at sea', in the ship, the Devils are on *terra firma,* with 'their feet on the ground'. This is the dogma. There is no doubt. And no choice.

Yet the ship still allows us dreams. The ship is there, full of fools. The Venetian ship led by Carafulla, full of meaningful fancies..

In the Devils, the danger which was within as 'folly', and outside, vaguely in the weather, the wind, the sea, the world at large, is not just 'danger' any more, but definite theological evil. The Devil is the active enemy, recognized and defined. As a defined, and definite, concept (and representation) it can therefore be contained, and used, by authority (the Church).

Furthermore, apart from those wider considerations, here, in Florence, near in more than one way to the seat of the temporal power of the Church which has structured the management of salvation by way of precise hierarchies, an indefinable vague *dementia* or folly, is not sufficient. This is a civic and institutional occasion which demands a wide resonance. Here the devil, an institution itself, is haunting and driving the fool, to remind him (and us), even in the reversal of values, of hierarchies, and power.

Between devil and fool, we have traced distinctions and a division of tasks. Devil and fool are, however, still aspects of the same object – the dark face of the world, that unknown zone which, when called instinctual evokes, indeed, the devil, while when called irrational evokes the fool. That unknown zone that is not limited or explained within concepts in which reason can circumscribe it – a vast and unknown zone, dangerous because un-mapped and un-legislated. Like the sea where one cannot discern any path. The devil has however been better defined, somehow, as in all monotheistic religions, the Devil is 'the other'. And that's it.

Yet the ship, still allows us dreams

And both the devil, and the fool, are elements of the language of imagery and concepts whereby one tries to express what one seems to catch only glimpses of. In this sense – as instruments of knowledge, as well as imaginative tools – they are elements of great value.

Even in the different modalities in which they appear – one relatively well defined and close, the devil, the other more open and un-defined, the fool – devil and fool are signs of 'danger' – and are aids to knowledge.

Another ambivalence and reversal of this game of mirrors, is that the devil, although definitely damned, nevertheless appears in different guises, a mask, with horns or a cockscomb (fig.9), cock, bear, goat, man, he changes, yet is well defined and characterized. He is damned, irredeemable, his home is in hell. No doubt there.

While the fool, in iconography at least, has a fixed appearance, is always the same, in his hood with cockscomb and ass's ears which camouflage much of his features, a cloak or cape which covers the body. Yet the fool is left undefined, neither man nor woman, indefinite, fleeting – as dodgy as doubt – and itself doubtful indeed. But the fool goes on ships.

Nevertheless, that devil and fool are two aspects of the same symbol is also evident. It is evident from the fact that they both carry the same, or analogous, signs: the cockscomb and cock's feet, horns and ass's ears, the counterpart of the sceptre of command, the club full of wind and the *marotte,* and , last but not least, the bells [45].

III.4.ii. *The distinguishing sign of devil and fool. Club and bauble.* Vanitas vanitatum *and self-knowledge.*

The leather clubs full of wind have a common descent, with the fool's bauble *(marotte)*, from the ritual bladders full of wind (soul) of the Winter festivals, as seen for instance in the *Rapresentatio Herodis in nocte Epiphania* Medieval play of Padua (see III.3., and note 32), they contained "soul", as were the souls of the damned in the show of 1304 told by Villani. A practical origin is also in the credence that "animal souls" were limited in number, and therefore, to preserve the species, as for the pigs for instance, since they were killed in Winter, their "souls" collected symbolically in their bladders, were shown in the Winter festivals (Carnivals).

In the club, as well as the soul association with the theme of the air/wind, there is a recalling and a bridge to the most feared unreason of lower gross instincts, thus the phallic shape. The Fools as well as the devils are constantly connected with it [46].

The fool's bauble has on occasion been represented as clearly phallic (fig.6), although that is not the common representation, as is understandable, the fool being not necessarily defined in gender[47]. The symbology of the fool's bauble can be kept in the realm of knowledge – rational <u>and</u> irrational. On the other hand for the Devil, he being dogmatic, punitive, patriarchal, the phallic emphasis (and we should not forget his direct descendance from club-footed Pan) predominates. Therefore here are those clubs made of leather filled with wind.

The leather clubs are connected also, with implications both on the manifest and the latent planes (the leather and its use), to a motive coming from the fertility rites (and a faunus/goat godhead – Pan again), as is given in Ovid's explanation of the ritual in the Roman *Lupercalia*.

On explaining the origin of the Lupercalia, Ovid [48] tells that the Roman men,had found themselves unable to generate, because the wives they had stolen from the Sabine tribe would not conceive, not even with the help of prayers or magic formulas: '*nec preces nec magico carmine mater eris?* – why do you not become mothers, either with prayers or magic formulas?" they ask the women (l.426). So they go and ask Juno's oracle for help and advice. The Oracle's reply was '*Italides matres, inquit, sacer hircus inito* – Italic mothers, she said, go to the sacred goat' (l.446)

The Romans interpreted the oracular suggestion in a manageable way: they sacrificed the sacred goat and, initially perhaps, took to wearing the goat's skin [49]. Subsequently, however, they used the skin to make leather strips, which they used, as they ran naked through the streets of Rome in what became the feast of the *Lupercalia* (12th February), to strike the women, also naked, the result being, in some way, of making them fertile:

'Ille caprum mactant; jussae sua terga puellae
pellibus exectit percutienda dabant.
Luna resumebat decimo nove cornua motu
virque pater subito, nuptaque mater erat.'

'They kill the goat; with the skins taken from its back
they strike the young women.
As the moon entered her tenth cycle
the man became father, and the mother was married.' (ll. 445-448)

This is how Ovid explains the origin of the February *Lupercalia.* It is an obvious mythologizing of events otherwise difficult to understand (impregnation), it is a ritualization with magical connotations to propitiate fertility, and also possibly with expiation purposes, as seen in the use of prayers, magic formulas and the need for the prescriptive intervention of the oracle.

Whatever the value of Ovid's explanation, it seems to be clear that something like clubs made of leather was in ritual use in Rome at the time of Augustus, and the origin of those leather clubs was already legendary then [50].

The filling with 'wind' of those clubs the devils wield around the *Fusta* in Florence in 1514 indicate them to belong, through submerged and surface connections, in iconography, legend and fiction, to the tradition of the fool and the festivals in the whole of Medieval Europe [51] (illustrations and note 'follis', III.3. n.23)

The iconography of the Fool in the North of Europe, referring in particular to the woodcuts for *Das Narrenschiff* by Dürer, those by Holbein for Erasmus' *Praise of Folly*, and in the production of Hieronymus Bosch, is rather rich and clearly characterized.

We cannot say the same for South of the Alps. Here we find devils instead.

There is, nevertheless, a precious example in a fresco by Giotto in Padua, in the famous Scrovegni chapel (fig.8). This is an allegory of Folly, *Stultitia*, who wears attributes common to the fool and the devil. These are a sort of cockscomb-cum-crown made of feathers and bells, a belt also decorated with bells, a sort of skirt with a long train seemingly representing a cock's tail [52]. She carries a club, of a similar shape to those of the devils by Agnolo Gaddi in Santa Croce in Florence (fig.9), holding it aloft, as if it was not heavy at all, perhaps just full of wind, it is held, in fact, upright, like a fool holds his bauble.

The devils in the painting by Agnolo Gaddi are also of much interest. They exhibit the same model of club as Stultitia [53], while their features resemble those of the devils in Botticelli's drawings for the *Divine Comedy* – these being nearer to the timeof our *Fusta*. They are similar in their bodies, nearly human, in their feet (some have goats' hooves, some cocks' feet, and/or talons), in the rudimentary wings, as well as in their features. Gaddi's devils seem taken from human models wearing a mask (the one with a bull's mask is particularly revealing) as they may have been seen in the masquerades for the Carnival and other feasts in Florence, and whom Gaddi may ave used as models. These devils have also very big ears, like ass's ears – like the Fool. Unfortunately Gaddi's fresco is very high over a chapel in Santa Croce, Florence, and I had difficulty in obtaining a good photograph.

As for devils in a ship the nearest example, both in time and meaning, to the *Fustapiena di matti* is the demonic boat of Charon, and even better the one of the devil Flegiàs – as he is carrying people – and they are not fools, nevertheless they are on a quest, they are searchers – while Charon, in the picture is rowing alone. These are drawn by Botticelli for the Canto VIII of Dante's *Inferno* [54]. The drawings by Botticelli (ante 1481) are earlier than any for Josse Bade's *Stultiferae Naves* (1502) where there are some nascent devils at the oars (see figure 10), and earlier also than the ship of fools in the frontispieces to *Das Narrenschiff* (1492) and its translation. The boats have in common, however, an important detail, they all have some people hanging out of one side of the boat breaking the line of the side of the ship, or boat, which is thus revealed as not properly enclosed, therefore unstable and un-concluded. More on the (un-enclosed) ship soon.

The club/truncheon, and the fool's bauble, counterpart of the sceptre (in the fool's bauble combined also with the globe), and of the pastoral staff, is found unfailingly in the hands of the devil, and the fool, in all ages, from the strips of leather in the Lupercalia, and, on the stage, as the clicking palette of Harlequin [55].

Harlequin's 'palette' (sometimes a double piece of wood) has lost the 'wind', is not a filled bladder, but has preserved the clacking noise – this was a noise (a 'raspberry') produced by buffoons and fools who made it with their mouths, with a strong emission of 'wind' called also 'buffa' – wherefrom the name 'buffoon', or from the filled bladder on the stick and it was a reminder of the 'wind' or soul escaping from the anus, and so a reminder of death.

From the leather strips of the Lupercalia, themselves a memory of phallic symbols in the rite of Dionysos, the path to the 'palette' carried by Harlequin runs through the various versions of clubs and baubles, the *marotte* of the Medieval Carnival Fool, and the clubs of the devils.

The fool's bauble could also actually be the bladder of the pigs killed in Winter, around the Feast of St. Anthony (17th January) filled with the pigs' 'soul', where it was preserved in order to avoid the extinction of the species, since animals' souls were believed to be limited in number [56].

The soul of the world, the souls of the dead, the devils, the supernatural. Therefore, some reversed, the *divine*. However, the bladder full of 'wind' (a 'nothing'), is also an indication, a mention, a warning of *vanitas vanitatum*: the vanity of the world, the vanity of the sceptre (power), the vanity of man who invests in them, and the void in his foolish skull (or head). In fact the filled bladder, the fool's bauble appears, in some instances, as a mirror, where the fool sees himself. He can also turn the mirror towards someone near him, who will see his own fleeting reflection perhaps mingled with that of the fool. This evolves also into a miniature of the fool's face: the '*marotte*' name comes from the face of the 'Marie', a figure of some French Carnivals, where Marie is the caricature of the Mayor, le Maire, and reversed, dressed as a woman, Marie.

The mirror, and the miniaturized face of the fool on top of the bauble leave no doubt as to the reference to self-knowledge, fleeting, fleeing self-knowledge, ever unreachable, yet an ever present search. The only salvation is in its pursuit, yet when found, the result might well be a grinning fool's face in cap and bells. And it comes as a bladder filled with air, a puff of wind, or a mirror capable only of a fleeting ephemeral reflection.

Yet all this has also a realistic basis. R. Klein reminds us that "*la marotte notamment derive de la massue dont on les armait comme defense contre les passants qui leur gettaient des pierres* – the '*marotte*', or bauble, derives from the club or stick, which they, the fools, were allowed to carry as personal defense against the public who threw stones at them". [57] A simple club, or stick, was all that was permitted to the fool, constitutionally defenseless and innocent. The excluded fool carried a little parcel where he kept his worldly possessions, probably attached to his stick, a miserable bundle which was his *ubi consistam*. Similarly, the jester he has become carries the bladder filled with 'wind', or a mirror, or his own portrait, at the tip of his "*marotte*".

It all means that all we have in the world, and that we can carry with us, is nothing but a bladder filled with air, or our soul which is a puff of wind, or a fleeting reflection in a mirror, or indeed the grimacing face of a fool in a hood, with a cockscomb and ass's ears. The fool teaches us. And this is why he is chased away by 'civilized' society. On the other hand he is retained in the courts of kings – we see King Lear, having two, to speak truths that he could not see, or could not say. At court the fool is the entertainer, yes, but also the mouth of truth. He has license to say what nobody else dare(s) say, to and for whoever is the power: the King, the Church [58], the Bishop [59] , those in authority in general[60], to the Pope in Rome[61]. And it may well be for their benefit as well. Should they happen to listen

The head of Government, the *Signore*, holds the seat of power, but he can also be a prisoner in it, because he may have everything to lose. The fool has nothing, and nothing to lose. So one calls on the the fool, to let him say what one can later pretend to ignore. One does not have to take reponsibility for what that irresponsible fool may say. After all it was said by a foolish face half hidden in a hood, by a grinning mask atop a stick, the image of all and everyone. And all that is behind that mask is only a puff of wind.

> *'E la plebe pur ride a tan spectaculo'*
>
> 'and the people yet laugh at such a performance',

the people perhaps only temporarily foolish, but wise, like the fools. They do know something is going on, it is bigger matters, and laughter is the only release.

Or we can read deeper, and one finds the mirror, and 'what was in jest turns into reality': it is us who are that mask over the puff of wind, and the fool speaks to and for everyone.

III.5. *The container that does not contain, the open-ended container. The flaw in the ship ('unenclosed' ship) and unstable passengers.*

All the three ships we have in our sights – the *Fusta piena di matti* of 1514, the one designed by Botticelli (*ante* 1481) for Dante's *Divine Comedy*, and the ones in the illustrations to *Das Narrenschiff* and its translations, are open to exchange and social commerce with the external surroundings. A breach, a gap caused by a body, is kept open on the side of the boat.

The first one, the one by Botticelli for the Canto VII of Dante's *Inferno* has a demon at the oars (Flegiàs) and carries two figures who are heading to the other side of the muddy lake. '*Piú non ci avrai che sol passando il loto* – you shall have us only for the crossing of the Virgil announces to the devil who thought he had two new damned souls in his power. They don't pay a fee or a forfeit, either. One of the figures, however, is leaning out of the side of the boat, as if addressing another figure in the water, with whom he is in contact by the arms. He is pushing it away from the boat, but the gesture is not dissimilar to one that would be needed to help it on board. In any case, the figure of Virgil leans out, and opens a wide breach, in the drawing, in the side of the boat, on the left toward the stern (fig. 12)

Exactly the same effect is displayed by Dürer's boat (see figg. 3 and 4), where on the left, at the stern, a fool is seen holding (or pushing?) another who seems to be falling overboard – someone who pushes out of the margin, breaks the limit(ation), transgresses, spills out. There is a breach in the side of the ship, and some "commerce" with the outside.

It is not clear whether the fool half in and half out is in the process of falling out of a boat too crowded and confused, or whether he is being saved (having previously fallen out from another boat heading to Narragonia), or whether he was late and is trying to catch up by swimming, or whether, in the pushing and shoving of a crowded and confused departure he had been overtaken by someone smarter than himself – all or any of these things being possible for a foolish fool.

In classical Rome too provision was made for disorganized fools. The *Festa stultorum*, the Feast of Fools, was held on the last day of the festivities for the fertility rites. It was kept for those who were so foolish that they could not read, or had nearly missed the banns, therefore they arrived late, when the festival was nearly finished. And so, the last day was officially dedicated to them[62].

Perhaps for one or some of these reasons the 'Ship of Fools' carries a figure half hanging out, breaking the line, making a breach on the side – this makes the ship incomplete, open – if the fool was a late arrival, then the ship was incomplete – if he was one too much then the ship was overloaded – in either case disorganized and ill managed from the start – inconclusive, un-enclosed, precarious, open ended.

And finally, in the Florentine *Fusta* there is the 'assumption' of Giovanni Tancredi, much more foolish than Carafulla, he was so foolish, they say, that he had never even thought of being called Maestro like Carafulla, and who, in fifty years had never changed his trade. He too is half in and half out, not in time, and/or taken by force. And he will be made to pay. Different among the different. Yet even more the same.

It seems a wise choice, and it is, for a Fool to take on someone even more foolish, in a basket, [63] a hanging, swinging, miniaturized ship, a 'Gulliverized' *fusta*.

Giovanni Tancredi in a basket is to the fools in the fusta what the bauble *marotte* is to the Fool.

As '*la marotte est le double du fou, sa propre image en miniature; elle met le fou en abîme, elle est le fou du fou, son miroir et son reflet* – the *marotte* is the double of the fool, it is his own image in miniature; it puts the fool "*en abîme*", it is the fool of the fool, his mirror, his reflection'[64]. So Giovanni Tancredi in the basket is a de-multiplication of Carafulla the Master and all his "*fusta*", his miniaturizing mirror, his *mise en abîme,* his reflection.

As the fools in the ship are surrounded and goaded by the devils, so Giovanni in the basket is now in the fools' power. And as in that basket the *Fusta piena di matti* has its mirror and its miniature, so in Gio. Tancredi Carafulla has his mirror and his *marotte.*

The image of the *fusta* with its fools replicates itself, as well as acquiring the connotations added by Gio. Tancredi, and the added intensity of the miniature thanks to the most foolish of the fools.

Giovanni Tancredi, with his name in odour of knighthood and Crusades, and his pre-falstaffian fate of being 'tossed in a basket', is a figure to which Cambi gives a certain relief. We shall see later that he is probably a *dramatis persona*, a created character, interpreted by an actor [65] (the young Barlachia, see IV.5)

The pageant of the *Fusta piena di Matti* which opened the procession on June 22nd 1514 must have been furnished with a mechanism of pulleys with a basket ready to be let down to collect someone from the public, more or less pre-established and condescending, to be prey of the tomfoolery and the jokes of the fools, jesters or buffoons. It was usual in the pageants to make use of elaborate engineering works for lifting, moving, hiding. The apparatus for lifting somebody from the crowd would certainly be available to the *fusta*.

Masi's version, even though it is less detailed that Cambi's, says just that 'they caught someone and if he wanted to get off they made him pay a forfeit'[66] . This could indicate that this was a game that could be repeated along the way, a game with rules. We are not told by Cambi whether Gio. Tancredi was let off. Gio. Tancredi must have been a special case. Indeed he was.

The chaotic festive ambience where the *fusta* catches some new or late fool is the sea with which all the Ships of Fools have an exchange or commerce.

Back to the ship. This is not a safe ship – it is a ship of fools, indeed – it has a breach, a wound on the side.

In all three cases, however, here is a ship full of excluded beings. It contains, rather precariously, beings that are different, that are excluded, – or free – prisoners or escapees. The ship is in some way flawed. It is at the same time so desirable that its very desirability makes it precarious. It is passing through a chaotic environment, mobile, uncertain, from which one needs protection. The protection, and the salvation, is a ship with a flaw.

The whole, however, is set against an area of stability, the land, '*terra ferma*', order from which the dis-order of the fools is (intended to be) excluded, controlled, caged, removed. But not completely, we have seen. It is also an example. A mirror, reversing and distorting, but a mirror.

On the one hand there seems to be dis-order, the incomplete, the un-organized, the search, too, the journey, the quest. On the other is order, law, certainty – as well as the finite of the dry land that is 'still', is dry and does not move. In the *festa*, the game, the play, (the *ludic space*), one can attempt these distinctions. In reality, in real life (which has movement) the boundaries are not always as clear or constant. Here perhaps is the need for the breach, for 'the flaw'.

The ship is the point of distinction, of separation, and of encounter, together. The ship isolates, but she also transports and connects.

Our ship not altogether 'concluded', with a breach on its side, is a symbol, ambivalent, and necessarily so – a container that holds but not completely – bursting at the seams with fools who are prisoners but free – intended to maintain the separation between the two areas – even though its manifest aim was simply to exclude the fools by enclosing them. The ship has a side that is open to exchange.

Perhaps we may have a case, here, of 'involuntary symbolism' [67] in this breach on the side of the ship which seems nevertheless to hold course unperturbed. The apparently senseless commerce between ship and its environment which these 'containers' seem to allow does carry the symbolism in each, and in the three, of a double ambivalence.

In the breach of our ships, it is not a single artist that has put there 'the signs that form his work'. I see, however, a collective expression and the emerging from the collective unconscious of a symbolism that can be read from the signs that form the collective 'work', when 'the intention of the observer' is attuned to them. Mine is, it seems. I see the breach very clearly and consistently. In the several and different ships, imagined by different authors at different times.

On the one hand, in each we may read the suspicion, the suggestion, of a precarious ship because of the breach (although they do not give signs of lack of balance), of not having the capacity to 'hold water'. Nevertheless they are on the sea that, we know, is perilous and of unstable humour.

On the other hand, to recognize the same sign in the three different examples (plus Bosch), a sign of precariousness and instability, is precisely to recognize one of the distinctive signs of the symbolical stability of this open container, its magnificent hold as a symbol.

The breach in the side of the ship, in its ambivalence, is one of the elements of coincidence (of correspondence, co-value) between the three distinct expressions of the tradition under scrutiny.

The three expressions which we are connecting together, have manifestly dissimilar intents. Botticelli's drawings are of boats of the dead, neither ironical, nor festive. Dürer's intends to illustrate a didactical-ironical poem, anti-festive and moralistic. The *Fusta piena di matti* is a burlesque pageant for a festival – and the breach made by the basket being lowered and lifted, is indeed the jest within the jest, the *mise en abîme* of the *Fusta* itself. Its essence.

It seems that precisely in the breach, in the commerce with the outside, in the relationship between seafarers and 'swimmers', between included and excluded, between enclosed and free, between the fools in the ship and the crowd on dry land, precisely in these comings and goings, we can read also an important point of contact and exchange both *within* each of the three pictures, and *between* the three of them, as they come to form the symbolic system of a 'ship of fools', no matter which the geographical or *genre* tradition [68].

And a last word about *Das Narrenschiff* which has sailed in a wave of popularity over most of Europe during the last years of the XV century, there is 'no evidence' that it has been found South of the Alps in the years near or around these festivities of 1514. This is also the conclusion reached by Lefebvre in his chapter "*La Nef à l'étranger*" (the Ship abroad) [69]. It may well have been heard of, but it was not riding on waves of popularity. And, as a model, well, it was not needed.

So we can return to the Florentine iconographic model, to the Botticelli boats for Dante's work (the latter taking us back to 1300). These boats have already provided a connection in time to the other important reference points: the *'festa'* of 1304 on the river Arno, and the *'festa'* in the swimming pool in *Momus* by Alberti.

Now with the reading of the 'involuntary symbolism' in the several ships, and with the game of capture of someone and who will have to pay a forfeit for being let out of the *fusta*, the boats of the souls of the damned return to being in the forefront and to highlight, so to speak, 'the shadow'.

Botticelli's drawings were in existence, before 1481 – date of the publication of the engravings in a famous Dante edition of 1481 – available to be seen well before the publication of *Das Narrenschiff*, and before the first visit of Dürer to Venice (1494-95). He may even have seen them there.

It is certain, however, that the drawings propose a precise source, *in loco* and in accordance with our *Fusta piena di matti*", therefore those are being adopted as the most direct model for the *Fusta* our ship of fools, turned Venetian, that went for S. Giovanni in 1514.

The iconographic source of the "*Fusta dei Matti*" is in the drawings of the boats of the dead by Botticelli, as her reason of being rests on a long and coherent festive tradition of Florence. The question od the Venetian qualification, is a matter for later.

1 *Carnasciale* had returned, promoted to public office, as was observed (Chapter II, notes 7 and 11, as well as note 18 below), and the official festivals had been frequent, for Carnival and S. Giovanni from the Autumn of the restoration in1512 and well documented (See Masi, Cambi, Nardi, Vasari, as already indicated.)

2 See full discussion about the *Fusta piena di matti* as spirit of the *festa* in the Fifth Chapter, at V.1.

3 PICO della Mirandola, (1463-1494) *De dignitate hominis.* written in 1486 as an introduction – *Oration* – to 900 theses or *Conclusiones,* for a conference in Rome, cancelled and prohibited by pope Innocent III, published postumously in 1496 , also as *Oration,* come to be known as *De dignitate hominis*. It appears commented upon as 'what could be called the original myth of humanism' – or 'if there was such a thing as a manifesto of the Italian Renaissance Giovanni Pico della Mirandola's 'Oration on the Dignity of Man' is it'.

4 Leon Battista ALBERTI, *Momus seu de principe* cit., pp.286-287.

5 See Carafulla in Chapter IV, at IV, 6, i.

6 *Istorie di Giovanni Cambi cittadino fiorentino*, cit., already quoted also earlier in the introductory 'The Stage' .

7 The six of the Merchant Guilds '*I sei della Mercatura con le loro Capitudini, che andaron il primo giorno, dopo la processione grande* (who went the firsr day after the principal procession – this is a record for the San Giovanni of 1454 – to take the offers [to the Church] of all the elected to the government', in: Cesare GUASTI, *Le feste di San Giovanni Batista in Firenze, descritte in prosa e in rima da contemporanei*, Firenze, 1884, p. 22 . See also Goro DATI, *L'istoria di Firenze dal 1380 al 1405*, Norcia, 1904, pp.156-157.

8 '*Andare a hoferta*': was the procession to the cathedral. It was originally meant to take offers to the church, mostly in the form of large wax tapers, which became more and more lavishly ornamented. But the 'offerings', or *doni*, i.e. gifts, given by the Magistrates and by the representatives of the territories belonging to Florence, developed also into the pageants, the *trionfi*, the displays of armed men, and dancers. This year, with the *Trionfo di Camillo* Sanudo *(Diarii, XIII,* p. 313) records that there followed a '*moresca di 31 uomini con la livrea del Magnifico, con la spada a do mani'*, Lorenzo's men, dancing the *moresca*, in his livery and carrying two-handed swords, obviously of the *Compagnia del Broncone*. See also *La canzona di Firenzuola: 'le dame con gli amanti...questi doni balleranno'*, and my article in *Il teatro dei Medici* cit., p.128.

9 As a matter of fact his 'nickname' was *Carafulla,* and *soprannome* was intended for 'da Vespignano', a sort of 'surname' from the nearby town of his origin.

10 The traditional distinctive headgear of the fool is the fool's hood, often with the cock's comb with ass's ears and often bells : 'the cap and bells' of the buffoon and jester. See W. WILLEFORD, *The Fool and His Sceptre*, London, E. Arnold, 1967; Maurice LEVER, *Le sceptre et la marotte*, Paris, Fayard, 1983; also illustrations in Joël LEFEBVRE, *Les fols et la folie* cit.; as well as the illustrations from Dürer and others in this essay. It is a really uncanny coincidence that Carafulla's trade should be that of a maker of hoods.

11 Giovanni CAMBI, *Istorie*, cit. See the devils tormenting the souls of the dead with forks and hooks in the episode from VILLANI above Chapter I at I.3. .See the tattered cloak of the exiled *Carnasciale* above in Chapter II, at II.1. and the black tattered cloak of the *Compagnia del Mantellaccio* which will be discussed in Chapter IV, at IV.6.i. Other relevant footnotes are note 33 below, and at Chapter V, note 20.

The matter of the cloak torn off the fool's back (similarly we should refer to Carnasciale's cloak, torn by someone who scorned him, at II.1., and note 9) is an important matter also with reference to the fool-as-heretic, since we have a definite evidence of a custom, probably widespread on such occasions, perpetrated on Fra Dolcino, condemned as a heretic in 1306. Fra Dolcino (ca 1450-1307) was the leader of a 'sect' first started by Gerardo Segalelli (of whom see note 59 below, and IV.6.i. for the episode of heretic-as fool) against whom a n actual 'crusade' was launched by pope Clemens V, and after months of fighting in the mountains of Piedmont Fra Dolcino was captured and taken to Vercelli to be burned at the stake. On the way to the stake he was tortured by having his very flesh torn off him by people with red hot pincers (on the way to the execution, a brazier with hot coals carried , so that the perpetrators could have the pincers always red-hot ready). See also note 33 in this chapter, below. .

12 Bartolomeo MASI, *Ricordanze*, cit., p. 142. The *ordini* presumably are all the complements of a ship, oars, mast, 'castle'...etc.

13 Cesare GUASTI, *Le feste di S. Giovanni Batista* cit., p. 33

14 So we have the Prince of fools in the forecastle, and the crew of fools all around. Maestro Antonio is the leader *(il Duca),* and he also leads them all into a recalling of Carnival because being Carafulla's real life name Antonio, Master hood-maker, he connects, by way of this uncanny coincidence of his real name, with another Antonio, S. Antonio Abate. S. Antonio Abate – one of the most ancient a prestigious saints of the Christian church (the hermit founder of monasticism, and the one of 'the temptations', apparently died on 17 January 356 AD, and has been grafted to the Winter agricultural festivals. So he, in the calendar, initiates the Midwinter Carnival. S. Antonio also carries the bells or *tintinnabuli* and the 'pastoral'. He carries a wooden stick with fire at the tip – a legend from Sardinia reports that Sant'Antonio had gone into the underworld to gather fire to fight the Winter cold (repored by Filippo VALLA, *Prometeo e S. Antonio Abate*, quoted from Annabella ROSSI e Roberto DE SIMONE, *Il Carnevale si chiama Vincenzo*, cit., p.62). The bells and stick-clubs are carried by the devils, and the *'marotte'* of the fool, who also carries bells – devils and fools are reciprocal doubles – they all carry a sceptre, pastoral. So S. Antonio carrying the fire from hell can be considered 'devil connotated' too, while Antonio Carafulla is definitely Fool connotated. S. Antonio is associated with Winter fire, stolen from hell, with the pig (and he is patron saint of breeders and domestic animals), and with the bells or *tintinnabuli,* or *sonagli*, probably warning the people that he was approaching. Giotto's *Stultitia* is abundantly adorned with bells, and so are the *Narrenschiff* woodcuts, in one of which a fool has even a bouquet of them in his hand. Bells were carried by lepers, by the devils of the '*Mesnie Hellequin*', and by the 'goat men' of Barbagia (Sardinia). See Piero CAMPORESI, *Il paese della fame* cit., a p. 33, note 27. Interesting bells are to be found also in a 'will and testament' by Carnival, who leaves his bells as a legacy to those who don't have any, so that they can do a Moresque (a Morris dance, indeed) for the fools : *'Item, lassa a quei che non han sonai. Che i faccia la moresca per i bai'* – from Giulio Cesare CROCE, *Lo sbandimento, esamine e processo di Carnevale*, in Piero CAMPORESI. *La maschera di Bortoldo,* cit., p. 314. These warning and fools' bells – indicating folly, disease, difference, alteration, red light- are also attacheded to women, see Bernardo GIAMBULLARI, *La conditione et costume delle donne, Intitolato al Sonaglio*, which concludes with '*Finisce il sonaglio delle donne'* by Bernardo GIAMBULLARI, (somehow carrying the '*sonaglio*' himself) Firenze, 1495, in Savonarolian hood (B.N.Fi. P. 6,2)

15 As a matter of fact this *fusta* was echoed in a – probably later – carnival as mentioned by ARETINO, in *Il ragionamento delle corti* (edition consulted: Lanciano 1914 1914, pp. 93-94) where Carafulla in his hood and cloak also appear, as well as the gastronomic-carnivalesque '*Caldaie di maccheroni' cauldrons of food.* Or it was just a fantasized memory used in a *ragionamento* of his own.

16 Mars was the ancient Patron god of Florence (see Dante, *Inferno*, 143-145*)* and had a feast, the Roman *Quinquatrus* at first on March 19th, together with Minerva Mèdica.. Both feasts were then shifted, at the time of Augustus, to 19th June, Midsummer. The position of Patron Saint

of Florence was later given to St. John the Baptist, with a feast at the same time of year, Midsummer. In the distribution of solstices, the Church has given the Winter solstice – the new sun, and therefore hope -as well as taking over the birthday of the god Mitra – to the Christ, while the solstice of decadence – the beginning of the descent of the sun – to the 'feral twin' the Baptist. There is also another St. John, the Evangelist, that is celebrated on December 27th who is a further double. In fact S. John the Evangelist was also related to June 24th , but had been shifted to represent the Church as Bride of Christ, next to Christmas (see Claude GAIGNEBET, *Le carnaval,* cit., p. 45 and notes from the *Legende dorée*), and as a Confessor next to the Martyr (S. Stephen) and near to the feast of the Innocents. Piero CAMPORESI on the other hand, in *Il paese della fame* cit., p. 30, seems to offer another interpretation of the opposition between the two feasts, as he proposes that it was the Baptist who was shifted to June 24th in an attempt to Christianize and absorb the pagan celebration of vegetation and animals. This agrees also with the view of the Baptist as the 'Wild man' or the 'Green man', and as patron of the animals (see also a Jean de l'Ours, in GAIGNEBET, cit., pp. 110-114, for 2nd February). The two possible shifts are in consonance with Church policy to adapt Christian Saints to the pagan gods and rituals of the agrarian cycle.

17 With which we are dealing fully in the second part of this essay.

18 In the *Capitoli della compagnia del Broncone,* edited a cura di G. PALAGI, Firenze, 1972, chapter first we read that the '*nobili e gravi sopradecti giovani*' young of the principal Florentine families faithful to the Mèdici '*hanno due intenti principali: uno , essere uniti e concordi tra loro quanto è possibile, l'altro di dilectare la città generosamente…et questo pensano sia la loro conservazione* – have two main.purposes: one was to be united and in agreement among themselves, the other was to manage generously festivals to please the city…and this they thought was needed to preserve their power.' (p. 10)

And Bartolomeo CERRETANI in the *Sommario e estratto della sua storia* (MS. Magl. II, IV, 19, in the Biblioteca Nazionale di Firenze, carta 17r) records how Giuliano, as soon as he had re-entered the city in 1512, collected the young people of the families whose fathers used to be in the *Compagnie dei Magi e dello Zampillo* of Lorenzo in the XV century and formed the *Compagnia del Diamante*; Lorenzo his nephew formed the *Compagnia del Broncone*, in collaboration and competition for the festivals, but with precise political aims of alliance within power, and the intent was that these *compagnie* should govern the city. Cerretani declares that Aalready no one was made a magistrate that was not one of ours 'and thus the *compagnia* was to govern the city'.

19 See my article dating the collection *Canzone per andare in maschera per carnesciale* to 1515, in *Il teatro dei Medici*, 'Quaderni di teatro' anno II, n. 7, marzo 1980, at pp. 114 – 134, by the rather unwieldy title *Un'occasione in cui la storia detta il canto alla festa*. In it the history and development of the *Broncone* emblem – from being a burning log when it belonged to Piero, to a branch of laurel sprouting leaves for Lorenzo his son, indicating also a renewal of the Magnifico's image – can also be found.

20 See chapter I, at I.3., '*il gioco da beffe avvenne col vero*' and '*mostra che Iddio volesse*' and the prescription of : A*noli plus sapere quam opporteat*' .

21 The souls of the dead in VILLANI as described in PUCCI *Centiloquio (see* Chapter I, I.2.) are '*camicie di paglia ripiene e vesciche di bue piene di vento*','A shirts full of straw and bulls' bladders full of wind'. Wind is soul. See also *Lupercalia* at III.4.2.

22 Jacopo NARDI, *Istorie della città di Firenze*, a cura di A Gelli, Firenzo 1858, vol.II (VI, xix), p.27.

So Carafulla was well known, he was a maker of *cappucci* (hoods), which must have been the common Winter headgear for those who did not wear hats, and also as an eccentric character ready to propose semantic-onomatopoeic etymologies. Benedetto VARCHI, in his dialogue *Ercolano* (published posthumously in 1570) -quotes examples which he calls' modern Tuscan etymologies'. They come from his interlocutor who reports that 'Maestro Antonio Carafulla was never asked by anyone, mad as he was considered to be, without immediately replying..... If he was asked why the *Girandola* was so called, he replied immediately, because it turns, burns and swings, '*gira, arde e dondola*', and having been asked from where the *Bombarda* had its name, he answered without hesitation, because it resounds and burns, '*perchè rimbomba e arde*' edition Firenze 1730, at p.199. CAMBI in the passage we refer to defines him 'a little foolish but smart of tongue and amusing'.

Pietro ARETINO (1492-1556) also remembers Carafulla, or of him, in his *Ragionamento delle Corti* (first published in Venice in 1538 – text consulted: edited by Fulvio Pevere, Mursia, Milano 1995, p.95) – as '*un meschinello che faceva cappucci ed essendo il ricetto degli scioperati, davano di petto nella sua bottega provisanti, astronomi, alchimisti, dottoresse, medicastri ed altre spezie di chiacchieroni, e...le nuove del prete Janni, del Sofí e del Soldano si scaricavano tra loro.*' (a poor devil who made hoods, and being the friend of all the time wasters, in his workshop improvisers, astronomers, alchemists, female doctors, quacks and other types of chatterers let out hot air, and news of the priest Janni, of the Sofí and of the Sultan were exchanged among them – stories of the Crusades and tales of chivalry – quite up to date, if we think of Pulci, Boiardo, Ariosto, Tasso & co.). Aretino uses Carafulla as an example of those 'ruined by the Courts', infact he says Carafulla 'had been put out of joint' by the Court (he was in fact also a professional a court jester for the Medici) and he remembers that Carafulla liked to act out being a king, holding court and talking by himself, as if with his counsellors and advisers whom he then sent off to be hanged. Aretino might have met him in Rome.

Carafulla is also well known to Bernardo Giambullari (see E. ORVIETO, *Un poemetto inedito di Bernardo Giambullari,* in 'Bibliotheque d'Humanisme et Renaissance', Genève, 1977. See also at Chapter IV, IV.5. of the present study. Marin SANUDO, in *Diarii* cit., Vol. XVIII, p.313 knows him and mentions him as *el Carafulla* (the well known Carafulla).

23 *Follis* being a leather bag which in Classical Latin meant 'bellows' C. BATTISTI and G. ALESSIO, *Dizionario etimologico italiano*, Firenze 1950). *Buffone*, and buffoon, from *buffare*, to blow, by blowing out the cheeks, and from the ancient Italian *buffa*, a strong gust of wind, sudden, not continuous, (see also the Italian *bufera*, a violent storm). The fool, central figure of Carnival, in his person with the characteristics of an unstable and psychic state, therefore shamanic, and in his attribute of the bladder on a stick, full of wind, and the 'windy' pranks and jokes, is invested of the (connotations surrounding) constellations of spirit-soul-death-wind, the invisible world, world-and-other-world. In the depth of Winter, when in fact Carnival and the *Feste dei Folli,* in Rome there was a door called *Mundus*, it was a slab of stone in the centre of the city which, lifted, opened the way to the souls of the dead who could then ascend to the ethereal world, the final destination of the soul which is of divine nature, after it had completed its terrestrial cycle. (See GAIGNEBET et FLORENTIN, *Le carnaval* cit., p.60; with regard to the circulation of the souls, see also pp.11-16, pp.26-32, p.52, p.58, and the whole of chapter VII: '*La circulation des souffles*') Piero CAMPORESI, *Il paese della fame* cit., at pp 18, 31, 32, 34, and 48 also touches the event.

Both the fools, and the devils, are figures of the Carnival who celebrate as well as exorcise 'the spirits', the souls of the dead, they represent them and transmit to us the experience, therefore the knowledge. This is the reason for wind, winds, and flatulence jokes (see M. BAKHTIN, *Rabelais and his World*, Cambridge, M.I.T., 1968, p. 131. And RABELAIS himself, obviously)

24 Bernardo GIAMBULLARI, as seen in: E. ORVIETO, *Un poemetto inedito di Bernardo Giambullari*, cit., v 12.

25 See note 10 above, and illustrations. The coxcomb on the hood indicates the realm of instincts, and refers to lust in particular. In the Medieval traditional *Ludi del Testaccio,* in Rome, at the time of Gregory VII, (1073- 1085) the custom was to 'kill a cock symbol of the lust of our loins' (DE BARTHOLOMAEIS, *Le origini della poesia drammatica italiana* cit., p.107). The fool's hood of illustration n. 5, with the coxcomb and ass's ears only just hinted, and a button under the chin, is not greatly dissimilar from the normal hoods we see in Leonardo's sketches of grotesque figures .

26 See later in Chapter IV, at IV.6.ii, the political value of the term '*cappucci*'(hoods or cowls), or the definition '*Cappucci*' referring to political factions.

27 Jacopo NARDI, *Istorie della città di Firenze*, cit., vol.II, ... , xix, p.27. This was happening early in 1513, having Leo X been elected on March 10th (although the news arrived in Florence the following morning, and is generally reported as of the 11th) , see Luca LANDUCCI, *Diario*, (a cura di Jodoco del Badia, Firenze 1883) p. 336, and NARDI cit., vol.II, vii, i., p.63.

28 CAMBI, *Istorie della cittá di Firenze*, cit., see above at III.1., note 5 (and *The Stage*, n.2)

29 Vespignano is a village in the Mugello hills, part of the 'comune' of Vicchio, at about 40 kilometres from Florence. Carafulla was Antonio *di Pierrozzo da Vespignano*, whether he was born in Vespignano, or whether his father was, or his family, I have not ascertained. It is also the birthpalce og Giotto.

30 DATI, Gregorio, *L'istoria di Firenze dal 1380 al 1405*, a cura di Luigi PRATESI , illustrata a pubblicata secondo il codice stradiniano, Norcia, 1904, p. 143 and 145.

31 *Idem,* p.145

32 DE BARTHOLMAEIS, *Le origini della poesia drammatica italiana* cit., pp.151-152, and p. 210. Here we find also the 'blown up bladder', like the fool's bauble, and particularly significant for our devils' clubs made of leather filled with wind, and their being used to beat people up. See also Piero CAMPORESI, *Il paese della fame* cit., p.28.

33 The black cloak will have also a connection to the a recent festive expression in Florence, as it recalls the *Compagnia del Mantellaccio*, as discussed later in Chapter 4, at IV.6.i.

From a ritual point of view, however, the aggression of the devils on *Carafulla*'s cloak reflect a known practice in the treatment of condemned heretics who, on the way to the scaffold, to the fire, were carried through the city on the executioner's cart, and were subjected to the torture of having their actual body scratched and torn off their very back by hot forks and pliers: we have an example in the story of Fra Dolcino and his followers, condemned as heretics reported by ANONIMO SINCRONO in his *Historie* which I quote from E. ROTELLI, *Fra Dolcino,* Torino 1978, p.51: '*fatti salire i condannati sopra un carro...che percorresse tutta la cittá...e che di tanto in tanto, si lacerassero ai rei, con infuocate tenaglie, le carni'* – the condemned were put on a cart and taken through the city so that their flesh could be torn off them with hot irons along the way.

34 With the club which corresponds to the fool's bladder-bauble, self portrait and mirror of the fool, as well as counterpart of the sceptre, symbol of the taunted power.

35 The hooked instrument, pole, is the counterpart of the bishop's crozier, like the stick and bauble-bladder of the fool are of the king's sceptre. They both carry also phallic connotations.. See W. WILLEFORD, *the Fool and his Sceptre,* cit., and Maurice LEVER, *Le sceptre et la marotte,* cit., pp. 53-56, as well as illustations 5, 6 and 9 in the present study.

36 Although it is a well known derivation, one can see James HILLMAN, *Saggio su Pan*, Milano, Adelphi, p.18

37 For more about the devils, it is interesting to examine fig. 6, the reproduction of the *fresco* by Agnolo GADDI (end of XIV century) in Stanta Croce in Florence, one of the many Temptations of St. Anthony. There the devils surround St Anthony and threaten

him with clubs and sticks. They have cloven hooves, and some have cocks' feet (equivalent to the cockscomb on the fool's hood). Cocks'claws for feet are also on some of the devils BOTTICELLI drawings for DANTE's *Divine comedy,* for example *Inferno* XXII and XXIII. Coming back to GADDI, some of is devils show clearly masks on their faces, as if the painter used human models but with masks on, or even remembered carnival figures. From them we can draw information as to the festive devils. As for festive-ritual tradition realtive to cockrels, DE BARTHOLOMAEIS, in *Le origini della poesia drammatica italiana* cit., p. 107 reports that in Rome, in the *ludi del Testaccio*, in the XI century (the times of pope Gregory VII, 1073-1085) they 'kill a cockrel symbolizing the lust of our loins', '*uccidono un gallo simboleggiante la lussuria dei nostri lombi'*.

38 R. KLEIN, *Un aspect de l'hermeneutique à l'age de l'humanisme classique. Le thème du fou et l'ironie humaniste*, in *Umanesiemo e ermeneutica,* Padova, Cedam, 1963, p. 17.

39 See fig.10. This is clearly the *hortus conclusus*, now excluded, and turned into a boat. The counter Earthly Paradise.

40 The prominence of the musician is also interesting, as music – except for church music – was always sinful, and a marker for damnation . See R. HAMMERSTEIN, *Diabolus in Musica*, Bern and Munchen, 1974. It is therefore also indicative that it should be the pipe-player to be in charge of the 'communal' *marotte*, as we see in the illustration (fig.4).

41 The *Encomium Moriae,* that is *The Praise of Folly*, was written in 1509, ostensibly during a journey from Italy, as Erasmus claims in the introduction, or probably in the house of his friend Thomas More to whom it is dedicated. It was published in Paris in 1511, and re-issued some sixty times during the century. So I want to claim it as an important backdrop to the subject in hand, as well as a contemporary expression.

42 Erasmus, in his *Encomuium Moriae*, by making his Folly the daughter of Pluto redeems, in a stroke of genius, also that Greek god that Chistianism had demonized. He presents Pluto in a warm light, and altogether free of sinister implications: '..and the father who generated me, remember, is not that that old and blind Pluto as described by Aristophanes, but the one still young and vigorous, and not only because of youth, but more thanks to that nectar he had drunk in abundance, and not thinned with water, in the banquets of the gods' ERASMUS of Rotterdam, *The Praise of Folly*, [7] .

43 See Chapter or stanza 66 of *Stultifera Navis* (1494) where the roundness of the earth is not admitted .

44 They are not adrift, searching. They have been captured. Captured by their double, the Devil. We may also add that the boats drawn by Botticelli of devils transporting the souls of the damned (pre-1480) may well be the *source* of those in the woodcut we find in the *Stultiferae navis* of Josse Bade (1498)

45 The devils surrounding the *Fusta dei Matti* of 1514 carry *'cierti oncini e campanelle in mano'* 'certain hooks and bells in their hands' (Bartolomeo MASI, *Ricordanze*, cit., p.142). In Giotto's fresco of *Stultitia* in the Cappella degli Scrovegni in Padua (see fig. 8) the crown she has around her head is made of long (cock's) feathers strung upright on a headband that contains also bells: if she does not have a proper cockscomb, certainly the odd skirt she wears has a sort of train like a cock's tail. The gender of the figure is not exactly clear, although the grammatical gender is feminine, naturally, an ambiguity consonant to the fool, like her name. The club she carries is however of the kind of the devils use in Gaddi's picture (in S.ta Croce in Florence. In a high position difficult to photograph) – see fig. 9, as well as n.4 of figure 6. And indeed the *bastoni di cuoio pieni di vento* of the devils around our *Fusta* must have the same appearance.

46 We think it suitable now to remember the connection between club, wind-filled bladder,

and the bells (either as traditionl bells with a hanging ringer, or as those bells that are a sort of sphere containing rattling objects inside – the *grelots* – as worn by the Morris dancers). On the one hand we may have Saint Antony (Sant' Antonio Abate) and his walking stick or better his pastoral or shepherd's hook which he was supposed to have dipped in the fire of hell to bring the warmth of fire to men in the depth of Winter (his feast is 17 January and is the beginning of Carnival – see also above, note 14) He is also carrying a bell, whose 'banger' , is also transposable into the small dried objects enclosed into the round globular bells (the *grelots*) in use in festivals, let's say the Morris Dancers's bells. We can recall the irrational represented in the stone of madness – see Enrico Castelli, *L'umanesimo e la follia,* Roma 1971, ill. Tav. VI-XVI, which reproduces surgical operations to remove the 'stone of folly'. The bladder carried by the fool atop his stick, was often found to contain dried peas, which shaken made a white noise, like a rattle. This was the empty head of the fool, filled with stones of folly, and also a ritual rearrangement of elements. See Maurice LEVER, *Le sceptre et la marotte*, cit. 1983, p.51: *'Ces sonnetes discordantes qui s'agitaaient en desordre nous renvoient à la matièere inorganisée, au chaos primitif'*. We travel therefore, from the *marotte* containing the stones of folly as in a vacuous head, to the globe bells, the *grelots*, miniaturized heads, as far as the small globe-world containing the four elements which are shaken and thus allowed to rearrange and regenerate a world fallen into deathly *'stasi'* for instance in the ancient Egyptian rituals of Isis – Esther HARDING, *Mysteries....* [it trans Astrolabio Roma 1973, p. 188 and notes)

47 The Christian devil is clearly male (as the counterpart of the male god presumably – presumably women were not great enough to be involved in the supernatural...) The fool, on the other hand is genderless, covered up in coats and hoods. Giotto's *Stultitia* is unclear, although she tends to look female, and being an allegorical figure is grammatically female. The other female fool, is Erasmus of Rotterdam's Moria, Folly. And the French name for the fool's bauble, which at times is his portrait, is *marotte*, diminutive for Marie. (See Maurice LEVER cit., p.54, 84 and following. The festivals were naturally occasions for disguise (see in France the *Compagnies de la Mère Folle*), and in iconography the fools are not distinguished as either male or female.

48 OVID, *Fastorum Libri Sex*, Book II, 445-448

49 GAIGNEBET, *Le carnaval*, cit., p.23, rightly observes that it '*fait honneurà la sophistique latine, mais elle ne peut tromper; il s'agit de l'origine de deguises carnevalesques en bouc-loups (luperques) qui fecondaient les femmes*', and the representation of rigid instruments made of leather must have been meant to be phallic, to carry the mimetic-magic connotation propitiatory to fertility.

50 So, rigid and turgid clubs made of leather filled with wind are seen in the hands of the devils, in the XIV centry frescoes, and are in the hands of the devils at the foot of the *Fusta*.

51 See figures 6,7,8,9. In particular the rare and precious example of Giotto's *Stultitia*, with his/her airy club held high, the cockscomb made of feathers, the bells that decorate it. See also note *follis*, note 23 above.

52 The headgear that *Stultitia* wears is almost identical to the one sported by the blue devil with cock's feet in the fresco by Andrea da Firenze (1365) in the *Cappellone degli Spagnoli* in *Santa Maria Novella*, in Florence.

53 Although theirs are held as weapons, not trophies. They are used menacingly and have the appearance of being heavy and able to hurt.

54 The date of Botticelli's drawings is not precisely known. The engravings which illustrate the 1481 edition by Cristoforo Landino are said by the critics (from Vasari) to have been

done by the engraver Baldini on Botticelli's drawings. (*Inferno*, VIII) See figures 12 and 13.

55 As for illustrations of Harlequin, see for instance: DUCHARTRE, *The Italian Comedy*, New York, 1966.

56 C. GAIGNEBET, *Le carnaval,* cit., pp. 62-63

57 See R. KLEIN, *Le thème du fou et l'ironie humaniste*, cit, in *Umanesimo e follia*, cit., p. 12

58 Erasmus uses the mask or *persona* of Folly very skillfully to express his thought (see for example Ch XVII), and to protect himself from punishment from the Church (see J. LEFEBVERE, *Les fols et la folie*, cit., pp.258-268) or answer to censoring theologians. One can say unpalatable truths under the mask of Folly. This is what the *Fusta piena di matti* does.

59 As we have found in the cloak torn by the hooks of the devils a parallel with the torments of the heretic (Fra Dolcino, on the way to the stake and the fire), we may find the example here of Gherardo Segalelli (1240-1300), example of heretic-as-fool. Fra Dolcino's precursor. Gherardo Segalelli was condemned by the Church as a heretic (he was 'a roaming 'minimal' and unauthorised Franciscan, founder of a 'sect' of alternative Christianity, based on poverty, equality, and direct personal contact with God , irregular preacher,) and, at first, imprisoned. Some say that rather than as a heretic, he was initially condemned and imprisoned as a madman and thus spared death. He was however soon taken by the sympathetic and secretly supportive Bishop of Parma, Obizzo Sanvitale into his own palace. He licensed Gherardo Segalelli as a fool or jester and actually had him to eat at his table. ' he Bishop laughed at his words, not taking his talk as being about religion but just as senseless and vacuous chatter' (from Salimbene de Adam, *Cronichetta*, quoted in Elena ROTELLI , *Fra Dolcino* cit., p.30). It is the fool's dress that saved Segalelli's life, for a time.

Having established the connection between heretic and fool, including their poverty, we must add that Gherardo, having been persecuted by several popes (Gregory X, Onorio IV, Nicolò IV), after been saved by Obizzo for a time, was imprisoned once more in 1294, escaped, and eventually he was finally secured by the Inquisitor (Manfredo da Parma) under Boniface VIII and burned at the stake in Parma, on 18 July 1300.

60 See Maurice LEVER, *Le sceptre et la marotte* cit. All of it!

61 The *Fusta piena di matti*, this indeed is what the present essay is about. See the Second part, in particular, and the Epilogue.

62 See GAIGNEBET, *Le carneval*, cit., pp. 22-26

63 The basket carries two relevant messages. One is the link with Carafulla, who amused himself with sending his counsellors to be hanged. But even more relevant is the symbolical value of a miniaturized ship, the 'gulliverized' *fusta*. See DURAND, *Le structures anthropologiques de l'imaginaire,* cit., pp286-289.

64 Maurice LEVER, *Le sceptre et la marotte*, cit., p.54.

65 See at IV.5 below and notes.79 . The Barlachi hypothesis.

66 Bartolomeo MASI, *Ricordanze*... cit., p.42. Gelasto had been in the power of Charon, because he had no money to pay his passage, a sort of forfeit. But Vergil and Dante (*Inferno* VIII, 19-21), the wise men, the saved -more or less- they go free.

67 *Simbolismo involontario* is the definition given by the eminent philosopher Enrico CASTELLI in *Umanesimo e simbolismo involontario*, to '*quel simbolismo sui generis...che affiora in funzione di una certa 'intenzione dell'osservatore', più che da una manifesta tesi dell'artista, nonstante sia dovuto anche all'affiorare di un'immagine presente nell'inconscio dell'artista stesso che dopotutto è colui che ha messo tutti i segni che fanno la sua opera* – involuntary symbolism is that symbolism *sui*

generis ...which emerges in accordance with a certain 'intention of the observer', more than from a manifest thesis of the artist, neverthess it is due to an image present in the subconscious of the artist himself, as it is he who has put there all the signs that make his work.' The specific example given here by CASTELLI is the reading, in the folds of the mantle of the Virgin Mary, of a grinning skull, in Michelangelo's *Pietà*. Elsewhere Castelli brings as an example of an altar made with certain marbles veined so as to let figures of devils emerge in the front of the altar.

In the breach of our ships, it is not a single artist that has put there 'the signs that form his work'. I see, however, a collective expression, and the emerging from the collective unconscious of a symbolism that can be read from the signs that form the collective 'work', or conception, when 'the intention of the observer' is attuned to them.

In this breach on the side of the ship which seems to hold course unperturbed. The apparently senseless commerce between ship and its environment which these "containers" seem to allow (present) does carry the expression (symbol) in each, and in the three, of a double ambivalence.

On the one hand, in each we may read the suspect, the suggestion of a precarious ship because of the breach (which does not, yet, give sign of real lack of balance), of not having the capacity to hold in the high seas,on the water that, we know, is perilous and of unstable humour.

68 Also in the table by BOSCH of the *Ship of fools* at the Louvre, a relatively late but fundamental icongraphic example of the tradition under examination, there are people in the water who collect, one with a cup, others with their hands, things, food, that falls from the table of the fools on board. One of the people in the water is holding on to the boat, so that he manages to break the line of the side of the boat with his two arms, aided, so to speak, by the habit of the friar, which spills out over the border a little. This is the 'usual' breach towards the stern, on the left.

69 Joël LEFEBVRE, *Les fols et la Folie*, cit., pp.161-163 remarks that the absence of notices in Italy may depend on the fact that the censure of the so called 'worldly follies' may be contrary to the Renaissance culture or spirit. I would like to suggest that in Italy, it is the devil that takes care of the blame for 'worldly follies' and it is the devil who is the collective scapegoat.

Interlude

In Florence

Up to now we have reconstructed the '*Fusta piena di matti'* as a text, the text of a feast. The text is the description by those who have seen the performance. Complete as some of the reports are, the inside instructions, the actual script, the stage directions, the intention of the authors and producers, all have to be guessed, or deduced, from those records . Those records are the text which is our point of departure. It is not a literary text, it is a pattern nevertheless, (*un canovaccio*), it is the record of the collective production of a phenomenon shaped within the rules of a ritual feast as we have traced from various sources in Chapter One, and found clearly recorded in literature and written history.

We have scrutinized a festive tradition of which we have testimony from several angles and times; the indirect mention of the 'cart of fools' in Poggio Bracciolini, the games in the water of 1304 and in the *Momus* by Alberti. We have drawn a line of distinction from iconographic and literary elements which have developed in parallel, with which we have noticed analogies and oppositions, but not derivation – the tradition of *Das Narrenschiff* by Brant, the Northern or Gothic tradition.

Now, however, having a full 'text' of the entity '*Fusta piena di matt*'" in the details of its theatrical and festive structure, the task is to investigate the political and historical *humus* which has supplied the pre-text to the event, and the motives which have dictated that particular choreography.

First of all, the container of them all. Why a Venetian ship? Then the characters, the masks, what and who are they? Carafulla is also a real person, he has a history, which comes to aid. Gio. Tancredi del Quartier di Santa Croce has a name which speaks volumes, we shall see. And what do costumes, namely cloak and hood add to the story?.

Consequently, in the second part of this study the object of scrutiny will be the 'historical sources' into which we try to read the 'plot' on which the pageant has expressed the text, that text which has been read in the first part as creative expression, as an entity, complex and complete in itself, lived one evening in Florence, but yet to be examined relative to its anchors in the reality of topical (immediate) motive and causes.

The time has come to ask, on the local historical plane, why on that day, in that *festa* a '*fusta*', precisely a Venetian ship, was chosen to parade Carafulla in his hood and cloak as a captain of fools, with Gio. Tancredi citizen of Santa Croce, more foolish than all the other fools, tossed in a basket? Did the devils have a function beyond the traditional 'decorative ' one in a festival?

What were the Florentines, there and then, wishing to expose with that '*fusta*', and why, the evening of 22nd June 1514?

From Venice

The real Venetian *fusta*, being a small swift galley, may have been used in action for swift sudden sorties. It was not heavily armed, but just two or three guns could still do some damage. Because of it size and low profile it could approach other vessels by stealth. For this reason the *fusta* was a ship favoured also by North African corsairs. But in Venice it is recorded as being used mostly, in reality, as a messenger. From the *Bacino di San Marco* it carried messages, supplies and personnel to the main body of the fleet collected at sea outside the harbour. As a messenger it is perfect for us.

Apparently at the end of the XVI century, the *fusta* fell into disuse, being substituted more and more by bigger galleys, and finished its life at anchor as a ship for convicts and madmen in training for the sea. Apart from a rather simple example of fusta, rather small too, in the *Museo della Marina* in Venice, the only pictures I have found are in some paintings by Canaletto of the *Bacino di San Marco*, where the *fusta* appears covered by a large awning in red and yellow stripes at anchor in front of the Doge's Palace. Apparently it was still there in 1740 as shown in the painting of the Reception of the French Ambassador of that date.

Archive documents reveal that the *fusta,* or a 'disarmed' ship of the *fusta* type, was instituted as training ship for convicts, by a law passed by the *Maggior Consiglio* in 1545 [1] . The first convicts had started being used at the oars in the Venetian fleet since 1542 . The voluntary crews used at the oars until then were becoming scarce . Therefore, when no more in active duty in the fleet, the *fusta* had become a training ship for convicts, among whom, up to the XVIII century were also madmen – since madmen were still kept together with common criminals in ordinary prisons [2] as we know, not only in Venice.

In Florence, for instance, we find them in the prison of the '*Stinche*'. Madmen, disturbed people, fools, were kept there, sometimes also as fee paying 'guests' when families with means found it impossible to look after them in their own homes. In the history of the '*Stinche*' we find mention of a special sector for the mad, called *la pazzeria* – the madhouse The presence of madmen mixed with ordinary convicts was a normal occurrence up well into the XVIII century.

As a matter of fact Vanzan says that 'the first documentary evidence of the presence of madmen in the (training) *fusta* is of January 19, 1727' [3]. Although they must have been there long before considering the *fusta*'s status as a training ship since 1545. If it trained convicts, the madmen could would be there as well. As before the XVIII century, the fools and madmen (when they were not left to wander outside the walls of the cities) were 'contained' in the ordinary prisons together with the common criminals.

Madmen, *pazzi,* were just sentenced by ordinary law tribunals 'to be held for a number 'x' of years *come pazzi* – 'as mad'. It was not a medical diagnosis that defined someone a fool or mad-man/woman, but, at least up to the XVIII century, legal proceedings could be incurred by those who were perhaps eccentric or 'vague' and had found themselves unable to look after themselves or, careless of their material possessions and estate, had became destitute. (women were a different question, they mostly are found having fallen foul of the law because of 'infanticide'). Citizens then were judged by the law to be mad or *pazzi* as included in the category of '*Furiosus vel Prodigus*', (Mad or prodigal) according to Principle V of the XII Tables of Roman Law which informs the concept of madness in jurisprudence.[4] This until when medical 'science' will take over the jurisdiction of mental illness.

However, the Venetian *fusta,* no longer in active service in the fleet, had started being frequented by convicts and fools to be trained as rowers since the middle of the XVI century. Later, anchored in the '*Bacino di S.Marco*' it must have been used simply as 'containment', a special prison were men were trained at the oar. This, however, only *later* than the time when its name and form is being used in the pageant '*Fusta dei Matti*' in Florence in 1514. It became officially a training ship for convicts, and fools, by a law passed only in 1545, as we have seen. Not much later, but later nevertheless.

So the festive '*fusta*' of Florence had unwittingly captured exactly the spirit of the small and agile Venetian ship, used when in service for swift sudden action (incursions) and, more normally, as a messenger from the city to the large powerful fleet at sea. And the premonition of it becoming a training ship for convicts and madmen seems prophetic.

An intuition, in the game, of a destiny. A destiny, evidently, dictated by the very nature of the *fusta*, that elfin vessel, ready for mischief, and carrying a message.

1 VANZAN MARCHINI, Nelli Elena, *La follia, una nave, una città*. Storie di pazzi e pazzíe a Venezia nel '700. Mira (VE), Brenctana Editrice, 1981.

2 *Ibidem*, pp. 14-15

3 *Ibidem,* pp 20 and 26.

4 As we find still in use in the XVIII century, as seen in Marcantonio SAVELLI, *Summa sententiarum*, Venezia 1748 (from XII Tavole, the XII Tables of the Law, V) see notes at II. 1, n. 10 (*Carnasciale*); at IV. 5., n. 73 and n. 84.

Second Part

(The historical moment.)

CHAPTER IV

Rome, Florence, Venice.

IV.1. *The Holy See (the Court of Rome); Spring 1514.*

When Giovanni de' Medici was elected to the papacy, on 10th March 1513, the Medici family had just recently returned to Florence and to power (31st August – 1st September 1512) after eighteen years of exile. There had been eighteen years of 'republic' in Florence, beginning with the four years of Savonarola's regime (1494-98) at first, then a more normal republican regime with Piero Soderini '*Gonfaloniere a Vita*', and ended by the armies of the Holy League of Pope Julius II, when after a very bloody and brutal 'sack of Prato' [1] by the Spanish troops, Florence was again in the hands of the Medici, who entered it and were restored to the *Signoria* of the city on 31st of August. Giuliano is reported by Landucci to have entered on 1st September [2]. Cardinal Giovanni, who was *Legato* of Julius II also entered Florence, one of those days. Piero Soderini became in his turn an exile (in Rome). The Medici had also inside armed supporters who helped them take the Palace of Government, the *palazzo della Signoria*[3].

Giuliano (son of Lorenzo the Magnificent '*il Vecchio*', and brother of Giovanni now pope Leo X) and Lorenzo (son of Piero, their brother, who had died, so grandson of Lorenzo il Magnifico '*il Vecchio*) had only had a few months to consolidate their restored position at the head of the Government of Florence, when, at the news of (brother and uncle) Giovanni's rather unexpected election to the papacy, everybody goes to Rome[4] (and see IV.2. below and n. 15) Suddenly. In order to carry their congratulations to the new pope, for the public festivities, for the solemn "*possesso*' – taking possession of the Lateran, the palace and church of the Bishop of Rome. They came to proclaim their friendship and devotionin the hope of obtainings positions and favours. Giuliano goes, Lorenzo goes, and a large number of relatives, friends, and 'all sorts of Florentines who are or make themselves his relatives', 'hundreds' of citizens of Florence, take the way of Rome

Piero Soderini was already in Rome, in exile, and there will be more Florentines also in exile. But also many of those who have been just recently reinstated in Florence, also of the Medici family, just returned from exile saw now new prospects in in Rome as the Holy See was now headed by a Medici. Not all of them will be able to stay in Rome, nor are they all well accepted by the new pope. Jacopo Nardi, official historian, will in fact relate and publish comments, uttered in public, by Leo X, referring to the hundreds of Florentines seeking favousr and positions at the papal court thus showing themselves not at all devoted to the city of Florence which ought to be the principal object of their care and attention [5].

Young Lorenzo was sent quickly back to take care of the affairs of Florence and was not very pleased.[6]

Giuliano was to remain in Rome, and so was Alfonsina, Lorenzo's mother. Another Medici in Rome was cardinal Giulio (later Bishop of Florence and future Clemens VII). He was the illegitimate son of Giuliano (the brother of Lorenzo the Magnificent *Il Vecchio)* who had been killed in the Pazzi Conspiracy of 1478.

Piero Soderini, the former '*Gonfaloniere a vita*', ex-head of the fallen republic of Florence, was also in exile in Rome where he had joined his brother Francesco, a powerful Cardinal.

Even though the Medicean restoration in Florence was only strengthened by the election of the Medici pope, there were nevertheless certain aspects of foreign policy of those first years of the papacy of Leo X that were not well seen in Florence. Certain alliances, established or *in fieri,* being planned at this moment, and precisely in the Spring of 1514, could have given occasion to disillusionment, worry, jealousy perhaps, 'emulation', and may not have seemed altogether advantageous to those 'sent back' to look after Florence.

Among the activities and the policies of Leo X in the Spring of 1514 there are facts, alliances, proposals in which the pope was involved, that put the Florentines 'circles' in opposition to the Roman 'circles'.

Very near to Leo X in Rome, in this Spring of 1514, is Giuliano his brother, and a number of Venetian dignitaries and diplomats – Pietro Bembo (secretary to Leo X), Cardinal Cornaro, Tommaso Giustiniani, and Pietro (Vincenzo) Querini (we shall see rather a lot more of them later) – and cardinal Francesco Soderini, brother of Piero. Furthermore, appearing to represent a faction clearly opposed to the one now in power in Florence, there was a singular character, Francesco da Meleto, a merchant, traveller, prophet [7] of Savonarolian colour, who had been called to Rome from Florence in March 1514, financed probably by cardinal Soderini, but housed as a guest of the Venetian Pietro Bembo (secretary to the pope), in close contact of political-spiritual projects with the Venetians Querini and Giustiniani. Giuliano de' Medici [8] was also close to all of these.

The political-spiritual projects mentioned related to a 'catholic reformation' and to an alliance with Venice and perhaps France. Both were anathema in Florence. Too near to the disasters of 1494 and the recently fallen anti-Medicean republic .

The 'catholic reformation' was a very 'hot' subject as is to be expected. But strongly felt in Florence especially, not necessarily for doctrinal reasons (apart from the memories of the fanatic reformer Savonarola), but for financial and political questions no doubt, and generally relating to the power games within the Medici family, as we shall see.

Both the catholic reform (which involved conversion of 'infidels') and the dealings with Venice were connected with the possibility of a new Crusade, to which the new pope seemed to look forward with a great degree of enthusiasm (see IV.4. and note 29), and which implied an alliance with Venice that was to supply the ships. Venice was a 'hot' subject too, also because of her alliance with France, which was felt as a threat for Florence – memories of 1494.

IV.2 *Florentines in Florence and Florentines in Rome. (The) Way back for some travellers.*

Among those who had gone to Rome in 1513, young Lorenzo di Piero was amongst those who had to go back to Florence, perhaps not altogether happily. He was the one sent back to take charge of the government of the city.

It may seem strange that with the restoration and the enthusiasm for the renewed power of the Medici in Florence we should speak of disillusionment. But Rome was the bigger centre, and the papal court with a Medici pope seemed to offer greater opportunity of fame and glory than the city of Florence. The Holy See had become a power centre for the Medici too.

In the *Cronichetta sopra le ultime azioni di Lorenzo de' Medici Duca d' Urbino*, the Little Chronicle on on the last actions of Lorenzo Duke of Urbino (who is the Lorenzo di Piero with whom we are dealing now) by Bartolini Salimbeni, who was the treasurer of Lorenzo, we read of his discontent at this point:

> '*Di poi che Papa Lione fu assunto al Pontificato, nacque fra il Magnifico Giuliano Duca di Nemours, et il Magnifico Lorenzo emulatione grande perché ognuno voleva avere luogo appresso sua Santità, et havendo ottenuto il Duca Giuliano el Capitanato generale della Chiesa … al Magnifico Lorenzo non restava altro grado che pigliare cura delle cose di Firenze la quale da Papa Lione etiam con consenso di Giuliano gli era stato concesso* – After Papa Lione was elected to the papacy, great emulation had been born between the Magnifico Giuliano Duca di Nemour (brother of Leo X), and the Magnifico Lorenzo (their nephew), because each wanted to have office near to His Sanctity, and having Giuliano obtained the office of Commander in chief of the Church, no other resort was left to the Magnifico Lorenzo than the taking care of the government of Florence, which had been assigned to him by the pope with the consent of Giuliano…'[9].

As a matter of fact we may also take into account that Lorenzo had grown up in Rome, as an 'exile' since the age of two; and it would therefore be understandable now that he may feel at least ambivalent about being sent away from Rome, although to lead the government of Florence.

Lorenzo had been made a honorary citizen of Rome, together with his uncle Giuliano. The granting of the citizenship was to be celebrated in September 1513, but Lorenzo was ordered back to Florence on August 10th [10] so as to miss out even on the celebrations for this honorary title. In Florence he 'got himself elected, by the Magistrates, *Capitano Generale*', thus making up for some of his lack of honours, in part [11].

Nevertheless the historians agree that 'the Government of Florence depended for everything from Rome'[12] , quite officially, via Cardinal Giulio, and that Lorenzo was not at ease in the situation[13].

Cardinal Giulio was in Rome and sent regular instructions by letter to Lorenzo on how to behave in order to attract the benevolence of the Florentines, especially those that counted, supposedly. He wrote, for instance to:

> ' *offrire qualche cerimonia exteriore di affabilitá et gratitudine di parole da le quali ne saria liberale con quelli ad chi più se ne convengono et che ne son più desiderosi … intrattenere … quando uno et quando un altro ad mangiare seco non solo nella città ma in villa…* – do offer some external expression of friendship and gratitude of words, with which to be liberal with those that are more useful and who seem to desire them…entertain them…sometimes one, sometimes others at dinner and not only in the city but also in the country residences…"[14]

Lorenzo's mother, Alfonsina, was also similarly generous with her advice.

Alfonsina was in Rome, were the young Lorenzo himself (now 20 years of age) had grown up. She sent him very frequent letters, she warned him not to trust the Florentines, not even for his teams in the jousts [15] (no wonder he did not feel too comfortable). She asked him to report to her almost daily[16], she managed his communications with Leo X, to the point of withholding from the pope certain letters from Lorenzo where he made demands or observations she judged inappropriate or un-diplomatic [17]. If the reports she received from Lorenzo were not sufficiently detailed or clear, she wrote back to him that '*meglio sarebbe che non l'aveste scritto* – it would have been better not to have written it at all"[18].

Giuliano was in Rome, while the Magnifico Lorenzo had 'no other choice' than taking care of things in Florence – and follow advice.

Many Florentines had hoped to find benefits or 'a post beside His Holiness': Leo X himself had spoken in public expressing his opinion on the subject. He betrayed a certain impatience towards the great number of Florentines who had gone to Rome on the occasion of his election with the obvious wish of obtaining some personal advancement. All these Florentines had come with the pretext of celebrating the pope's election, but were in reality intent only on their own interest. Nardi records Leo X's comments in his *Istorie*:

> '*In tanta moltitudine di parenti e amici e d'ogni sorte di Fiorentini che l'andavano a visitare e fargli riverenze col baciargli i piedi, disse adunque papa Leone che fra tante centinaia di cittadini, non ne aveva trovato se non uno sommamente savio (e quegli era stato Piero Soderini) e uno sommamente matto (e questi era stato un maestro Antonio cappucciaio chiamato il Carafulla) i quali soli, lasciando da parte I propri interessi, gli avavano raccomandato istantemente la città di Firenze sua patria* – in such a multitude of relatives and friends and every kind of Florentines who went to visit him, and kneel to him and kiss his feet (slipper), the pope Leo then said that among so many hundreds of citizens, he had found only one of great wisdom (and that was Piero Soderini) and one notably mad (and this was a maestro Antonio maker of hoods, called also 'il Carafulla'), these two alone, leaving aside their own interests, had recommended very specially to him the city of Florence his homeland'[19].

In this short passage, which has already been quoted elsewhere in this essay, it is evident how there was a certain impatience on the part of Leo X with the Florentines, or many of them, anyway. He must have spoken aloud, and he must have said it to be reported, with repetitions, 'the multitude, the hundreds, the relatives, and the friends, and all sorts' their servile attitudes, and among the so many not one that he could begin to appreciate, to trust, because they had only their own interests at heart, not one except ... except whom? Except Piero Soderini and Carafulla. The ex *Gonfaloniere* of the Republic [20] whom the pope terms as 'exceptionally wise'- even though he was of the opposite side to that of the Medicean Florentines now in power and who were his relatives and his friends, those who came to visit him and kneel to him and kiss his feet.

Together with Piero Soderini, now in exile in Rome, the pope can find only one other exception to those self-serving Florentines, and this – notably mad – was maestro Antonio maker of cappucci (hoods)[21], *cappuccetto* himself[22], il Carafulla. And all those Florentines, relatives and all sorts of acquaintances[23] 'who are or make out to be, his relatives' are put into place, publicly judged and slighted: the only good examples being these two: a rival of the Medici faction in Florence, and the eccentric Carafulla.

Notwithstanding the advantages and protection gained by Florence thanks to the papacy of a Medici, at the moment of exultation and hope, many had their sights on Rome, but they were sent back empty handed and not a little humbled. Nor could they draw much consolation from the unflattering observations and the comparisons we have read in Nardi's *Istorie.*

IV.3 *Better luck for other travellers.*

Perhaps those who had managed to stay in Rome, and to find favour and 'posts next to His Holiness' were therefore in a position to attract envy (like the 'emulation' felt by Lorenzo towards his uncle Giuliano as reported by Bartolini Salimbeni), and also to be blamed for their lack of loyalty towards Florence. It was not unlikely that some would run the risk of being made the aim of satirical thrusts (for fun, in the games). As it happens, however, the aim of the satire will not be generally directed to the many, but to some well selected few instead.

With irony and satire much can be said, without risk (only the risk of not being understood), and satire can be seen as a chance to influence (hopefully) politics. Irony, satire, and political message in disguise have a proper traditional place in festival play.

The '*festa*', used in these first years of restoration as celebration, propaganda, glorification, and therefore with openly political ends, had, however, in its traditional roots also the language of 'reversal'. In this language, structures are acted and messages are expressed by opposites – this language is most apt to satire, political satire in this case.

We must also say that, even though the possibility was there, in this particular moment, in the enthusiasm for the restoration, satire is not normally found. Indeed it seems that the *'fusta piena di matti'* is the only burlesque episode in the official celebrations [24] . And indeed the burlesque is the style of traditional/popular, rather than official, festivals. Official celebrations have the power to make their point directly. It is the powerless that must resort to covert and oblique references.

Or those who have something to say that is not exactly safe in the circumstances. Like now.

In Florence there were families, and Lorenzo himself, who were watching those that should have been considered 'the vanquished' have a better place and more influence than themselves in the court of the Medici pope. It cannot have been a happy sight.

Piero Soderini has been singled out by Leo X as most wise, and praised for his loyalty to Florence. His brother, Cardinal Francesco (whose "*vicario*" at Volterra, Antonio Zeno, had been instrumental in inviting, and funding Francesco da Meleto to Rome [25], enjoyed a high position in the Holy See, since the beginning of Leo X's papacy. This was dictated perhaps also by 'the desire on the part of the Medici, to allay any possible opposition to their restored *Signoria* in Florence'. Another of the Soderini brothers, Pagolantonio, had also close connections with Venice.

Furthermore, in Rome there were other characters who were certainly not there to recommend to the pope 'the city of Florence his homeland', but were apparently working to make him build alliances that were considered dangerous for Florence, namely the alliance with Venice who was allied to France[26]. The circle of Giuliano de' Medici, as well as cardinal Francesco Soderini (and consequently perhaps Piero), included the Venetian humanist Pietro Bembo, that Leo X had made his secretary, and Vincenzo-Piero Querini, former Venetian diplomat, now a 'hermit' (on leave obviously) of the Camaldolenses order. Querini had been called to Rome in the Spring 1514 by Leo X, and was rumoured to have been offered a cardinalate [27]. He was very close to His Holiness, so much so that 'not a day passed that he was not received, and not briefly either, by the pope, and alone, or more often in company with Bembo, and at times also of the Venetian ambassador Piero Lando'[28]. He also accompanied His Holiness to the Magliana – the papal villa where Leo X was fond of going hunting.[29] Among the other Venetians mentioned there was Tommaso (Paolo) Giustiniani, author, together with Querini of the *Libellus ad Leonem X* – a plea and and project of reform of the Church [30]. The reformist thought, as well as the 'prophecies', included intentions for the conversion of the 'infidel', which must have been considered an important support for the plan of the Crusade which we shall see was close to the pope's heart. Although the proposals in the *Libellus* – better selection and education of the clergy, translation of the liturgy and of sacred texts into the vernacular, reformation of the Curch away from politics and temporal power, towards a renewed spirituality, and a better control on published materials (later leading to the *Index* of condemned books) remained dead letter – Leo X must have felt some interest for Querini's ideas, and perhaps hoped to gain support for the Crusade. The question of 'reform' however, was really hot stuff, heresy perhaps, for the Florentines with fresh and unpleasant memories of Savonarola. Gio Tancredi di S. ta Croce will deal with this matter.

With Querini and Giustiniani, close to Giuliano must have been also powerful cardinal Cornaro, another Venetian, that we shall see in Florence, visiting uninvited and in disguise with Giuliano for the very feast of San Giovanni 1514. (See next chapter V. 2.).

The circle of Giuliano, these cardinals and these Venetians so near to the pope, as well as the other reformers connected with the condemned-as-heretic Savonarola, were a very good reason for feelings of 'great emulation' in Florence, and impotent hostility towards Rome.

Not forgetting that Florence had always felt 'great emulation' towards Venice – Venice was the successful republic, as opposed to the unsuccessful one in Florence – not to speak of the Medici faction which was altogether uninterested in republican ideas, and of course opposed to any that might come from Venice. [31] We must say that the lack of sympathy was reciprocated (see quote form the Venetian Ambassador Marco Minio, above, note 31).

Great travellers, these Venetians, and their ships are now on the move. Lucky now also on their way to Rome, together with Giuliano, luckier than Lorenzo, on the way to Rome. Good traveller also Piero Soderini, although an exile, better accepted and appreciated than all those Florentines friends and relations, and his name made to resound in praise by the pope, side by side with that of Antonio, Master maker of hoods, *el Carafulla*. Except for this last one, they had all happily landed at the court of Leo X. While Carafulla will be in Florence, and will speak for the Florentines.

So what thoughts would the Florentines be entertaining about all this? Those who had been sent back, with not much choice but to look after the running of things in Florence? While Venetians, reformers, dodgy counsellors stayed, were summoned even, to be near to the pope.

In the Spring 1514.

IV. 4. *More journeys by sea.* 'Navicelle' *on the way, as the* fuste *are ready.* [32]

In Rome much talk was heard of a new Crusade, and of the Venetian fleet, in the Spring of 1514.

Talk came from the Venetians, especially perhaps Bembo, certainly Querini, perhaps Francesco da Meleto, so let us not forget this obvious link with Savonarola's doctrine which, also, included the conversion of the 'infidel' and the Jews.

But talk notably came from pope Leo X himself. He was still talking about it so convincingly that in August 1514 Baldassarre Turini writes to Lorenzo:

> '*N.S.…non fa che ragionare della impresa contro turchi; et dice ci vuole andare di persona; et disegna tanto bene le cose che non ci manca che lo andare per havere la victoria* – His Holiness talks of nothing else than his enterprise against the Turks; and he says he wants to go in person; and he represents things so well that it is as if we (he) needed only to go to achieve instant victory' [33]

To be so enthusiastic and convinced Leo must have talked and planned for some time, indeed at least since the Spring, when he had collected the 'reformers' and the Venetians.

In fact, at the beginning of the papacy of Leo X, the 'Catholic reform' was a prominent subject. There was talk, and there were writings. The 'magna charta of the catholic reform' was later going to be the *Consilium de emendanda ecclesia* (1537). At the moment it was the *Libellus ad Leonem X*, written by Querini and Giustiniani [34], that must have interested pope Leo. So these two were called to Rome, and notwithstanding their *piagnone*, or reformist, leanings, were too close to Giuliano de' Medici and the new pope for the Florentines.

So the Crusade was intrinsic with the reformist thought. And the agenda of Christian expansion included converting the infidels in the (near) East, the unification of churches, the conversion of Jews and expeditions to the newly discovered lands in the West.

That the dreams of such a 'reform' possibly favoured by this papacy were kept in mind, with disapproval, in Florence (where Savonarola had ruled, preaching similar ideas, and where he was excommunicated and then tried, condemned and executed as a heretic in 1498, with the intervention of a popular uprising) is also evident in the comment by the historian Giovanni Cambi, who remarks, on seeing the cardinals coming from Rome with Giuliano

– on horseback, armed, and in disguise – for the San Giovanni '*Sicché ci davano buono exemplo e a questo modo si riforma la Chiesa. Iddio lo perdoni loro* – And so do they expect to give us good example on how to reform the Church. May God forgive them' [35]. (See more about this below at V. 2.)

In the Spring of 1514 this matter of reform had started to move with the calling of Querini to Rome, the summoning of Francesco da Meleto, and then the embassy to Venice by Querini and Bembo (who was Leo X's secretary).

Because Leo X dreamt of a Crusade, the Venetian fleet was in focus. It was the Venetian fleet that would be hired. Hence the reason of the '*fusta*', a Venetian ship, no doubt. And the important thing was the money. of course.

Because the pope was not only "dreaming", but he was doing, he had actually started to pay. He had already sent money to Venice. And money was a very serious matter . This was the subject of talk, too, and of letters.

The money minted for the treasury were the '*fiorini da camera*'. These were also called '*navicelle*' little ships, as one side carried the engraving of the ship of salvation, St. Peter's ship. In a poem by Bernardo Giambullari [36] we find stated that the pope was taking '*navicelle*' out of his very pockets, in this case it was to give to jugglers and jesters'.

Yes, and now also to send to Venice. Leo X's *navicelle* were sailing to Venice.

On the other hand from Rome they were writing to Florence, where Lorenzo was expecting funds from Leo X , that in the coffers of the pope '*non ci è uno quattrino manesco* – there is not a penny in hand', indeed 'there is not a penny to hand', as is repeated twice in the letter[37].

Two years later the Venetian ambassador refers to the general, endemic, and well known [38] situation of the pope's finances writing in a letter to the Senate that Leo X 'has no money – *non ha contanti*', because he is generous (*liberale*, perhaps prodigal?), and is unable to keep his money; and also the Florentines – *che si fanno e sono suoi parent i*- who claim to be and are his relations, do not let him have any money' [39].

Nevertheless we know, from letters by Bembo and Querini to the government of Venice, that, after having undertaken to pay 20,000 ducats, and after several times promising to send them, on May 9th – only six weeks before we see the *fusta* in Florence – the pope has actually sent 3,000 ducats, and a few days later, on May 12th another 2,500 '*per non tenere questa patria pasciuta di parole* – so as not to keep that city fed on words only'[40] . For which, in exchange, he obtains from the Venetians to have '*l' armata veneziana veramente per mare* – the Venetian fleet actually at sea' [41].

Not bad for someone like pope Leo X about whom it was said that '.. it was so possible for him to have one thousand ducats together as it would be possible for a stone to fall upwards – *quanto è possibile che una pietra vada in alto da per sè*.' as the historian Vettori puts it. [42] No wonder (once we accept to 'look into other people's pockets') that there might be complaints from Lorenzo who was expecting funds for Florence..

Because between Florence and Rome too, the talk was about money. And the talk was not sweet. '*Parole pungenti* – stinging' words were exchanged. Lorenzo was *adirato,* angry, he was *alterato*, upset, and letters from him when these moods were apparent were not shown to the pope. Lorenzo too was expecting money, and to him it was not forthcoming.

There is a letter from Baldassarre Turini da Pescia – secretary to Lorenzo's mother Alfonsina – who kept the letters going between Rome and Florence, to Lorenzo, about money, dated 16th June, only a few days before the feast of San Giovanni. It all becomes clear now. Here is the passage relative to the money, the '*navicelle*'[43] that were going to Venice but not coming in the direction of Florence:

> 'About the money I will not reply to your highness, because I see how upset you are bacause of what I already wrote to you, as ordered by the Cardinal [Giulio], and indeed as His Holiness Most Reverend had told me to: and do not think that my Lady or myself have added anything: but I simply wrote what the Most Reverend had told me to: and I did not say that he did not have the 2,000 ducats: but that he did not want to give them to you yet: because he intends to give you a bigger sum: but I only said that they were needed for ends that His Holiness had established, and since we see that your highness is angry, with this letter we are sending a letter of credit to Lanfredini for 1,000 golden ducats from the treasury, and the other 500 remain in the hands of my Lady who will send them to you in a month and a half. Your letter has not been shown to His Holiness, nor to the Most Reverend Monsignor, because it has not seemed suitable to my Lady with reference to the several 'stinging'- *pungenti* words that were in it, and she did not want them to think that such things could come from you – *Delli denari non replicherò altro ad V. S. Per che vedo quanto la sia alterata di quello che gli scripsi per ordine del Cardinale et in verità S.re Mag.co S.S. R.ma me commisse cosí: et non pensi V.S. ne che Madonna ne io ce abbiamo misso del nostro ma meramente scripsi quanto Mons.re R.mo mi aveva decto;....* -' [44].

Lorenzo is angry, it is about money, he writes harsh words, but those do not arrive where he wanted them to be heard.

This discontent can be expressed in other ways, though, less harsh and direct, such, however, that reach the pope and make him aware of the problem. It can be expressed through irony and satire – obliquely yet unmistakeably. By way of a ship, perhaps, a Venetian ship, why not..

There are ships, little ships, '*navicelle*' , big ships, whole fleets, that come and go ways between Rome and Venice that do not seem to bring much good to Florence.

Querini had obtained the money (an advance on the agreed sum for the lease ofVenetian ships), notwithstanding the resistance of theTreasurer General cardinal (Dovizi da) Bibbiena (who was a Tuscan, not a Venetian), the only one in this court who seemed to want to put obstacles against an alliance with Venice, and against openings towards France, with which Venice had recently signed an alliance. But everyone has a price, obviously. Bibbiena had a brother in Venice, who had recently died, and the cardinal had made a request through Bembo about some assistance for his nephews in Venice. Now Querini had sent a reminder (in a latter letter to his brother of 19th April 1514) to be passed on to the Doge saying diplomatically : 'Remind the Prince that it would be very useful at this point to satisfy the Cardinal's [Bibiena] request – '*Aricordate al principe che gioverà assai far in qualche parte contento il Cardinal S.M. in Portico [Bibbiena] per li nipoti soi* ', the request that had already been made by Bembo on the Cardinal's behalf...[45] And in May the pope found the money to send to Venice.

'A valid help to Querini in all these negotiations was, besides Bembo, the Magnifico Giuliano, who was to wed Filiberta of Savoy, and was favourable to the friendship with France'[46]. In any case the Venetian ships were needed for a planned 'impresa italiana', to conquer the kingdom of Naples for the very same Giuliano.

As a matter of fact 'the Venetian fleet already on its way' this time was to be used for the 'Italian undertaking, that is to say for certain (designs) plans Leo X had on the kingdom of Naples, that he would have given to his brother Giuliano. Querini writes to Venice (31st May 1514) [47] that Giuliano talked to him freely of being intent on activating that plan, meaning to conquer the kingdom of Naples for himself.

So it was not a question of Crusade after all yet, although the theory and the talk about it were bubbling on, as we have seen.

And Giuliano was not thinking of the good of Florence by any means. Nor was Leo X either. Neither the Venetians nor the French (who had invaded Florence in 1494) had much to recommend them to the sympathy of the Florentines[48] (see also V.1 and Camillo)

While in Rome 'they' were conferring with the Venetians, and dreaming of setting sail on reckless enterprises. And – a serious matter indeed – they spent real money on all of this.

So perhaps in Florence the need was felt to say something or do something to correct the course of Leo X politics and plans? Perhaps they felt the need to say to Leo X that those plans to set sail on senseless voyages are foolish things, to point to him that he is surrounded by evil counsellors who want his ruin, by inciting him to mad and dangerous journeys by sea.

It was not unknown that events in the *festa* might represent certain realities not aired openly in the everyday official world.

That the atmosphere of 'reversal' of the festa could also forebode or represent real danger for the established order, was also well known in Florence (as elsewhere). That the festive reversal of values, and the limited period of license and play could bring about some real turbulence was never too far from the mind of those in power. The holiday, the exterior pomp an play did also mean that the palace of government, the centre of power, would remain empty and unguarded. During the previous regime, for instance, on the last year of the republic, the S. Giovanni of 1512 had not been celebrated by the Magistrates, for fear of disturbances – the Medici were on their way back from exile, the armies of the Holy League were not far away, the authorities were fearing a *coup*. The Magistrates and the "*Gonfaloniere*", the head of government, Piero Soderini, did not join the festivities 'because he had been warned not to go [to public ceremonies] as he was going to be cut to pieces by those who wanted to put the heirs of Lorenzo de' Medici back in power in Florence' [49] (C.Guasti…)

And now, precisely these very 'heirs of Lorenzo de' Medici', in the person of his grandson Lorenzo (while his sons Giuliano and Giovanni were looking over from Rome) were in Florence, certainly not unaware that in the festive 'disguise' one can do and say things which seem playful, but can go well beyond a jest.

The 'diversion' connotation [50] that we can read into "*divertimento*" means just that. Furthermore, on certain occasions, like in a *festa*, it could be something in a precarious balance between to 'divert' and to 'subvert'.

In the episode quoted from *Momus,* discussed earlier [51], we have seen how clear the understanding of the mechanism of subversion under the guise of play- *divertimento* is, where the playful action in the *festa* is only a pretence, and the diversion results in real subversion. Although *Momus seu de principe* had been composed in the middle of the previous century, it was not forgotten, and it may have gone out of print just about at this time. It was going to have, in fact, two re-prints, in Rome, in 1520 [52].

One is not suggesting that in the case under observation, the San Giovanni 1514, there should be a proper conspiracy, there was no necessity of one (yet), and if there was a problem, as we suspect, it was not within Florence. The problem was between Florence and Rome. It was perhaps ealted to the protection and support which were coming, and not coming, from Leo X. It concerned his allies and counsellors. That's where warnings were directed, that's where attention was demanded.

The Medici were in Florence, and the Medici pope was the nearest friendly power. As a matter of fact, Giuliano, although otherwise engaged, was the real governor of Florence, while young Lorenzo had been sent just 'to take care of things in Florence'. Although young Lorenzo was the son of Lorenzo's eldest son, Piero, in some respect he was 'first in line' . Yet such dynastic correctness may not be expected as necessarily appropriate. Or, yet again, young Lorenzo may not have had a strong political personality, nor a good managerial mindset. In any case the seat of real power was Rome and the papacy, and therefore in the hands of Leo X. The consequence was dependency for Florence.

And, considering it as a family politics sort of situation, all that could be done was to indicate that Leo needed a nudge, a warning. Instead of thinking of the good of Florence – an attitude he had praised in Carafulla – now he let himself be involved in matters too big and strange, he befriended reformers, he paid for the Venetian ships, but ships can be dangerous, they may take ruinous routes, fit only for fools. And as for the matter of a Crusade, and setting sail himself, the fate of a certain Gio.Tancredi would show him what could happen.

Besides, the danger was not only related specifically to Venetian ships . There was another ship, even more important, whose captain was threatened by dangerous counsellors, real everyday devils: it was the *Navicula Sancti Petri* (the one that also appeared on the coins minted for the papal treasury), it was St. Peter's ship of salvation, the Holy Church itself. Leo X was its captain in real time, he was the present pope, and was responsible for its right course. Leo X, besides, knew the symbolical value of the ship, the *Navicula Sancti Petri,* and we can see that he cultivated its resonance with the *Navicella* belonging to his own church.

Leo X as cardinal was titular of the church Santa Maria in Domnica, known also as '*della navicella*'. He had engaged the young Jacopo Sansovino to restore the church and to reconstruct an ancient Roman ship found on the Celio hill, near his church. In Sansovino's books, the *Libretto dei ricordi – 1513* we find records of payments made for works (a new pedestal, and reconstruction of the *nave*) regarding the *Navicella*. These records are in a section up to 16th April 1513, and one for works from the 6th to the 31st of March 1513. Leo was elected pope on 10 March 1513. and it was as soon as he was elected that he had started the restoration of the ancient ship, entrusting the work to Jacopo Sansovino [53], to make a monumental fountain that still exists today.

The ship-fountain was a traditional symbol of imperial Rome, and in this restoration of the ancient ship Leo X combined the Roman pagan tradition with that of the Christian church, the *navicula* of Saint Peter.

It thas been proposed [54] that this *navicella* combines elements of the classical tradition of ship-fountain, with the Christian symbol of the ship of salvation. There is not much room for doubt, in my opinion, that the *navicella,* and the *Navicula Sancti Petri* are closely and symbolically connected.

Not much later when Raphael prepares the cartoons for the *Miraculous Draught of Fishes*

the ship of Saint Peter and Cardinal Giovanni's church are also connected. In the 'strip history' below the main scene, in fact, as Giovanni travels from the river Arno of Florence to the Tiber of Rome, to become Leo X , he passes by the church (shown as not yet fully restored) of S.ta Maria in Domnica. It cannot be chance that this image, from others that could have been found to represent episodes of recent history, should be chosen to underline the great allegory of the the boat of St. Peter, the Ship of Salvation.

Giovanni de Medici's safe landing[55] in Rome was certainly worthy of a special 'votive' ship, and the *navicella* restored in front of the titular church of Giovanni de' Medici was a very appropriate, timely and deeply symbolical monument. Certainly the antics of a ship for the San Giovanni in Florence would communicate something of significance to someone sensitive to the idea of ship, the *navicula Sancti Petri* and the *Navicella?*

So 'ships', little ships, *navicelle,* the *navicella* of the Church Santa Maria in Domnica, the *Navicula Sancti Petri* and the Venetian ships, are very much in the limelight. Hence the *fusta*.

The ship of Saint Peter, the ship of salvation, was it being launched on crazy crusades, perhaps turned into a Venetian ship, goaded by diabolical advisers? Even Charon, the wise boatman, careful of his own safety, takes care of his boat better than this waster of *navicelle,* the prodigal pope who lets his treasury money, his *navicelle*, slip out of his pockets, to go to fools and jesters, or to Venice. And what about that friend of his, this Maestro Antonio *cappucciaio*, also mad and prodigal, who forgets his own interest and remains poor?[56]. All he deserves is to be made captain, for a day in the festival, of the *fusta* the (Venetian) ship of fools, in Florence.

So who could also be chosen to be the mad mock-captain, irresponsible but recognizable, someone who could be able to say so much even while saying nothing, who could mimic one in power, speak on behalf of, and to, those in power, and who could then be minimized and disowned once his games were done, if not this same friend?

This suitable character happened to be at hand. He was uncannily well suited. He was someone who enjoyed to act out being a king and being called Your Majesty [57] (see IV.6.i) He was a well known colourful character in Florence, and known in Rome too, where he had enjoyed an admiring mention from Leo X reported by the historian Nardi [58]. This was Carafulla, that very same Maestro Antonio *cappucciaio*: who else could have been better at impersonating a madcap captain of a ship, who, with other fools, and goaded by devils, could take over a Venetian ship and set sail for who knows what sensless and perilous journey by sea?

It seems that there were not many fools in Florence[59], but foolish characters there were, and two in particular, the second even more foolish than the first.

Carafulla, the one to be established at the head of the *fusta* full of fools, 'foolish but swift of tongue' could in fact find another, even more foolish, and together, as real court jesters of the *festa*, they could say so much, they could say everything, without even opening their mouths. And those who can, will understand. Let the wise understand what the fool says.

IV.5. *Gio. Tancredi, whose humble trade is to carry the wool. And those good turncoats who wear silk, and perhaps a cardinal's hat.*

'Gio Tancredi, ciptadino per artefice [60], del Quart. di S. Croce, che portava[61] la lana ed era piú sciocco assai…perché non sapeva far altro che portar la lana[62], e dessere mai maestro non pensava, che in 50 anni non mutó mai arte – Gio. Tancredi, citizen and manual worker, of the Quarter of S. Croce, who carried/wore wool and was much more foolish…because he did not know any better than carrying (and wearing) wool, and never even thought of being a 'maestro- master', as in 50 years has never changed his trade' is captured by the devils, the fusta sends down a basket and they pull him up, he is put to rowing, and further beaten by the devils.

Gio .Tancredi represents, at the level of the obvious, a poor devil who has an unskilled job, carrying the wool, a menial job in some minor guild, or indeed attached at the edge of the major Arte della Lana, and who had kept to the same trade for fifty years, without any advancement in his career. He simply carried (and wore) wool, he had no ambition and no career. He had never even 'thought' of becoming 'maestro' .

Even Carafulla was Maestro – he was 'Maestro Antonio da Vespignano', a master craftsman as a maker of hoods with his own workshop – and 'signori and Gran Maestri' were the cardinals [63] we shall see coming from Rome, in disguise, to gate-crash Lorenzo's celebration of this San Giovanni. Cardinals would wear the purple robe, even though they come to Florence in disguise, dressed in black in the Spanish fashion (not in cloaks and hoods, we notice) in capes and hats'[64]. The cardinals are Gran Maestri, they have made a great career, and if here they do not wear purple-red on this occasion, they will wear at least silk.

The principal connection with Santa Croce reinforced by the name of Tancredi carried by Gio. Tancredi di S.ta Croce must be made with the idea of a Crusader – as 'of Santa Croce' could well mean bearer of the Holy Cross, from which Crociato-Crusader comes – because of the known rumours of Leo X, Giovanni, fretting to become a Crusader himself (see letter IV.4. and note33). That he wished to become 'a Tancredi' himself is implied, a hero like the leader and great hero of the first Crusade. Tancredi is the subject of a widely known chanson de gestes, the Gesta Tancredi by Roul de Caen, one of the historical sources of the first Crusade. The chansons de gestes were well known, broadcast by storytellers, most likely performed for popular entertainment, and discussed, perhaps even in Carafulla's workshop, as we read in Aretino (see III.3., n.22, Carafulla).

The name Tancredi is a clear indicator of the Crusade connection. The pointer would be revealing for anyone. Tancredi the Cross bearer, the Crusader.

A more sinister connection for Santa Croce, although perhaps a slight one, may be the one with the visiting Inquisitor, who would be hosted by the Franciscans (possibly being a Franciscan himself) seeing the recent disgrace of the Dominican Savonarola. Although Dominicans were usually Inquisitors, not in Florence certainly, after the experience of Savonarola, the Dominican convent of S. Marco was discredited in consequence. Business of the Inquisitor could be with 'reformers'. It was not a forgotten subject in Florence if Cambi, seeing the cardinals in fancy Spanish dress, thinks of the reformers when he says 'and in such a way they reform the Church may God forgive them'(see V.2.).

Finally the Franciscan convent annexed to Santa Croce had a school, religious naturally, which had been attended by the young Giovanni de' Medici already destined for a career in the Church.

As for Gio. Tancredi, the question of the ambiguity of '*portava la lana*' meaning both to carry and to wear is difficult to play with in the English language. But I still think it might be intended as such in Cambi's text, especially taking into account the fact that Gio. Tancredi's is a scripted character and probably Cambi was given by the organizers a well thought out 'press release' with a full ad hoc description (see later in detail at IV.5 n.80). So this ambivalence is very likely to have been 'planted', like the other elements in the construction of the character.

Gio. Tancredi's dress is not described (no hood or cloak mentioned), but that he wore wool is moslt likely meant because a kind of wool, certainly humble and simple, was also the habit of the friars and the poor people. This will come to matter also as a political connotation with reference to the the cappucci, and also the *popolani* political factions.

There is a Tuscan proverb to the point. It says '*se non puoi portar la seta, porta la lana* – If you cannot wear silk, just wear wool" [65] meaning, obviously, that those who can, wear silk, popularly considered a finer material for rich people, but those who can't, wear wool. There were very fine wool materials indeed produced in Florence, they were the pride of the city, and were exported all over Europe. But there was a lower grade of wool which was dark and would not take the purple dye of the finer wools. This was used for the humble dress of poor people and friars.

The Battaglia Great Dictionary states how in normal popular parlance the generic "*lana*- wool' is the marker of humble dress. The friars, the peasants, the poor, just 'wore wool'. So one can wear silk (or purple), if one is good (rich) enough, but if one can't, one must 'wear wool'. So Gio. Tancredi is in the humble clothing [66], in wool, while there are those who get to wear silk, if they can, and even the purple robe, if they can. But Gio. Tancredi wore wool, and in fifty years had never changed his trade nor his humble manner of dress. Presumably.

This argument of the fifty years in the same trade (and most probably dress) and no career is also a significant allusion. It is to be taken into account, because there are those, instead, who are so much 'cleverer' and experienced at changing trade, profession and habit, for the sake of a good career. There are many, in Florence, but especially in Rome, who in these last years have changed their trade, have changed their party, have progressed in their careers, and wear much better than humble wool. Many had taken the wool, and then had to change it for something better.

There are first the many conversions in Florence (change of habit), when to follow Savonarola seemed desirable or expedient [67] (Trexler) and even among the humanists several had taken the holy orders, and friars of other orders had changed to Dominicans. The inflamed preaching of the Dominican friar had put the fear of God into everybody, indeed.

But there are two specific cases of conversions, and change of trade or profession that are particularly relevant to the arguments in hand. They are in Rome, now. They are resounding examples, and they are near to the characters populating the events of the days before the celebration of the San Giovanni 1514. The characters in the Fusta are their mimics, their 'spitting image'.

One is Querini, who had changed not only his profession, but also his name. Vincenzo Querini was a Venetian nobleman in the diplomatic career, he had taken holy orders of the Camaldolite hermits (a branch of Benedictines, in the vale of Camaldoli in Tuscany), with his friend Giustiniani. He had changed his name from Vincenzo to Piero, and although he was supposed to be a hermit, is now in Rome, very near to the pope, expected to be made a cardinal shortly[68]. Querini, even though he may wear the humble habit (even to go hunting at the Magliana?), is expected to wear purple shortly, to don the cardinal's hat. He attends the pope's court daily, more frequently than the Medicean correspondents themselves. He goes hunting to the Magliana with the pope, as Baldassarre Turini reports with some 'emulation' in his letters to Lorenzo.

Perhaps we should allow for the fact that some of these may be rumours and gossip. But it is the rumours, especially those in the letters from Alfonsina and her secretary to Lorenzo, that count to set the moods of these days before the S. Giovanni.

Alfonsina's secretary, Baldassarre Turini da Pescia, is the correspondent from Rome from whom we gather the information as to what was going on in Rome, or rather, how what was going on in Rome is possibly relevant to the affairs of Florence, and how that was translated to Lorenzo, and therefore how that could be perceived by him and by those we call 'the Florentines', the families allied to the Medici in Florence – those that are the ones responsible for the organization of the celebrations for San Giovanni in 1514. We have seen his letters and noticed their relevance before.

One of these letters from Baldassarre Turini da Pescia contains a strange yet clear sentence in mixed languages, about Querini at the papal court: "*Querini tratta qui oltre che le cose dei Viniziani, cose grande, ed est apud hos nosotros maxime auctoritatis* – Querini deals here, beside the Venetian affairs, of great things and is, among us, of great authority', showing more than a hint of irony, with his bit of Spanish and his bit of Latin (from Rome, May 11 1514).[69]

Piero Querini (or Vincenzo), so near to the Holy Father that he was received by him daily, and accompanied him on his trips to the Magliana [70] for hunts and entertainments. He was close to Bembo, Soderini and Giuliano de' Medici, he was cardinal in pectore, pushing 'reform and who knows what other '*cose grande* – big things'. This Querini was one who had gone farther than many, in the eyes of the Florentines, at least. It was Querini who dealt with the matter of the Venetian ships. Hence the relevance of S.ta Croce and the Crusade project[71], of which Querini was taking care, and for which he had obtained money from Leo X for Venice. Inquisition threats because of ill thought 'reform', instigated by someone who had changed a lot and furthered his career.

Another outstanding case, also reaching to high places, although of a different quality, and nearer to the level of the jesters – too well loved by the Medici pope nevertheless – was Fra Mariano. This is someone who has changed trade (often), profession (enough), with remarkable success in his 50 years of working life.

Fra Mariano Fetti had started his career as Lorenzo the Magnificent's barber. After the death of Lorenzo and the exile of the Medici to Rome, he is found in Rome, a jester for Julius II. Now he is one of the new Medici pope's jesters, very near also to Alfonsina, Lorenzo's mother (we see him mentioned often in her letters, with requests of favours also from Florence). He had been granted by Leo X the lucrative office of '*Piombatore*' (Master of the Seals).

To this very desirable office, lucrative and prestigious – before him it had been held by Bramante, (Benvenuto Cellini would apply for it to no avail after Fra Mariano's death when the office passed to Sebastiano del Piombo). Fra Mariano had been appointed to it in April 1514, only two months before the San Giovanni in question [72] therefore it was known he had certainly well progressed in his career.

To arrive where he got to, Fra Mariano had gone through several changes of trade. He had been the barber of Lorenzo the Magnificent (*il Vecchio*), had then become a Dominican friar (as many found it suitable to become at the time of Savonarola), then had become a jester for Julius II, first, and for Leo X, later, in Rome. Those are not the only changes in his progress, he also had to change from being Dominican to becoming a Cistercian friar, because the office of 'Piombatore' was a prerogative of the Cistercian order. He managed however to keep the use for life of the Dominican church and convent of San Silvestro, another source of income. So he ended up being both a Dominican and a Cistercian.

Fra Mariano, as opposed to Gio. Tancredi, in about fifty years (he was born in 1460) has certainly changed trade, profession and order several times, to good profit and advancement..

As well as Lorenzo, Pope Julius II and Pope LeoX who employed him now, Carafulla also must have known fra Mariano very well, at least for 'professional' reasons.

Carafulla is the other character in a satirical poem of 1515 (manuscript copy dated 1515 ascribed to Bernardo Giambullari), dedicated to fra Mariano himself. In it Carafulla is introduced as:

'*...un omacino strano*
che non l'avresti stimato una frulla
e non pareva abate nè piovano
Maestro Antonio chiamato Scharafulla
che disfinisce e dischiara ogni dubbio
e par pur de dotrina e non à nulla'
(ll. 100-105)

'A strange little man
you would have not valued a feather
and did not seem either abbot or priest
Maestro Antonio called Scharafulla
who (dis)defines and clarifies all doubts
and seems a learned fellow, but he has nothing'
(ll. 100-105)[73]

Maestro Antonio is inside the poem, but is also one of the two characters who, in a brief dialogue, open it: Biagio and Tonio (Antonio, obviously). Tonio is the one '*con il chapo pien di grilli e di zampognie* – with the 'head full of whims and puffs of wind '(l.12) . And Biagio is Biagio del Capperone, Giambullari himself. This burlesque poem consists of a series of grotesque 'triumphs' as 'doni', i.e. presents, offerings, that Lorenzo offers to Fra Mariano. It has no title, but a sort of address, or dedication, made to sound like the banns of a town crier (*banditore....*)[74]

'Appresso sarà nota del presente
mandato dal Magnifico Lorenzo de' Medici
a Fra Mariano dell'ordine di....' (sic)

'Here follows the notice of a present
sent by Magnifico Lorenzo de' Medici
to Fra Mariano of the order of.......(sic). [75]

Fra Mariano is named as of an order without a name. Naturally, because he has two, as as we have seen, Dominican and Cistercian. So the order is left a blank on purpose, as a hint, surely.

Giambullari here, addressing Fra Mariano, parodies and also collaborates with Carafulla, by making a sort of punning caricature of his name[76] (according to what at III.3, n.22 is reported being the character of Carafulla as known to Nardi, Varchi and Aretino)

An 'accusation' of penury, and not only of an empty head, in the line 'he has nothing' is also a likely accusation. Aretino too calls Carafulla '*meschinello'* a poor little man. Furthermore Maestro Antonio wears a threadbare black cloak and hood, because he was poor (Cambi), even as captain of the *Fusta*. So Giambullari makes an altogether congruous observation. At the risk of belabouring the point, Carafulla (and later we shall see Gio.Tancredi di Sta Croce) is poor owing to being foolish, or prodigal – *furiosus vel prodigus* – [77] irresponsible, blameworthy, highly censured, and thoroughly a Fool – in a threadbare black cloak and hood as he well deserves.

Carafulla is poor because he is a Fool, and that he is a Fool is proved by the fact that he is poor.

Giambullari echoes Carafulla's own words, when he gets Tonio (obviously Antonio, but made into a peasant name, as of a clown[78]) to say: '*O Biagio, onde viem tu? Che sie impichato!* – O Biagio, where are you coming from. May you be hanged!' in the first line of the poem, as they meet. It was a little game of Carafulla's, as Aretino remembers, to demand to be called Your Majesty, and to send his imaginary subjects to be hanged [79] .

Fra Mariano and Carafulla are in ideal (and at times indeed real) competition as alternative representatives of the courts of Rome and Florence. Their competition will be clearly expressed and reported the following year, when, in 1515, for the ceremonial presentation of the '*Bastone'* – the mace of office- to Lorenzo, who was already Captain of the Militia. Fra Mariano will ask to be sent from Rome to take part officially to the celebrations and carry the '*bastone'*, be the mace bearer. His application must have been unsuccessful, as the record in Aretino reports Carafulla 'in white cermonial dress' in the pageant of the '*bastone* [80] (E.V. Thompson and Aretino *Ragionamento* cit. pp.93-94.)

In Florence now the theatricals of the festival are a celebration of Lorenzo (not Giuliano or Leo X), and it is Carafulla, to have the counter-centre of the stage.

It is reasonable to assume, in view of all the 'competition' and 'emulation', which we have had the opportunityof discussing at length in this chapter (see above IV.2. and IV.3), between those who stayed in Rome seeking advancement, and those who were in Florence, that Fra Mariano, the one successful in Rome with his Roman patrons, would be, at Jesters' level, one to be satirized. As well as being given to Carafulla for a hanging, in the basket, in the composite figure of Gio Tancredi, the most foolish of all.

Carafulla, we are told, amused himself by summoning his imaginary cousellors, 'pretending to be a Gran Maestro' and then giving orders that they should be hanged. Now he is head, chief, governor of the *Fusta* from which someone is lifted up in a hanging basket, and that one, we know, is a poor devil who wears wool, and still carries the wool, because he in fifty years he had never changed his trade and does not even think of being called Maestro. Fra Mariano was fifty four years old, had changed his trade (and religious order) several times, and had reached a good position.

Carafulla, in Florence, however, although he is nothing, is way beyond, now. He is the Captain of a very important ship, and he can swing people in a basket.

****

These two, Carafulla and Gio.Tancredi, must be really foolish, as they do not hanker after power. They are able to jest about it, deride it instead. One leaves aside his own interests and thinks of the good of Florence rather than himself, and consequently remains poor – like Carafulla. The other never changes his trade and sticks to the wool – like the even more foolish Giovanni. It would be sufficient to go to Rome, change your trade according to the more profitable trends to obtain real power – great authority *apud hos nosotros* – words perhaps echoing ironically some Spanish cardinal's household – to obtain rich offices, revenue of churches and convents, to change from wool to silk, and perhaps also to a cardinal's purple robe.

Furthermore, considering that this is a satirical piece of very public civic 'theatre', organized to comment upon (among other things) a certain foreign policy which carries also a project of Crusade at the head of which the pope himself, Leo X, whose name is Giovanni, dreams of sailing, it does not seem at all improbable that a figure called Giovanni, with a surname Tancredi like one of the chiefs, and hero of the first Crusade, and citizen of Santa Croce [81] might well be a character created *ad hoc* by the organizers, the Medici

Compagie[82]. This Gio Tancredi is a composite figure, but also precisely defined, pointing in sevearal directions.

That he might be a character created on a script is also suggested by the fact that Sanudo's correspondent has spotted an actor in the *Fusta* among the sailors/fools.

Although this is mentioned only in Sanudos *Diaries* [83] among the buffoons in the *fusta* there was a certain Barlacchi. Barlacchi, or Domenico Barlacchia, or Barlachia, was a young employee and friend of one of the better known masters of the revels, Filippo Strozzi. He was an actor, a comic actor who specialized in old men parts, even as a young man. He went on to have a long successful career and became very well known[84]. He may well be the one be the one who played the rôle of Gio. Tancredi del Quart. di Sta Croce.

Gio. Tancredi by his name and the allusion to a Crusade impersonated a recognizable caricature through which the Florentine contingent could express, indirectly, what they thought of what was going on in Rome: there was someone in high places who did foolish and crazy things, who led a Venetian ship of fools, the *Fusta piena di matti* headed by someone as mad as a hatter, and that someone, even more foolish, at the core of it all, represented a Crusader. The were all driven by devils, evil counsellors all.

If the figure of this Giovanni Tancredi of Santa Croce is, as it seems to be turning out, a script interpreted by an actor, this being a servant and friend of Filippo Strozzi, one of the principal *festaioli,* we have here a fairly clear indication of a definite intention, a proper plan, in the setting up of the *Fusta piena di matti* and the characters in it.

This fool, Gio. Tancredi, Giovanni and Crusader, much more foolish than Maestro Antonio, caught up in a basked, put to the oar and beaten by the devils, sums up in a nutshell what is the direction the comments of the *fusta* are taking. And the question that he is a scripted character does not leave doubt as to the fact, already indicated by the abundant circumstancial evidence, that the *Fusta piena di matti* is not a simple burlesque, but a well aimed and focused creation.

Gio. Tancredi del Quart. di S. Croce is however an 'appendix', so to speak, as well as a validation, of Carafulla, the principal carrier of symbols and recollections – the Golden Age, the wider political situation and so forth. So we must proceed to round off the Carafulla figure.

IV.6.i. *Maestro Antonio di Pierrozzo da Vespignano. Maker of hoods.*
Head of the Fusta. *Governor of a Company. Prince of Fools.*

Carafulla, Maestro Antonio, was a Master of his trade, but also, as a jester or fool, impersonator of himself as Grande Maestro, important person in authority, with a following of imaginary counsellors. He spoke to himself, gave himself the answers, and telling himself 'Your Majesty should have done such and such, send them to be hanged, such and such. [85] He was a character capable of collecting in himself, and expressing, a number of symbolical motives based, nevertheless, on real facts belonging to his actual life and person, his trade and his actions, altogether extraordinary in the apparent normality of famous 'nobody'. It is uncanny how well suited his reality is to his symbolical *persona*.

Carafulla, chief and governor of the *fusta*, who had disregarded his own interests (in this like Piero Soderini, we were told), and who, when the wheel of fortune turns towards Rome returns to Florence, now impersonates power as a jest and in the '*festa*' – a power, however, by which he is not owned, and which leaves him free to exterminate the counsellors he does not like, while still retaining a title of Your Majesty. He is back in Florence holding court in his workshop, making up puns and elaborate etymologies [86], and *making hoods,* that is his trade. Where can such a character lead the ship of fools if not on a mad journey to hell and ruin, to nothingness? -

Or to new and unknown worlds, to the Happy Islands of the Golden Age, perhaps.

And thus Carafulla, dear to Leo X who singles him out in a pair with Piero Soderini – the same Leo X who now holds the Soderinis and various other '*cappucci*' (hoods) dear likewise [87], and mends or improves their fortunes by giving them status beside him – is made an example and a symbol.

Carafulla with so many signs and signals of power (reversed) and folly, in the world of the *festa* in which sometimes '*il da beffe torna dadovero* – what was in jest turns up to be true' (perhaps for the will of God himself, at least in the *Trecento*, as in Villani) was a very good match. He was the right charachter to impersonate the pope, as governor of a ship (St. Peter's ship), a Venetian ship at that, the *fusta* – and as a prodigal aspiring chief of a Crusade on Venetian ships.

Carafulla wore a well worn black cloak and a hood, and we shall soon see that for one who frequents the palace, wearing a black cloak means that he is mad.

Carafulla, is on the *Fusta* in a black cloak '*chom usava vestire, che era assai consumato, perch'era povero* – as he usually wore, which was threadbare, because he was poor' writes Cambi. So he was poor – poor because prodigal perhaps, therefore mad [88] and the distinguishing mark of his situation is the black threadbare cloak. .

That the black cloak is a sign of poverty and madness is well explained in the burlesque poem (first published in 1489) *La Compagnia del Mantellaccio* – the company, or Fraternity of the Tattered Cloak) [89] . It may have been a stock symbol in carnivalesque culture In this poem we also find a *festa* structure (the hierarchies, for instance) and rôles who can be models for some of the aspects of Carafulla in this San Giovanni of 1514 – madness, familiarity with those in the seat of power, symbolical tattered black cloak.

The tattered black cloak can be worn as a 'costume' as we also may infer from the frontispiece of the published poem, where the figures, including Lorenzo *Il Magnifico,* wear tattered cloaks and, to make sure that they look 'poor', Lorenzo sports a patch on his hose. It is in doubt whether such a '*Compagnia*' existed in reality, yet the poem is a full description of an ideal festive fraternity, and as such it is used here to enrich and explain the traditional background of our festive characters. In the spirit of the returning Golden Age, we should mention, as well, as it comes from the Magnificent's times..

In the 'company' there was a Governor:

'*Simone del Mangano è Governatore*
Et per insegna porta un mantellaccio -

Simon Mangano [90] is Governor
and as insignia he wears a tattered cloak' [91]

The cloak of the title is the subject of a game carried on several three line stanzas. The Governor has an aid, Pier Fabrini [92] who goes around to collect the members of the company who, when assembled are addressed by the governor:

'*Cari frategli da poi che S.Godenzio*
le nostre prece non vuol esaudire...

Dear brothers, since Saint Gaudentius[93]
has not been listening to our prayers...'

the consequence – as a sacrifice, in order to appease the saint – shall be to be penitent and wear torn clothes and a tattered cloak.

Now since Simone's usual one is an expensive and elegant cloak, he will have to change it. He asks for another:

'Con uno dei vostri lo vorró scambiare
levi su chi questo vuole ubbidire...

With one of yours I will exchange it
someone take his off, to obey me...'[94]

The game, the fooling around turns on the characteristics of the cloak: it has to be black, then tattered and torn, and also being exchanged – it all applies to Carafulla and his cloak too.[95]

After lengthy fooling about over this cloak to be exchanged and offered to the governor, one of the company, Arrigo degli Spini[96] announces:

'Che nelle Stinche stetti ben trenta anni
non chel mantello tutti glia altri panni
scambiar voglio babbo reverendo

I was in the Stinche prison for thirty years
so that not only my cloak, but all my clothes
I want to exchange reverend father[97]

But if this was an offer, it is not taken up.

Then another interlocutor, Lionardo Dossi [98] says he cannot spare his one, but while explaining why gives us important information:

'Caro guardiano, io pratico il palazzo
et perchè ho un po' chativi lucci
col mantel nero sarei tenuto pazzo..

Dear guardian, I frequent the palace
and my cloaks are already not too good,[99]
but with a black cloak I would be held as mad'.[100]

But fortunately, at page four, finally Giovan Guiducci [101] arrives, it is he who:

'Che senza sconcio vi puó comodare
perchè egli ha due, e due cappucci.

.... can help you without damage
because he has two, and two hoods.'

So, Giovan Guiducci, the well guided, the well kept, has two cloaks, one to spare. ...But he also has two hoods... may there be some 'hood' or *cappucci* question here?

Carafulla, 'in a black cloak and hood ... that was threadbare', which will be torn further, and later he will be given a second one, has the insignia, and completes a ritual as a real 'Governor' in a *festa*, just as it is displayed in the Lorenzo's Company of the Tattered Cloak", *La Compagnia del Mantellaccio*.

The connection with, and possibly a revival of, the *Compagnia del Mantellaccio,* with the figure of Lorenzo *il Magnifico* on the woodcut on the frontispiece, is also consonant with the intention of the return of the Secol d'Oro, the Golden Age of Lorenzo. He sang '*le temps revient*', and now the revival of the emblems and times of Lorenzo *il Magnifico*, our Lorenzo's grandfather, is being remembered in this restoration of 1512 in all manners possible. Principally with the '*Broncone*' – used as name by one of the '*compagnie*' – the trunk of laurel which '*che rinverdiva le foglie per significare che rinverdiva il nome dell'avolo* – sprouted leaves to signify that the name of the grandfather was revived', with the repetition of Lauro, even with 'typographical fictions' when publications were printed, perhaps intentionally, to appear as of the XV century, but couldn't be, as they contained later material [102].

Everything concurs to reveal the intention of re-creating the *ambience* of before 1492 as if it were in the present. Trying to take the last years of Lorenzo over into this political restoration of 1512 and see it as a rebirth. Perhaps Carafulla is doing it also through the *Compagnia del Mantellaccio.*

IV.6.ii. *The* Apologia dei Cappucci, *and the recycled hoods.*

Cloaks and hoods are often paired, as when Giovan Guiducci comes over with his offer.

So we have spoken of the cloak, but the hood, *cappuccio,* deserves some attention now.

Maestro Antonio actually was a maker of hoods, (a sort of hatter), he had a workshop which was used as a meeting place of storytellers and assorted eccentric characters. He wore a hood, no doubt – both Cambi and Sanudo mention his headwear as a distinctive item. Of course it is also a matter of 'dusguise' and a matter of definition. It is a fool's hood. But it may carry also political connotations.

Jacopo Pitti was to write, in the second half of the XVI century, an apology of the so called republican period (1494-1512), and of Savonarola, in the form of a dialogue by the title *Apologia dei Cappucci* as a polemic against the historical views of the Medicean Guicciardini and what, according to Pitti, was

Guicciardini's 'slandering of the government of the Florentine republic, the people, and its best citizens" [103] .

He was writing polemically of 'foreigners' (those who did not like the Florentines, as we know) '*Eh, sì, noi siamo tassati da' forestieri di grande avarizia e soverchia parsimonia per non dire ispilorceria* – Oh, yes, we are accused by foreigners of great avarice, of excessive parsimony not to say stinginess" [104], because they, the foreigners, according to Pitti, the goods of fortune " they consume them all at the service of their bellies, and of the arrogance of being accompanied by followers and liveries without ever dreaming what is republic (res publica), universal good.. – *se li consumano tutti al servizio del ventre, della boria d'aver dietro codazzi e livree senza sognare giammai che cosa sia repubblica, bene universale*'[105]

After this he begins his defence of the 'republic', in the '*forma viniziana* – Venetian form' proposed, in Florence, by Pagolantonio Soderini (the third of the Soderini brothers – brother of Piero and cardinal Francesco) who was the theoretician for the republic of Savonarola.

Jacopo Pitti begins his anti-Medicean dialogue [106] with a virulent: 'the Florentines, having shaken off Piero de' Medici' in 1494', then introduces Pagolantonio Soderini [107] who was a republican political theorist and had proposed the 'Venetian form' [108] as the best type of republic. This was Aristotelic, opposed to a Florentine Platonic form of government. Pagolantonio Soderini 'not without some difficulty of being accepted by the citizens', it is admitted, advised fra Girolamo Savonarola 'to preach it ardently, for the common benefit'.

The choice, we see, although called 'democratic' was to be imposed on the Florentine citizens by the well known 'ardent' preaching – and what opinion the Florentines had of it was demonstrated in 1498, when the friar was captured '*a furor di popolo* – by an uprising of the people' to be tried and condemned. And what sort of fire Savonarola's 'ardent' preaching has lit up for himself is also well known.

However, Republic, according to Pitti, and Pagolantonio Soderini, has its origin in the republican idea and form proposed by Aristotle, and on which, in their theory[109], the Venetian form of republic was based. Comparisons between Venice, the successful republic, and Florence, forever failing to establish one may have also contributed to the feeling of competition and campanilistic animosity between the two cities.

While the idea of state, in the Medici's Florence, was elaborated by a culture which took inspiration from Plato and neo-Platonism [110] (Plato's Laws etc.).

Thus the '*cappucci*' of Pitti's title (often also called *popolani*) are 'republicans', but were also friars, and evoke echoes of Savonarolian heresy, and the form of republicanism represented by the Soderini brothers and (misplaced) loyalties towards them. Several "*cappucci*", failed or expelled from Florence are in exile in Rome, finding welcome and influence in the papal court, together with other reforming friars – Querini for one, with Giustiniani – renewed, refreshed, recycled *cappucci*. A sort of reversed return the Golden Age? Much as they celebrate and recall Lorenzo il Magnifico's Golden Age and show green branches and new leaves sprouting on the laurel log, the *Broncone,* in Florence – in Rome on the other hand the *cappucci* resurface as if recycled.

Piero Soderini, having lost his office of *Gonfaloniere a vita*, having been banned from Florence soon after the restoration of the Medici in August 1512, had ended up in Rome, and now is more welcome – at least in the minds of those who were sent back to Florence – and more powerful than themselves (including young Lorenzo). He has power and access to the pope together with his brother the cardinal, and all those Venetians, friars, cardinals and prophets. They are near to the pope who seems intent on renewing and recycling the fortunes of the '*cappucci*'.

Maestro Antonio il Carafulla had it as a trade, to actually make *cappucci*, and now he is on the *Fusta piena di matti*, Governor, in the *festa*, driven, instigated, jostled by devils.

Here Carafulla, in his aspect of maker of '*cappucci*'- hoods, can allude also to this aspect of Leo X, as one who recycles *cappucci*, while in his aspect of wearer of a hood he also alludes to Piero Soderini.

Piero Soderini, (not necessarily in person, but clearly impersonated), had appeared as a hooded figure in a *festa*, in a pageant [111], at the bottom of the Wheel of Fortune, in Rome, in the Carnival of 1513. The scene had not gone unnoticed, as we find it described in Sanudo's *Diaries*. In Venice Sanudo writes that in Rome, on 28th February 1513 (that is before the election of Leo X, which occurred on March 10, but after the restoration of the Medici in Florence, August 1512) there was a pageant (a carnival cart) with a great Wheel of Fortune (which was also a favourite emblem of Lorenzo Il Magnifico), with a '*marzocco*' (the sitting lion of Florence) on the rise, with a figure at the top representing the Medici, and at the bottom '*uno vestido con uno mantello e uno capuzzo in cao, si dice era il confalonier Soderini olim in Fiorenza* – someone dressed in a cloak with a hood on his head, said to be the Gonfaloniere Soderini once of Florence" [112].

That Carafulla was wearing a cloak, we have abundantly seen. But he was also '*in capuzo*'- in a hood, Sanudo adds, in the summary of a letter from Florence recording the *fusta*' of the San Giovanni of 1514 [113]

Here we have Carafulla and Soderini iconographically connected, as they are in discourse in the pope's remarks recorded by Nardi.

The information in Sanudo' *Diaries,* regarding the *Fusta*, is from a 'Summary of a letter from Florence'. Although the letter is summarized and the language is Sanudo's, a mention remains, of Florence, as 'this city of ours'. So the author was a Florentine. Perhaps one of the several Florentines followers of the Medici who had spent their exile years in Venice rather than in Rome.

The facts reported in Sanudo are substantially the same as those in the Florentine chronicles, but his informations seem more precise as to some detail: the information about the actor Barlacchi comes from him, and so do the costumes (marinary – sailor's liveries). Furthermore he is better informed than the others about the contingent of the Cardinals coming from Rome, gate-crashing, so to speak, the festival, a matter to be discussed in the next chapter, at V.2..

We do not get a description of the sailors livery indicated by Sanudo's correspondent, nor do we have it in the Florentine chroniclers who don't seem to have paid attention to it – it was probably more recognizable to a Venetian. However the mention of the 'livery' for the rest of the crew, and the mention of Carafulla '*in capuzo*', in a hood, and, as we know, in his black well worn cloak – both highly significant – separates him as a figure in a distinctive relief against the indistinct but uniform group of the rest of the crew of fools. Carafulla will have his miniature, his '*marotte*' [114] when the basket captures Gio. Tancredi.

That Carafulla was in real life also a maker of hoods, and a was a Master in his art, does not cease to amaze me. The coincidence with the idea of the ancient fool's hood, as well as with the political meaning of *cappuccio* in Florence, I find it a matter of wonder. He wears a hood, as well as making them, in an exceptionally conspicuous way, as a chief of the *Fusta piena di Matti*. Perhaps he is also good at recycling those *cappucci*, or rather impersonating someone who does, I should say.

1 See Luca LANDUCCI, *Diario Fiorentino dal 1450 al 1516,* edited by Iodoco del Badia, Firenze 1889, anno 1512, pp.322-325. The population of the surrounding countryside had taken refuge within the walls of the small city of Prato, bringing in their families and goods. The Spanish troops breached the wall and perpetrated a terrible massacre with, of course, raping and looting, on 29th August. Such was the ferocity of the troops that laid waste of the city, that a famine ensued, which is remembered and commemorated with a 'festival' to this day.

A translation from the Italian, by Alice de Rosen Jervis, of the *Diary* , published in London 1927 by Dent is also available,

2 *Ibidem*

3 These are well known events, as are the dates. However, because of the fundamental place of these events and dates to our investigation, we refer again to the basic sources: i.e. Luca LANDUCCI, *Diario*, a cura di Jodoco del BADIA, Firenze, 1883, pp.235 and 238, for that taking of the *Palazzo della Signoria* in particular, and William ROSCOE, *The Life and Pontificate of Leo X,* London 1846, vol I, pp. 285-286 for the election of Leo X. Of the three Medici brothers, Piero (1471-1503), the eldest, father of young Lorenzo, had died by drowning in 1503 in the Garigliano river during a battle.

4 L. PASTOR, *The Lives of the Popes,* London 1908, vol VII, p. 25, *passim*. William ROSCOE, *The life and Pontificate of Leo X* cit. Chapter X. With reference to the festivities in Rome and Florence see my article *Un' occasione*...cit. (Quaderni di teatro – marzo 1980), pp.121-124

5 See quotation from Nardi relative to this observation, at IV.2 below , and notes

6 -This is mentioned more fully in IV.2, note 5;

7 See IV.4. below. Cesare VASOLI, *La Profezia di Francesco da Meleto,* in *Umanesimo e ermeneutica*, Padova, Cedam, 1963, p.33. The 'prophet' Francesco da Meleto had been summoned to Rome in the Spring 1514, through the priest Antonio Zeno, who worked for Francesco Soderini, Zeno had provided him with funds, he had been invited by Querini, and in Rome he was a guest of Bembo. He was a 'fortunate traveller' (at least up to June 1514). His itinerary and presence in Rome proves the alliances of Soderini with the Venetians, the Venetian Cardinals., and the usual suspects of Savonarolian descent.

8 As for Giuliano there was a question of the kingdom of Naples – for which a Venetian fleet was being negotiated. He was also being organized with marriages of convenience, dangerous dealings with the French. Eventually he marries Filiberta di Savoia, who brings him the duchy of Nemours in 1515, but this is later. He will die in March 1516.

9 Edited by ILDEFONSO DI SAN LUIGI, in *Delizie degli eruditi toscani*, appendice, vol .24, p.2 BARTOLINI SALIMBENI writes: '*Di poi che Papa Lione fu assunto al Pontificato, nacque fra il Magnifico Giuliano Duca di Nemours, et il Magnifico Lorenzo emulatione grande perché ognuno voleva avere luogo appresso sua Santità, et havendo ottenuto il Duca Giuliano el Capitanato generale della Chiesa ... al Magnifico Lorenzo non restava altro grado che pigliiare cura delle cose di Firenze la quale da Papa Lione etiam con consenso di Giuliano gli era stato concesso*' Bartolini Salimbeni wrote his *Cronichetta* for Francesco Guicciardini, asked by the same Guicciardini; he declares that he will report all that he remembers from the time he was employed by Lorenzo, as he had been asked to do.

10 L. PASTOR, *Lives of the Popes* cit., vol VIII, pp. 167-168. The festivities to celebrate the granting of the honorary citizenship took place in September 1513, but Lorenzo was ordered back to Florence on August 10th (see PASTOR cit., vol.VII, p. 80 and Luca LANDUCCI, *Diario*, cit., p.341)

11 Gherardo BARTOLINI SALIMBENI, *Cronichetta* cit., p.3.

12 L. PASTOR, *Lives of the Popes* cit., vol. VII, p.81, as appears very clearly also in Bartolini

Salimbeni quoted at note 5 above.

13 *Ibidem*, and note. See also W. ROSCOE, *Life and Pontificate of Leo* X cit., vol.I, p. 375, *passim*.

14 Cardinal Giulio was the son of the murdered Giuliano (Congiura dei Pazzi (26th April 1478, Santa Reparata, during the Mass), he will be the future Clement VII. See letter ASF, MAP, Filza CXIII, febbraio 1514. From Giulio and from Alfonsina's secretary the letters are very frequent, also two per day, with replies *a giro di cavalcata* – by return of ride. The letter mentioned suggests to him to be liberal with entertaining and being affable with those that are to be attracted and to entertain them both in town and in the country: '*qualche cerimonia exteriore di affabilitá et gratitudine di parole da le quali ne saria liberale con quelli ad chi più se ne convengono et che ne son più desiderosi ... intrattenere ... quando uno et quando un altro ad mangiare seco non solo nella città ma in villa...*'

15 ASF, MAP, Filza CVII, carta .35.

16 *Idem*, carte 42 and 43

17 *Idem*, carta 38

18 *Idem*, carta 45

19 Jacopo NARDI, *Istorie della città di Firenze*, cit., vol, II –VI, xix, p. 27. It is actually possible that Nardi might have been instructed to take the comments down, as he was the official historian, or reporter.

20 It is also possible to read part of this observation in the context of the policy of 'generosity and clemency' towards the Soderini family as ROSCOE observes, and to please cardinal Francesco Soderini (ROSCOE cit, p. 305). Coupled with *maestro Antonio cappucciaio chiamato il Carafulla*, however.

21 Maestro Antonio was a 'jester', and pope Leo X *de' cianciatori, giocolatori e buffoni si dilettò... sempre troppo* – of chatterers, jugglers and jesters ... he always took too much pleasure (J. NARDI, *Istorie* cit., Vol. II, VII, I, p.63) so no wonder that he was singled out to be praised. Yet, the coupling with Piero Soderini on this occasion, is very interesting.

22 Jacopo PITTI, *Apologia dei cappucci,* in Archivio Storico Italiano, Tomo IV, vol. II: *'cappucci erano i popolani'*, as a political 'faction', but also, just 'of the people' as opposed to definable 'classes' the merchants, the noble families....... See also Benvenuto CELLINI, *Vita*, (ed a cura di Cattaneo, Milano, 1958, c.17, p.53

23 *'che si fanno e sono suoi parenti'* who make themselves to be, or are, his relations, as the Venetian Ambassador writes – see note 27 below.

24 Richard C. TREXLER, *Public Life in Renaissance Florence*, 1980, pp. 507-509. He refers to the *Fusta dei Matti* of 1514 as a singular and only example of burlesque in official celebrations (1300-1530). And indeed the burlesque is the style of traditional/popular, rather than official, festivals. Official celebrations have the power to make their point directly. It is the powerless that must resort to covert and oblique references. Neverthelss, both in Florence and in Rome it was public knowledge that the *festa* can change a political situation, as demontrated in ALBERTI's *Momus seu de principe*, as discussed in I. 2. *Momus* must have circulated these years, and indeed had to have new editions in 1520 in Rome. Had it gone out of print because much sought these days?

25 Cesare VASOLI, *La profezia di Francesco da Meleto*, cit., p.33.

26 Florence had very bad memories of the French, who had been instrumental in the fall of the Medici Signoría in 1494, which allowed the reign of terror of Savonarola, and the subsequent 'republic' just overthrown. Venice now was pressing for a French alliance. There were also webs of campanilistic and cultural rivalry between Florence and Venice, in both directions.

27 Cesare VASOLI, *La profezia* cit., p.34. See also letter from Baldassarre Turini da Pescia '*apud hos*

nosotros...' ASF, MAP, ... He had indeed been offered the cardinalate, but because of his early death, in September 1514 , he will not be fully nominated and will not receive the cardinal's hat.

28 Vittorio CIAN, *A proposito di un' ambasceria di M. Pietro Bembo,* in *Archivio Veneto*, vol. XXX (1885), p.362. Lando and Querini kept regularly informed the government of Venice. (Archivio di Venezia)

29 *Idem*, p. 371. And see letter from Baldassarre Turini '... *apud hos nosotros...*' ASF MAP, filza CXVII, n.23 also at note 57 below.

30 (Cesare VASOLI, *La profezia...* cit., p.34)). It was probably as a result of the *Libellus* that Querini was called to Rome, he was offered a cardinalate, but was still only *in pectore,* and would become Cardinal upon nomination, which he could not receive because of his untimely death (note 28 above). See IV.4., note 34.

31 The third of the Soderini brothers, Pagolantonio, had been ambassador of the Florentine Republic to Venice from 1495 to 1498 (See *Commissioni di Pagolantonio Soderini e G.B. Ridolfi,* Venezia, 1901) Pagolantonio had been the theoretician of the Savonarolian republic, and there was a question of the *forma viniziana*. The Aristotelian, or Venetian form, was opposed to a Platonic form of republic, one that vaguely may have informed the Florentine ideas, and that was certainly extolled with reference to Leo X at his election to the papacy. when '*Sol Leo Noster'* appeared on triumphal arches, comparing new pope Leo to Apollo-Helios of ancient Greece. See also IV.6.ii... As for Venice as a model republic, see also Jacopo PITTI, *Apologia dei Cappucci* cit., Tomo IV, Vol. II, pp.271 ff. And IV.6.ii. of the present study. Later (1544) Gasparo Contarini, the third of Querini's friends from Padova University, was to write *De Magistratibus et Republica Venetarum*, where Contarini suggested that the secret of Venice's greatness lay in the co-existence of Aristotle's three types of government, monarchy, oligarchy, and democracy. In his opinion, Venice's *Maggior Consiglio* was the 'democratic' part, the Senate and 'The Ten' were the oligarchy, while the Doge represented monarchy . This was what was thought to be '*la forma viniziana*'.

That the lack of sympathy between Florentines and Venetians might be reciprocated is evident in this report to the Senate of the Republic of Venice by the Venetian Ambassador to the court of Leo X , Marco MINIO, on his arrival in Rome in 1516: '*Il qual Papa è fiorentino; tuttavia è buona persona ed ama questo stato [Venezia]... E questi [Leone X] per cagion di Fiorenza ha poca entrata per il papato.... Non ha contanti, perché è liberale, e non sa tenere i danari; e poi i fiorentini, che fanno e sono suoi parenti non lo lasciano mai avere un soldo; e i detti fiorentini sono in grand'odio alla corte, perché in ogni cosa son fiorentin'* – the pope is a Florentine, and nevertheless he is a good person and loves this state [Venice] And he [Leo X] because of Florence, does not have much income for the papacy... He does not have money because he is generous and is unable to hold on to money; and also the Florentines, who pretend or are relatives of his do not let him have any money; and the said Florentines are much hated at court, because they are Florentine in every way '- in: *Relazioni degli ambasciatori veneti,* ed. Albèri, Bari, Laterza, 1846, serie II, vol.III, p.63

32 *Fusta* was a small ship much used in Venice '*molto usata dalla repubblica di Venezia dal 1498 al 1570'* states the *Dizionario della marina medievale a moderna*, Roma 1937 cit. See also initial chapter of the present study, ***The Stage*** note 1.

Although the fusta was not exclusive to the Venetian navy as it was a swift ship with a low profile, and as such favoured by North African corsairs, for instance. Ariosto knew the *fusta* , in his *Orlando furioso* we find *fuste* as used in Egypt (canto XX, st. lxxv), and even on the Northern coasts and islands (cantoCanto VII, st.lx), as well as at Canto XXXIX, st.xxvii).

33 Letter from Baldassarre Turini da Pescia (Alfonsina's secretary) to Lorenzo, August 1514. (A.S. F., MAP, filza CVII, n.54) from: Cesare VASOLI *La profezia di Francesco da Meleto* cit., p.34, note 26.

I must say that a purpose or promise relating to conversion of infidels is one of the principles of faith to which a new pope is asked to adhere, as I read in Landucci's *Diary*, where three *Capitoli* are quoted from a list of thirty that were submitted the new pope, which he would be under oath to obey, including one saying that '...*fussi ubrigato a ragunare una congregazione di cristiani e ordinare la Santa Chiesa, e pensare contra gli Infedeli, e leggere due volte l'anno questi capitoli nella congregazione* . . . he was obliged to collect a congragation of Christians to look after the Holy Church and think of against the infidels, and read these chapters twice a year to this congregation' this in the *2nd capitolo* (*Diario* cit. p.338). And indeed, all the Crusades that were undertaken in the early centuries had that ideal as a basis. Territorial gains, profits from wars, plunder and so forth came with it as well. Like for all the following colonizations and missions. However, questions of Crusade were by now a distant matter, nor were they entertained by the secular, albeit Catholic, powers.. Offshoots of Crusading times, like the orders of the KnightTemplars for instance, had already been outlawed and eliminated by the Church and some states, like France. So a Crusade now was an outlandish thought, out of place and out of time. And in particular in very recent years, and precisely in Florence, it had been given a very bad name by inflamed preaching from an altogether disreputable source – the recently direly disgraced Friar Savonarola.

Nevertheless the pope may have kept tinking about the Crusade, Landucci (*Diario* cit. p.305) reports that on 4th May 1518, the custom of ringing the *Ave Maria*, at the *nona* – midday was started, 'for the Crusade, in order to have God favourable to it; processions and fasts wre also made'. We must remember that May is the month devotionally dedicated to the Virgin Mary, and it is not unusual to have 'special causes' entrusted to Her intercession. The XIX century editor, in a footnote to this entry says that the noon *Ave Maria* that was still rung in his time, was ordered by pope Leo, when he thought to 'persuade' the Christians to go against the Turks. The Turkish threat may still have been worrying the Christians. Vienna was threatened in the XVIII Century, and the North East of Italy too, where the star fortress of Palmanova was later built, to defend the territory from the Turks' threat.

34 Cesare VASOLI, *La profezia* ... cit., p.34. Most of the information about Antonio Zeno, the invitation to Francesco da Meleto, about the relationship between Soderini and the Venetians, their connection with Giuliano de' Medici are in this instance taken from Cesare Vasoli's study..

The *Libellus ad Leonem X*, of 1513, by Querini and Giustiniani was a letter to Leo X (the principles of which were later taken up also by the *Consilium*), regarding the necessity of reforming the Clergy, have more care in their selection and training, the language of the services, and translations of sacred texts, reformation of the Curch away from politics and temporal power and matters, towards a renewed spirituality, and a better control on published materials (later leading to the *Index* of condemned books). Nothing was really taken up until the Council of Trent. Yet the ideas had started circulating now. And Querini was summoned and entertained by Leo X, who also offerd him a Cardinal's hat (*in pectore* before his name could be published), although because of Querini's untimely death in September 1514 the proper nomination did not materialize.

35 Giovanno CAMBI *Istorie*... cit., vol III, p.48.

36 Bernardo GIAMBULLARI, *Sonetti rusticani di Biagio del Capperone*, città di Castello, 1902, p.

87, Sonettto XXVII: *'Adesso el papa dette di sua mano a Biagio 40 ducati, tutti della navicella'* – now the pope gave to Biagio 40 ducats, all of the *navicella* – and ...*'dalla scarsella cavastene quante navicelle ver' entro'* – from your pocket you took all the *navicelle* there were.

Navicelle were the *fiorini da camera*, that is the money coined for the treasury, coined both before and during the papacy of Leo X, having the *Navicula Sancti Petri*, or the *Navis Aeternae Salutis*, as called on the coin itself, on one of its sides. (E. MUNTONI, *Le monete dei Papi e degli Stati Pontifici*, Roma , 1972; for Leo X see tavola 24, number 3 and tavola 26, number 100)

37 ASF, MAP, Filza CVII, carta 58

38 Roscoe..... Pastor..... in Domenico GNOLI , *La Roma di Leone X*. Milano, 1938 p. 368, we find him defined '*scialacquatore*', a wastrel, which is not far from 'prodigal' and we know the juridical implications of that, see note 77, below. and Pasquino: *'nemo a Leone meo.indonatus abit.'*.

39 See note 31 above, from the Venetian ambassador Marco MINIO.

40 Quoting from Vittorio CIAN, *A proposito di un'ambasceria di M. Pietro Bembo...*, cit., pp. 369-370.

41 *Idem*, p. 371. The fleet this time was, however, it seems, for the *impresa italiana*, the Italian enterprise which involved an alliance with France (not well liked by Florence either) with the help of Venice and others. For the ambiguous and complex details of foreign politics, not strictly relevant here I refer to my source, CIAN, who refers to Guicciardini, by way of Muratori, who, he says, was right in writing : '*quali che fossero in tempi di tante discordie i maneggi e raggiri di papa Leone, chiunque bramasse d'essere pienamente informato, dee ricorrere al Guicciardini, storico provveduto di un buon microscopio per discernere le simulazioni e dissimulazioni della politica mondana dei principi....*- as far as what were the manipulations and circonvolutions of Pope Leo, in times of so many disagreememts, those who longed to be fully informed should make recourse to Guicciardini, a historian furnished with a good microscope apt to discern the simulations and dissimulations of the princes' worldly politics ...' (CIAN quoted above, p. 374, note 11). In the end, the question was that there was a plan to get the Kingdom of Naples for Giuliano, (p. 375) and that's why Leo needed the Venetian fleet now.

42 Francesco VETTORI, *Sommario della storia d'Italia,* in *Scritti storici e politici,* ed. by A NICCOLINI, Bari, Laterza, 1972 , p. 178.

43 Treasury money – not in bags of coins, perhaps, yet sailing away.

44 Letter from Baldassarre Turini da Pescia, to Lorenzo, from Rome, June 16th 1514, in ASF, MAP, filza CVII, carta 38.

45 Venice had provided hospitality to some of the Florentines during the 1494-1513 exile, so there were connections. A Venetian Nobleman, Gianfranco Valier was secretary to Bibiena. Bibiena had a brother in Venice, The brother had recently died and his children, Bibiena's nephews, needed assistance from the state. Querini writes to his brother, on 10th April 1514, with a diplomatic reminder, clearly intended to mollify the papal Treasurer: '*Aricordate al principe che gioverà assai far in qualche parte contento il Cardinal S.M. in Portico [Bibbiena-* there is a little problem here about S.M. in Portico, which was also Cornaro's titular church] *per li nipoti soi...*- remind the prince that it will be very useful to satisfy Cardinal of S.M. in Portico, regarding his nephews in some way' and this referred to a request by Bibbiena himself, transmitted by Pietro Bembo , : '*M. Pietro Bembo scrisse il desiderio del Cardinale, ben v'intenderà il principe-* M. Pietro Bembo wrote the desire of the Cardinal, and the prince will certainly understand' (Vittorio CIAN, *A proposito di un=ambasceria di M. Pietro Bembo*, cit., p. 366, nota 1).

46 *Idem*, p. 366.

47 *Idem*, p.371.

48 See V.1., *à propos* the *Trionfo di Camillo*, a Medicean apotheosis with a strong anti-French component.

49 Cesare GUASTI, *Le feste di S. Giovanni, Firenze, descritte in prosa e rime da contemporanei*, cit., pp. 24-25.

50 The accepted use of the word *divertimento* is, of course, an entertainment, amusement, but it derives from 'diversion', as diversion from normal everyday serious, useful, profitable action and thoughts

51 See above, chapter I.2.

52 L.B. ALBERTI, *Momus seu de principe*, Italian edition quoted, edited by S.G. Martini, Bologna Zanichelli, 1942, Introduzione, p. VIII.

53 LEHMAN etc. Andrea Sansovino notes are published by G. GIOVANNONI, in *Palladium*, anno V, n.1, pp.157-150. See also Appendix .... See also the present writer's article *Simbologia pagana e cristiana nella navicella di Santa Maria in Domnica,* in *Studi Romani,* XXXI, n.1, gennaio-marzo 1983.

54 See by Karl LEHMAN, *The Ship-Fountain from the Victory of Samothrace to the Galera*, in P. WILLIAMS LEHMAN and K. LEHMAN, *Samothracian Reflections*, (Princeton 1973) which proposes the idea, to which I too suscribe, that in the reconsturuction of this monument the symbolical images of the classical ship-as-state become fused with the ship-as-church. Lehman maintains that for the first time here elements of Hellenistic-Roman culture come to be re-interpreted according to Christian ideology. The *Navicula* of Sta Maria in Domnica assumes also the symbology of the Christian Ship of Salvation, the ship of Saint Peter.

55 It was said that Leo X election to the papacy had something of the 'miraculous' because it was wholly unexpected, and indeed it may have depended in part on his precarious state of health at the time. He was not expected to last long!

56 Much is made in this study of the connection between madness and prodigality, madness and poverty, as they are legally associated from a long tradition. The Twelve Tables that form the basis of Roman Law were the connection *Furiosus vel Prodigus* is carried in the Fifth table. See Marcantonio SAVELLI, *Summa sententiarum,* Venezia 1748, p. 338, par. 3 and p. 339, par 8. The assimilation passed into the *Codex Justinianeum*. See also the following discussion on the *Compagnia del Mantellaccio*, the 'Company of the Tattered Cloak', and notes following.

57 See Ch.III.3. and note 22 and 63 above, as well as Pietro ARETINO at note 65 and 70 below.

58 Quoted before, see IV.2 and note 15 above.

59 SANUDO did not think there were many: as he says '*furono raccolti i pochi pazi che si trovano in questa città* – they collected the few fools are found in this city' in *Diarii*, XVIII, p. 313.

60 Artefice: I suggest it must mean '*artefice manuale*' of those manual/unskilled workers who were collected in the Arti Minori

61 The great propblem of translation of this sections starts here: Gio. Tancredi *portava la lana*. This I took, at first to mean that he 'carried wool'. The *Arte della Lana* was after *Calimala* the most important of the Florentine *Arti Maggiori*, and Gio. Tancredi must have had a job of 'porter' carrying the bales of wool. There was a door in the walls of the city called *La Porta di Balla*. One of the doors of the Duomo of Santa Maria del Fiore, on the Via de' Servi, is also calle la *Porta della balla*. – The door where the bales of wool went by. But the Italian *portare* also means 'to wear' and for the interpretation of *portava la lana* as 'wearing wool', as well as carrying it as a trade, there is also a good case. The best bet is that this is an intentional ambiguity in the text. As we shall see later, see note 65, wearing the wool is the mark of a poor man who cannot wear silk., or of a monk, who is also poor. It

could also have a connection with the *cappucci*, see later at IV.6.ii.

62 That he 'was not able to do anything but ...' must mean that that was his trade and that he remained in a low position. That he was in a low grade is indicated also by the statement that he 'did not even think' of becoming a *Maestro*, which may have been a grade in the Guild, but also signified a high position in some circles....(see the following note). That in 50 years had not changed his trade is not necessarily demeaning, as any experienced craftsman or scholar could show – and, besides, someone like that would certainly not be one to board any old ship with a bunch of other fools, on the spur of the moment, to sail in search of the land of Cockaine. This may also indicate, though, that the passage deals with his trade (of carrying the wool), but it could equally apply to his poor dress, which also did not change (into silk – note 65) for all his 50 years of work.

63 As well as the grade of Master in the trades, Maestro could also be a an honorific title, for instance Giovanni de' Medici now the pope, had in the past been granted the title of Maestro d' ostello, by Charles VII, that is master of the household of the French king (Nardi, *Istorie*, vol .I, p.32

64 From ASF MAP, filza CVII, carta 32 , and the whole episode which will be discussed later , see V.2. with the reports by Cambi, Masi and Sanudo.

65 BATTAGLIA, *Grande dizionario della lingua italiana*, vol... *lana* anche '*abito confezionato con tale tessuto*, *veste umile dei religiosi*' habit made with such fabric, the humble habit of friars. Also '*panni vili, lini e lana*' cheap clothes, linen and wool'. Giovanni Tancredi di Sta Croce wears the humble wool, a less connotated garment than the more heavily connotated black cloak of Carafulla, who was also a Maestro. While Gio Tancredi only wears, and carries, wool.

66 Among the few mentions and descriptions of the *Fusta piena di matti*, Giovanni Cambi is the only one who has a detailed, as far as it goes, definition of Gio.Tancredi, including his name. I could not ascertain how he came to this knowledge, yet I strongly suspect he might have been given a 'hint', a planted 'leak' from insiders, a sort of personal press release. Because it is pretty certain to me that Gio.Tancredi, (omonimous of the Medici pope) is an 'invention', he is not a person, but a character most likely played by an actor (Barlachi), as we shall see later. See later at the end of this chapter, thanks to the testimonial of Sanudo.

67 See R.C. TREXLER, *Lorenzo de' Medici and Savonarola Martyrs for Florence*, in 'Renaissance Quarterly' XXXI, n.3, 1978, pp.293-308, where chain spectacular conversions of dignitaries and canons are mentined.

68 See Cesare VASOLI, *La profezia di Fancesco da Meleto*, cit., p.34 where Querini is defined *Cardinale in pectore*, these days of May-June 1514. Cardinale *in pectore* is someone who is expecting the cardinals hat, but has not had his name published and listed among the cardinals as some condition might be yet to be fulfilled.

69 ASF, MAP, filza CXVII, n.23

70 V. CIAN, *A proposito di un ambasceria*... cit., pp.361-362.

71 See IV.4. above and note 29

72 This summary of the events and career of Fra Mariano is based on the article by Etta V. THOMSON *Lorenzo de' Medici's Puzzling Present for a Papal Buffoon,* in 'Bibliotheque d'Humanisme et Renaissance', n.41, 1980, pp. 157-165 and relative references. The Fra Mariano history is also to be found in L. PASTOR, *The lives of the Popes*, cit., vol. VIII, , pp. 151-162, and it is substantially the same.

Mariano Fetti, barber and friend of Lorenzo the Magnificent, when Savonarola had started attracting some favour (or fear) during the last years and illness of Lorenzo, had taken part in the wave of conversions which had overcome the Florentine court, Academy and Cathedral had, like many, taken the Dominican habit. Following the Medici in exile to Rome, he had remained at the papal court after the restoration of 1512 and Pope Leo X's election of 1513. Not among those who had the Florentine interests at heart more than his own. In Rome he had obtained the office of *Piombatore* – the office of apposing the seals on the Papal bulls and decrees and letters – which seems to have been quite a lucrative office. This office, however belonged traditionally to the Cistercian Order, so he had become 'converted', to the Cistercian Order for this. He had kept to the Dominican Order as well, though, as he had been granted ot keep for life the church and convent of S. Silvestro which also was a source of income. After Mariano ...who must have died in 1517, the office of piombatore was given to the Venetian painter Sebastiano del Piombo.

73 See E. ORVIETO, *Un poemetto inedito di Bernardo Giambullari*, in 'Bibliotheque d'Humanisme et Renaissance', Genève, 1977 cit, pp,531-544

74 Festivities were announced by the town crier, who had to publish the regulations for the closing of shops, the special licenses, the number of days the festivities would run -see Bartolomeo MASI, *Ricordanze*, cit., pp.141-142. And we will find later that it is likely that a Fool , or the Herald, initiated the festivities, as SANUDO remarks '*come in destare il populo a festa* – as if to stir the people for the festivities'. See Marino SANUDO, *Diarii*, cit., Vol. XVIII, p.113.

75 This *Magnifico Lorenzo* is the present Lorenzo (di Piero di Lorenzo), as Magnifico was also a title equivalent to Signore, or the Ruler – while 'Lorenzo Il Magnifico' is his gandfather (Lorenzo di Piero di Cosimo). As for the omission of the denomination of the Order to which Fra Mariano belonged, ORVIETO, cit., (p.539. n.1) seems to ascribe it to 'not knowing', while D.E.V. THOMSON cit., ascribes it to the difficulty of deciding to which of the two orders Fra Mariano belonged . Naturally, being the poem a burlesque, the omission may well be a reference to the fact that he was in this peculiar 'unmentionable' position of belonging to two orders.

76 See above Chapter III. 3 and notes 22 and 23, pp.62-63. Notice *Scharafulla*, for *scarfuglia, farfuglia,* for confuses, mutters, stutters – he who was *sciocco ma verboso*, an experienced, if eccentric, user of language.

77 *Furiosus vel prodigus*... of the XII tables (table V), the foundation of Roman Law. See it still in the XVIII century as in Marcantonio SAVELLI, *Summa Sententiarum*, cit., p. 338, par. 3 and p. 339, par. 8. See also II. 1 note 11, p.35.

78 Giambullari had a prdilection for the 'rustic', he was the autor of *Sonetti Rusticani*, hence the Tonio

79 As for the joke about sending Biagio to be hanged, we have a reminiscence of Maestro Antonio, by Pietro Aretino, where he used Maestro Antonio as a a 'rovinato dalla corte – put out of joint by his frequenting the courts' (Aretino may have met him in Rome, in 1513, perhaps, although his *Ragionamento delle corti* is written, or at least published, in Venice some twenty years later). Aretino remembers the Carafulla liked to impersonate a King, wanted to be called Your Majesty, and sent imaginary followers to be hanged. See also III. 3, note 22 above. Aretino knew Fra Mariano well too. See Arturo GRAF, *Attraverso il cinquecento*, Torino, 1526, p. 313, *passim*. Above ch..III.3., notes 22 and 23, pp.62-63)

80 Fra Mariano's letter of application is in D.E.V. THOMSON, *Lorenzo de Medici Puzzling Present....*, cit., p. 158. As for Carafulla in white, he is in Aretino.

81 Santa Croce, for Cross bearer, Crusader. We may count also the fact that the Franciscan convent at Santa Croce was Giovanni de' Medici school. As for the Imquisition (matters of reform, prophets etc.) the Inquisitor visiting Florence would be given an office in S.ta Croce, the Dominican convent having run into 'bad times' because of Savonarola.

82 For Medicean *Compagnie* see Chapter III, note 18.

83 SANUDO *Diarii*, Vol. XVIII, p.313. We should remember here that Sanudo's record is the summary of a letter from Florence, therefore, the report of some emissary *in loco*, someone who saw for himself, a first hand report.

84 See Domenico Barlacchia, in *Enciclopedia dello Spettacolo*. See also A.SALZA, *Domenico Barlacchi, araldo, attore e scapigliato fiorentino del secolo XVI*, in 'Rassegna bibliografica della letteratura italiana', IX, 1901, pp.27-33. See also his biography, (by A.Zappori) in the *Dizionario biografico degli Italiani*. In the repertories he is mentioned as belonging to the *Compagnia della Cazzuola*, which is probably the Compagnia started by Giuliano which was known as *La Compagnia del Diamante e della Cazzuola*. Whether Filippo Strozzi belonged to one or the other of the Medici Companies, it is not at the moment clear to me. But he was a friend and *protegé* of Filippo Strozzi 'il primo dei festaioliper questo S. Giovanni 1514. (see the anonimous poem printed in C. GUASTI *Le feste di S. Giovanni Batista in Firenze, descritte in prosa e in rima da contemporanei, cit.*, (Firenze 1884) Filippo Strozzi was also to dedicate some sonnets to him, later, in 1529. The Florentine chroniclers do not seem to have noticed him on the *fusta* (and being Gio. Tancredi, he was not in the *Fusta* all the time). He was probably not very well known yet, as he must have been very young. As for Cambi, who described Gio.Tancredi del quart. di S.ta Croce in detail, I really think he must have been given a sort of 'press release' by the organisers, whose aim was to make clear what this character stood to represent. It is also possible that Barlacchi had been of the Medicean contingent which had just returned from exile (in Rome, and/or Venice) in 1512. So he had not been in Florence for long. And although Sanudo's correspondent seems to be a Florentine, he is also someone who had connections with Venice, obviously, and was probably one of those who had taken refuge during the 'republic', in Venice. Barlacchi wes very young, and only the 'insiders' knew him. The Florentine Cambi, I submit, must have been fed a 'press release' with the constructed character as if real.

Domenico Barlacchia became eventually a very famous actor of the *Comedie Italienne* in France. One of his great successes was his part in the play *La Calandria,* (Bibiena) in Lyon on the occasion of the great *Entrata* of Henry II and Queen Catherine de Medicis, in 1548.

85 See the often referred to note 22 of Chapter III, for Pietro ARETINO *Ragionamento delle corti*. [the basket lowered from the fusta as 'hanging']

86 As above. For ARETINO and VARCHI

87 Piero Soderini only the previous year, for the Carnival of 1513, on 28th February 1523, (just between popes) had been represented in a float which sported a large *wheel of fortune*, (an emblem of which Lorenzo il Magnifico was fond of using). This Carnivalesque *wheel of fortune* had a *marzocco* (The Medici lion) in the process of climbing up, a figure representing the Medici on the top, and below, '*uno vestido con uno mantello e un cappuzzo in cao, si dice era il confalonier Soderini olim in Fiorenza* – someone dressed in a cloak with a hood, said to be the gonfaloniere Soderini once of Florence' (SANUDO, *Diarii*, Vol. XVII, pp14-15)This Soderini has been praised at one with Maestro Antonio as we have seen (see III.3 and note 27 above), is now in Rome, obviously appreciated by Leo X, among the privileged Roman circles of Cardinal Soderini to which also Giuliano belonged. It is true that Cardinal Soderini was a powerful figure and the Medici, including the pope, would need his support. These circles involved also , however, 'reformers', *piagnoni* prophets, Venetians and their ships for hire. Piero Soderini, was he still wearing a penitential cloak and hood? Or was he a 'recycled' *cappuccio* in the political sense? As for the political value of *cappuccio*, see IV.6.ii., below.

88 *Furiosus vel Prodigus* of the XII tables (see note 10 at Chapter II above)

89 *La Compagnia del mantellaccio*, the compagnia of the tattered cloak. Burlesque *Capitolo*, printed in Florence in 1489, with a frontispice representing Lorenzo de' Medici, il Magnifico, with a '*compagnia*' or '*brigata*', a festive 'gang', all wearing tattered cloaks (and repair patches on their

hoses). From M. SANDER, *Le livre à figures italien depuis 1467 jusq'à 1530*, Milano 1942, n. 578. It does not seem to be known whether the *Compagnia del Mantellaccio* was a real fixture for the festivities (like the *Compagnia del Broncone* at present), or whether it was a literary invention, representative, nevertheless, of the festive spirit. The *Capitolo,* in verse, which presents it, was reprinted several times in the early XVI century. It is cited by the Accademia della Crusca and was edited, with a facsimile reproduction of the first edition, in Florence, by Antonio Cecchi, 1861. The characters in the poem which is in part a dialogue, go under pseudonims or nicknames (the *Compagnie* were formed also with a clause of secrecy as to the participants), and whether with a real life contingent or not, the *Compagnia del Mantellaccio* is an ideal entity of the Florentine festive society, and certianly also in this year 1514, as, like other examples, it is a document to be revived and used in the spirit of *le temps revient, the return of the times*, the Golden age of Lorenzo *il Magnifico*. See also Roberto RIDOLFI, in 'La Bibliofilia', n. 42, 1940, p 282, for the copy in his library. In any case, the frontispice is representing Lorenzo, in a similar way and pose as the forntispiceof *Canzone per andare in maschera per carnesciale*, printed not before 1515, but without date, and definitely in a format (the old typographical types, for instance, lack of mention of date or printer) suggesting an earlier time, the time of Lorenzo the Magnificent, what is now, in 1514, the Golden Age to be revived. For the dating of *Canzone per andare in maschera per carnesciale* to 1515 see the article by the present writer (Chapter II, note 11, above, and Chapter III, note 18.) *Un' occasione in cui la storia detta il canto alla festa*, in *Il teatro dei Medici*, monographic number of 'Quaderni di teatro', year II, n.7, (March 1980), pp.114-134.

90 We could read Simon Magus – but principally read the Mangano as *manganello*, i.e. a club (the baton carried by policemen is called *manganello*) which we can refer to the clubs wielded by the devils surrounding he *Fusta* and disciplining the rowers, as well as reading the obscene meaning : see *Manganus* ovvero *Il manganello*, XVI century satire in *terza rima*, against women and against marriage , edited by Diego Zancani, Exeter, 1982. It is anonimous, declaredly derived from Juvenal and Boccaccio's *Corbaccio*. Mistakenly sometime ascribed to Aretino, as it was first printed in Venice in 1530.

91 Verses and lines not numbered. Page 1.

92 Fabrini may refer to *fabbro*, i.e. blacksmith, and Vulcano, of the underworld foundry.

93 S.Godenzio, obviously, from *gaudere, gaudentes,* the patron Saint of pleasure seekers. RIDOLFI, in 'La bibliofilia', cit., n.42, changes it into S. Godenzo. S. Godenzo is also a village near Florence.

94 There are two rituals hinted at here: the brotherhood, in the exchange, and the submission, in 'obey me', we have examined them for instance in the 'rules of the game' in chapter I.2., when discussing the episode from *Momus* by L.B. ALBERTI, and specifically the central function of the oath of allegiance.

95 Carafulla's cloak was black and threadbare, then the devils will tear it still on his back, the *'chredo lo rivestirno poi di nuovo* – I think they gave him another afterwards', CAMBI, *Istorie*, cit., see Chapter The Stage. Carnasciale chased from Florence, too, wore a tattered cloak – see Chapter II. 1. And we like to remember also the heretic's torture, see Fra Dolcino see Chapter III, 3, and note 33. Fra Dolcino and his followers, condemned as heretics reported by ANONIMO SINCRONO in his *Historie* which I quote from E. ROTELLI, *Fra Dolcino,* Torino 1978, p.51: *'fatti salire i condannati sopra un carro...che percorresse tutta la cittá...e che di tanto in tanto, si lacerassero ai rei, con infuocate tenaglie, le carni'* – the condemned were put on a cart and taken through the city so that their flesh could be torn off them with hot irons along the way.

96 Can't offer a comment on this name, yet. Unless it is some reminiscence of the Guelphs and Ghibellinis factions in the XIV century.

97 *Babbo* was also some perhaps not altogether welcome familiarity. A phrase from Fra Mariano to Leo X is in a comedy by Andrea CALMO: '*Viviam babbo santo, che ogni altra cose è burla* – let's live (it up), holy dad, that everything else is jest'.

98 Nothing to offer, yet…unless Dossi being possibly 'back', some reference to sodomy???

99 *Lucci* for *lucchi,* rich and elegant cloaks, necessary to someone frequenting the Palace. Can we add a sexual innuendo referring to 'fish', *lucci.*

100 See the much repeated connection with *Furiosus vel Prodigus*, here too . Marcantono SAVELLI. In Summa Sententiarum,comments on the table V of the Roman XII Tables thus: Prodighi s'equiparano a furiosi e infanti…prodigals are equivalent to madmen or infants (p.339, par.8, and '*Che uno si possa dir prodigo non tanto rispetto alli beni, che al malgoverno della persona…* - that one can be termed prodigal no so much as to his property, but for the lack of propriety and the ill government of the person.', p. 338, par.3. So in the palace one would be held as a madman, if wearing a black cloak. So is Carafulla, so is Carnesciale, poor, mad, wearing black torn and tattered cloaks.

101 Guiducci, could be an indication to someone well guided (not at all misguided), well governed, on top of things. Or guiding: he is not a prodigal or a madman, he has two cloaks, no less, one to spare, and he has also two hoods, *cappucci* , perhaps he is a bit mad, as festive mood requires, but rich and double. That he should be called Giovanni should not be a reference, as the *Compagnia del Mantellaccio*, is supposed to be of the end of XV century. Yet, is it really? What if this was too of 1514, like the *Canzone per andare in maschera…?*

102 We are referring here to *Canzone per andare in maschera per Carnasciale*, already mentioned, see above note, 85 (as well as Chapter II, note 11, and Chapter III, note 19)

103 The *Apologia dei cappucci* is found in 'Archivio Storico Italiano'. Tomo IV, vol. II (1853), pp. 271 ff. Jacopo PITTI wrote the *Apologia dei cappucci* between 1570-1575; probably in an attempt to counteract the fortune of Guicciardini's historical works. Pitti wrote also some *Istorie fiorentine*, on which one cas see A. GIORGETTI, *Il Diario di Bartolomeo Cerretani, fonte delle 'Istorie fiorentine di Jacopo Pitti, in* Miscellanea fiorentina di erudizione e storia, I, 1886.

The editor of the *Apologia dei cappucci* defines, in the introduction, *cappucci* as '*nome già dato in Firenze ai seguaci della fazione democratica* – name given at the time in Florence to the followers of the democratic faction'. Perhaps he should have said of the 'anti-Medicean faction' as there was no 'democracy' with Savonarola, for instance.

However, as often in this essay, we are not entering in the merit of the discussion. What is important for me now is the evidence of this term, *cappucci*, found in the title, well remembered still , in the third part of the century, and shown to have been in use in our time, at the turn of the XV to the XVI century.

104 *Apologia dei cappucci* cit., p.273. We could compare Pitti's colourful defense of parsimony with the prodigal folly of Carafulla and the *festa*.

105 *Idem*, pp.272-273 . In a less colourful and rather spitefully censorious. The puritanical style of Savonarola.

106 *Idem,* pp.271 ff.

107 *Idem*, p.275. Pagolantonio was the brother of Piero and Cardinal Francesco, and was *oratore*-ambassador of the Florentine republic in Venice in the years 1494-1498.

108 The *Apologia* gives much space to the Venetian republican form, adding however, that as applied to Florence it should have '*tanto d'autorità da poter regolare quella repubblica (la fiorentina) tanto inferma e disordinata* – a certain authority such as to rule that republic (the Florentine one) so infirm and unstable' p.275.

109 (In 1544?) Gasparo Contarini (1483-1542) a fellow student at Padua University of Querini and Giustiniani, politician and Venetian diplomat, famous for his philosophical knowledgein

Aristotelian doctrine, and made a cardinal by Paul III, wrote his *De Magistratibus et Republica Venetorum*, where the Aristotelian form of republic, as applied by Venice is analyzed as supporting the success of the *Serenissima,* but Pitti does not refer to the 'foreigner', although Contarini's learning earned him fame, a cardinal's hat, and a seat in the Cardinals' Consilium for the Catholic Reform.

110 The Platonic idea of state becomes evident on the occasion of the election of Giovanni as pope LeoX, when the poem by the humanist Zenobi-Acciaiuoli, *Ode Acciaioli, qua leo X luminare maius ecclesiae soli sive Apollini comparetur* (Roscoe-Bossi *La vita e il Ponrtificato....)*, vol X, p. 368 – the Medici pope is compared to the High Priest of the ancient god Helios and the newer god Apollo together, in whose person (of the High Priest) the political and religious powers are collected as in the ideal Church-State as proposed in Plato's *Laws*.

This is also elaborated upon in my article *Un'occasione in cui la storia detta il canto alla festa*, in 'Il teatro dei Medici', monographic number of 'Quaderni di teatro', year II, n.7, (March 1980), pp. 114-134, quoted already.

As for *cappucci* and *cappuccetti* (Benvenuto Cellini, *Vita*, edited by Cattaneo, Milano 1958, ch. 17, p. 53) where he talks of '*certi arronzinati cappuccetti di quella fazione di Fra Girolamo*' see also note 18 above.

111 This was a Carnival in Rome, surely also celebrating the Medici Restoration, although in Florence they also were engaged in celebrating a great festival for the Carnival, with the theme of the *Ritorno del secol d'Oro,* described by Vasari (with some problems of dates) and by the historian NARDI who also wrote the *Trionfo del secol d'oro* which accompanied the pageant. See John SHEARMAN, *Pontormo and Andrea del Sarto*, in 'Burlington Magazine', civ., 1962

112 SANUDO, *Diarii,* cit., XVIII, pp. 14-15

113 SANUDO, cit., p. 313.

114 See (VI), EPILOGUE, below,

CHAPTER V

Performace and watchers.

V.1. *The* **Fusta piena di Matti** *as spirit (essence) of the* **festa.** *The* **Fusta** *as the collective Fool, or court jester.*

Sanudo's observation regarding the *Fusta* is that it was going '*per tutta la terra come in destare il populo a festa* – through all the land as if to call up the people to the celebrations'. A very interesting note. And then he adds that, '*tutto el populo e quanti forastieri vi si trovava* – all the people of the city, as well as what foreigners were present' [1] important foreigners, too. Sanudo is not the only one to perceive that the *fusta* has taken up a function of town crier or Herald. The people, Florentines and foreigners alike recognize it, acknowledge it, gather around.

The *Fusta* is also the (collective) jester who actually indicates that the revels have started, it gathers the people to lead them to the centre of festivities, so that it is a guide, as well as a catalyst, for the spirit of celebration. It is spreading the news.

Going through the city, whether or not on an established route ('through all the land', the Venetian diarist says), the jester, the Fool, elicits the participation of the people.

The Fool in the traditional *festa* teaches the people his art of jester, as he accepts – it's his job, his function indeed – to be made also the object of jokes and taunts by the people, so that the people become 'actors' also, not just spectators. The people could eventually act the same free script, precisely the jests and jokes which are the jester's art. The people in a *festa*, that is in fact a ritual, are not just spectators of a show, but part of it. This is the *festa* [2].

The model here, however, is more controlled and organised, as it is part of an official festival. The people, as far as we can read, remain spectators. And the choreography, as we are finding out, is well studied and intentional.

The *Fusta dei Matti*, the only example of"burlesque" [3] in the official festivals, represents still something with a popular function, something reminding of the festive spontaneity, still functioning at least as interface between the solemn pageant, and the festive crowd , as Sanudo has observed. It has the function of the jester, in so far as the crowd is made to follow, to participate, as it appears also, in a small way, when someone is caught and hauled up to join the fools – even though in the case of Gio. Tancredi it was a prepared someone, not just anyone. In any case the festivities before the serious celebrations of the following days, are heralded by the *Fusta* Jester.

We can surmise that a Fool had often the function of calling the people to the merrymaking by running through the city the day before, and Sanudo's ascribing such a function to the *Fusta* seems to show that he was seeing a character that was traditional and recognisable. Furthermore, as the *festa* now, in the XVI century, is gradually turning into theatre, that part of it that remains in the city square becomes the '*Commedia dell'Arte*'. The troupe of the *Commedia* keeps the tradition of detailing a couple of characters among the more comical, and sending them to run through the city and call the people to come and see their shows in their quarters (*alle stanze*) For example we find, in a *Canto Canascialesco* by Anton Francesco GRAZZINI dettto il Lasca, the *Canto di Zanni e Magnifici*, that a Zanni and Pantaloon, the two extremes of acrobatics and pomposity, wise-fools, Harlequin and the bumbling Pantaloon, go through the city to announce that the (strolling) players, the actors of the *Commedia* are in town [4]. These two are the buffoons, and the heralds.

The *Signoria* (the Government), in Florence, used to employ an official Herald. Precise evidence of this office is found in the History of Florence (*Istoria di Firenze di Gregorio Dati dal 1380 al 1405*) by Goro Dati [5] . Tthere is evidence that the office was maintained, perhaps in a reduced, form, for ceremonial and festive occasions, also by the Medici.

The *Signoria* was elected every two months, beginning from January 1st (as reported by Dati for the XIV century), and the elected Magistrates lived in the Palace of Government (*e ivi mangiano e dormono* – and here they eat and sleep) for the two months they held office [6]. These moreover ' have a knight herald, a young man of great excellence and virtue, gifted with talent and imagination to find new things every day to give entertainment to the said members of government – *E più hanno uno cavalier araldo, giovane di grande eccellenzia e virtú, dotato di gentile ingegno e fantasia sopra il trovar ogni dí cose nuove e piacevoli per dare sollazzo alla detta Signoria*' . This Herald was a salaried official appointee: '*e ha per suo salario per ciascuno mese fior. 3, e dal Capitano e podestà ha l'anno la somma di fior. 60, sí che gli viene in tutto 'l'anno fior. 120* – he has a salary of 3 florins per month, .so that for the whole year he has 120 florins'. His office was established and structured during at least the XIV century. With office, salary, and at the service of a *Signoria* whose term of office lasted two months, the 'knight herald', although 'gifted with fine talent and imagination' is perhaps not the same as a 'court fool' whose statute is ideally of freedom, and whose presence is based on a personal relationship with an individual ruler. Yet the 'knight herald' was in charge of entertainment, and is found, in the XV century, to call himself "*Kavaliere di palagio over buffone* – Knight of the Palace or buffoon"[7] (Trexler). Later Heralds tend to be appointed poets as well *as* Masters of the Ceremonies – as for example G.B. dell'Ottonaio appointed as Herald for the Signoria on 25th February 1517 [8]There must have been cases in which the personality of the 'knight' in his function of 'herald' made him in reality to be a "buffoon", that is. a jester.

As for the function of town-crier we do know that the festivals were announced several days in advance [9] as the rules and regulations about dates, times, the closing of shops, special permissions of access to the city and so on, had to be published. There may well also have been also information intended to create curiosity and invite the population to take part in the festive spirit.

I am very fond of this figure of a town crier *cum* jester that makes of the *Fusta piena di matti* a collective court Fool, and it is with wonder and pleasure that I feel I can recognize it as a collective theatrical fool, as this is a piece of theatre as well.

It is as a mixture of town-crier and hawker, or juggler-jester, and a herald that the *Fusta* went through the city, '*per tutta la terra* – through all the the land'. And with what she carried and captured, the elements we have examined so far, she was an expressive and complete court Fool punctuating, indeed initiating, the great theatrical display, the great civic celebration of this San Giovanni of 1514.

This official civic feast organized by the new *Signore*, the young Lorenzo, proclaiming his glory in emulation and competition with the court of Rome, can be seen as a metaphor of a court, in a festive day, displaying its splendour, and as a proper court, it has its Fool.

As a collective Fool, the *Fusta* speaks in visual riddles, and the riddles are about uncomfortable, or dangerous, realities which nevertheless are in great need of being aired.

In the first part of this study considerations were made over the symbolism of 'self knowledge' carried by the fool, and it will be useful to focus again on the function he, the fool, fulfills, in his ambivalence, in his multiple symbolism, of being a *mirror* of reality, an elusive and allusive reflection of facts, reversed perhaps, but symmetrical and clear as in a mirror.

He, the fool, is a mirror, like the mirror he carries on his staff, which precisely by means of slight kinks, shadows, odd perspectives, and yet in a mocking fixity, brings to the surface aspects of deeper truths where social conventions would have drawn a veil of denial and hypocritical adjustment.

The court in its festive day and in ceremonial pomp, must express glory without the 'shadow'. Lorenzo, his allies and his dignitaries wear velvet, damask, ceremonial armour, uniforms, liveries. emblems are displayed, and classical figure chosen as metaphor of the Medicean rightful restoration and renewed power is celebrated. This is elaborately constructed – as will be clear in the next pages.

Yet we also know that for Lorenzo Florence was an obligation and perhaps a second best – we do know that for him 'there was no other choice than to take care of the things of Florence' as the historian says. Therefore beyond, or behind, the glory and splendour proclaiming certainties, there was a background of conflict, there were things, found only in private papers but not allowed to become public, there was, in fact also 'the shadow'[10].

The famous "*Trionfo di Camillo*", the principal item of political glorification, includes allusions to foreign policy. The anti French allusion was relevant to Venice, who had recently renewed an alliance with France. Leo X was too close with the Venetians and the Florentines saw that as posing a danger.

Camillo and his history stood for the Medici, and specifically for Lorenzo in Florence. It was the "*Trionfo*" which staged the return of a chieftain who, after being wrongfully exiled, was recalled because recognized as honest and worthy, and because only he could save his land from from a new invasion by the Gauls – who came from France.

The "*Trionfo di Camillo*" went as a pageant composed of seventeen floats each carrying a *tableau-vivant* portraying the several events of the story. The splendour of the staging was such as to making it difficult for the enthusiastic correspondent of Sanudo to express himself: 'now I do not know where to turn to find words for what we saw that evening, something never before seen, representing the triumph of Camillo, which were seventeed carts or triumphs – *Hora non so da che capo mi fare a dire quello che la sera haveno, cossa giamai piú veduta, ripresentando il triumpho di Chamillo qual furono 17 cari, over triumphi*' he writes. [11] This is the principal allegory meant to carry the celebration of the restoration and the the glory of the Medici, that is Lorenzo now in Florence, in this San Giovanni.

Camillo, as Nardi's poem accompanying the pageant says, is the 'liberator of his land, and her second father'. It was that Marco Furio Camillo (d.395 BC) who, having been *interrex* and several times a 'dictator' and having been banned to involuntary exile because of false accusations of embezzlement by his 'ungrateful' country, was vindicated and recalled to liberate Rome besieged by the Gauls who were already at the foot of the Capitol hill. He returned and repelled the invasion, thereby giving Rome new life. So 'because of you I am Rome' the city has to admit, as the poet says [12].

The 'legend' of Camillo suggests that he had been banned because thought guilty of embezzling public funds. A similar accusation hung over Lorenzo the Magnificent (our Lorenzo's grandfather). De Roover proposes 'that he may have appropriated public money in 1478 and later has been a question debated for a considerable time…it seems possible, however, that whatever proof there might have been must have been suppressed when the Medici, after eighteen years of exile, returned to power[13] . Whatever the truth about the accusation, the Medici themselves would want redress, of course, and the Roman Camillo's rehabilitation stands for this too, as well as for saving his homeland from the French.

Legend and history are represented in the seventeen *tableaux vivants* taken in procession on the triumphal carts of the processional *trionfo*. In evidence were war machines, Sanudo reports: 'First there was a cart with ladders, lanterns and other similar instruments to force a city…, then a ram ("*ariete*)" which in antiquity was used to breach the walls…', nor where the geese forgotten '*Seguiva ancora un caro dove era sopra una oca, che fu causa che i romani sentirono lo scalare del Campitolio* – there followed a cart with a goose, which was what had warned the Romans that the Capitol hill was being attacked'. [14] The geese in the Capitol had made a racket at being disturbed by the would be invaders, and warned the Roman defenders.

The 'canto' by the title *Il Trionfo della Fama e della Gloria* by Jacopo Nardi is sung or recited in the last and 'most than any other splendid *trionfo'* on which Camillo is carried in triumph. It celebrates without mincing words the return to the 'ungrateful' home which has had to repent of having allowed 'wicked envy' (of Savonarola and the republicans) to harm the 'great father' with its 'rage' and the 'ill conceived decision' which had 'relieved him of the burden' (of government) with the help of the French armies, in the case of Florence[15] . All is under the name of Camillo, and it all alludes to the house of the Medici.

During the other days there will be jousts, hunts, fountains pouring out wine in the Piazza della Signoria. But the *Trionfo di Camillo* was the one that celebrated a victory and the glory of Lorenzo and of the Medici on their returning to Florence to initiate an new Golden Age, as dreamt by Lorenzo the Magnificent, and dreaming of his time now. It was also to vindicate the expulsion of Piero (our Lorenzo's father) in 1494 on which occasion the Florentines suffered the French invasion. So this triumph of Camillo who had saved his city from the Gauls was meant to be a a glorification of the restoration, and a new promise of safety, with stability and prosperity. Not without, perhaps, some special poignancy for Lorenzo, in the memory of his father.

But then, how does one cope with the knowledge that the great power behind Lorenzo, that is the pope Leo X, his uncle, and the other two Medici, Giuliano and cardinal Giulio (who will eventually become Clemens VII in 1523) are in Rome fully flirting with the Soderinis, of that side which had opened the doors to the French and expelled Piero? Those powerful figures in Rome are flirting with the Venetians who are allied with the French [16] – the French portrayed by Gauls in chains in the *Trionfo di Camillo*. Money is short for Florence, but money is paid to the Venetians for ships. *Navicelle* are sailing the wrong way. The *Navicula Sancti Petri* is in deep waters. Can one just swallow all that and say nothing?

Leo X, with him Giuliano and Giulio, is not only keeping Lorenzo in Florence, but is playing with fire: the old republican enemies, the Venetians, the ghosts of the French haunting them all.

In Rome, Leo X has taken charge of the ship of salvation, the *Navicula Sancti Petri*, and is in the process of restoring the *navicella* in front of his church Sta Maria in Domnica[17] , he, with Giuliano, dreams, and plans, foolish and crazy voyages, he dreams of conquering the kingdom of Naples with the Venetian fleet already on the way, he dreams of a new Crusade[18] on which he wants to sail himself against the Turks. He is surrounded and driven by counsellors who are recycled cappucci, pro-French Venetians, devils incarnate indeed.

How does one deal with this, how can one admit it, how can one not be haunted by the 'shadow' of all this, in a context which has dictated the triumph of Camillo, with which one had proclaimed a great victory, a glorious certainty, and a promise to keep this safety for the days to come?

Of course, one has a fool to say it all . A fool, who is a ghost and mirror of a reality one cannot say, of the truths one cannot directly display. Or even two fools. The most foolish of the fools says it, the fool who wears humble wool in silence, without changing his job for fifty years, who does not acquire honours and does not even think of aspiring to be called maestro[19], and Carafulla says it, with his fool's face[20] and his 'head full of whims and pipe dreams', Carafulla who is fond of speaking in riddles, who speaks too much, and who may or may not not be taken seriously. He is the fool hidden under his hood, which is a revealing mask. He is hidden under a black cloak which is a mad thing to wear in the palace of power, as in the penitential-burlesque tattered cloak[21] of the Laurentian followers of San Godenzo – a cloak which in this *festa* is actually torn off him by the hooks of the devils like that of a heretic on the way to the scaffold, a cloak which is also, therefore, a revealing (dis) guise.

And then one had Gio. Tancredi, taunted by the taunted, the most foolish of the fools, a character probably invented with all the suitable characteristics, but so true (and well played) that even the historian Cambi thought him an ordinary citizen [22]. It is all said by the masks and ghosts in the crazy vessel (*bateau ivre*), masks and ghosts who, as a joke, as play, as theatre, evoke real ghosts and shadows present in the disturbing political (and in the case of young Lorenzo very personal) [23] aspects of the days of Spring to Midsummer 1514.

****

While from another direction a really ghostly cavalcade, earnest and altogether real, arrives in Florence these days, black clad and darkly menacing, clattering with their cavalry on the cobbled streets for the days of the festival. Certainly more threatening than the ephemeral ship of fools drawn on a cart by placid oxen for a short, if lively, evening.

V.2 *A troublesome cavalcade. Cardinals in black, their faces covered, 'with many horses and men'.*

There are ghosts, real ones, visible but elusive at the same time. They are the Cardinals from Rome. Landucci[24] has heard of four, but unknown. Cambi sees six, Masi says seven or eight, Sanudo seven, and he knows them all. Plus Giuliano himself, also masked and in Spanish black.

They come, uninvited, but (there was no choice) endured. Ghostly and threatening is the appearance of the cavalcade of cardinals from Rome 'dressed in black, in the Spanish fashion, with swords at their side(s)' [25], with their faces covered – *tutti turati* [26], '…and many unknown Romans with much cavalry with them'[27], a small army. They went through the city with covered faces, on horseback, dressed in black in the Spanish fashion, in capes, hats and (Venetian) silken sashes [28], with swords at their sides. They covered their faces so that they might not be recognized but all knew who they were.

It was the height of arrogance, and the ultimate insult to Florence, to enter armed, on horseback and masked, during a festival. This would be the Florentine view. The Romans could just have thought they were gate-crashing someone else's party, trying not to attract direct animosity, and supremely unconcerned with the smaller, dependant, city's rules. The Church was the highest power. and the festival just some fun. Some of these Cardinals were in their twenties – just a good bit of fun for them, abroad and in disguise.

In the letters of Baldasarre Turini da Pescia, Alfonsina's secretary, diplomatic correspondent and friend of Lorenzo, the story of the growing numbers the self invited cardinals and their train can be followed. The first note is of June 11th, in this they are reported as intending to come 'in four days, in disguise and with few servants…they will be about XXV horses, according to what I was told by the most rev. Monsignor Ferrara' [29] . At this point we could assume that the disguise could have been a sign of discretion, they were not 'pulling rank' in Lorenzo's festival. In the second note, of June 16th, the contingent has grown to four times as many: 'if they are not up to one hundred horses in all, they are not many less' [30] writes Baldassarre Turini to Lorenzo again, perhaps worrying or disapproving a little. It seems to amount to a small army. In fact the sense of disapproval, or worry, seems confirmed when he writes at the end 'they will be even a bigger number of horses and men than we wrote and said before' [31]. He is in fact sending what he knows may be unwelcome news of a small army descending, uninvited, to Florence.

Only a few days before they seemed to be just twenty five, and now about one hundred, and then more than that. Indeed they could be worrying news.

Florence had laws which forbid, during the *feste* (the festivals) to ride on hoseback into the city, laws that forbid to wear arms, and it was specially forbidden to foreigners to enter the city armed: it was also strictly prohibited to cover one's face in order not to be recognized [32] – all this because of the great danger of conspiracies, of unauthorized re-entry of political exiles, a danger in the confusion and precarious equilibrium of the *festa* – as well to prevent ther 'normal' dangers of brawls and disorders.

It was clearly stated in the Statutes of the city of Florence that armed cavalcades were prohibited[33]. The arrogance of the descent of the cardinals was indeed unbelievable, but it was true, it did not go unnoticed. But obviously nothing could be done. Lorenzo had even to have lodgings organized for them all.

The following year, on the occasion of the great '*Entrata*' of Leo X, on 30th November 1515, there will be another conflict of protocol resulting in the humiliation of the *Signoria* (all the government officials, Magistrates etc.) of Florence: the cardinals in the pope's retinue will enter the city on horseback 'the cardinals, in the order (in a line) of xvii, with all their grooms,…x archbishops. etc.…), while the pope's chair and canopy is carried by the *Signoria* of Florence on foot, and those same *Signori* – '*furono indiferentia con gli cardinali perché volevano andare a cavallo a paro loro* – were in conflict with the cardinals, as they wanted to ride like them: but the master of ceremonies obliged them to be quiet, both leading and following [34]. This was the following year, and it was a papal ceremony, for which one should make allowances, it is understood.

But this year, in the principal civic festival of Florence, the San Giovanni 1514, the cardinals obviously not even invited [35] – not even on foot were they included in the processions – with a sinister arrogance they arrive dressed in black Spanish fashion, with 'much cavalry', on horseback (on their high horses indeed), armed, with covered faces, in patent contravention to the very laws of Florence.

The Cardinals themselves, although masked, but known by all, were no ordinary foreigners, and exception may have to be made for them. But what about the nearly one hundred followers and many on horseback?

Sanudo, always well informed, reels the cardinals off one by one: 'Cornaro, Sauli, Bibiena, Ferrara, Cibo, Siena et Ragona and our magnifico confaloniere di Santa Chiesa' (this was Giuliano who was made the principal civil authority of the state of the church) dressed in black 'all with their faces covered, but we knew them all' [36].

Why should they want to go through the city, for several days, if not to make themselves obvious and yet ambiguous, sinister black eminences, in the Spanish fashion and wearing swords. These were the real ghosts – Landucci thinks he sees four of them, Cambi six, Masi seven or eight, Sanudo seven, by name, plus Giuliano.

Cambi, although he is not of the Medici party, recognizes the ambiguity of the shadowy armed cavalcade wearing black in the Spanish fashion (we might assume also bad memories of the Spanish Borgia pope) and is not impressed: 'So that is how they give a good example and in this way they reform the church. May God forgive them and make them repent of their errors.' [37]

These cardinals visiting uninvited, gate-crashing young Lorenzo de' Medici's party, flaunting the law, so overbearing in their number, impudence and impunity are the clear sign of where the real power lies. And power must bow to power. Those in power in Florence must put up with the cardinals' show, because Florence is the smaller power with much to lose.[38]

But there are some that do not need power, as they have nothing to lose. These are the fools who talk thorugh their hats (or hoods), and don't mind their careers. One is a master hatter, and maker of hoods. He calls himself 'Your Majesty' whenever fancy takes him, everybody has seen him holding court in his shop, and as a captain of the ship of fools he is king. He goes thorough the streets of Florence, and even without talking he has much to say. And to those black figures in capes, hats, silken sashes and garters in the Spanish fashion he speaks of *cappucci*, souls of the damned, evil power games, and of hanging Giovanni Tancredi di Santa Croce in a basket.

V.3 *'After the return of these most reverend cardinals from Florence ...'.*

We have no evidence of whether, and how, the *Fusta* was received in Rome. It is difficult to think that it might have gone unnoticed, as the letter reported by Sanudo records that all the people collected together behind the *Fusta*, included many foreigners from Rome and the seven cardinals: '*e quanti forestieri vi si trovava che da Roma ce n'è assai, fra quelli sette cardinali..*-...including the foreigners, of whom from Rome there are many, among them seven cardinals...'[39]. So they were about on the town, mixing with the people, they were seen. And certainly saw.

After the festival Giuliano remained in Florence. The cardinals returned to Rome. And I have found no direct comments about their visit. Nor have I found reports of possible negotiations or discussions in Florence.

A hint, however, that 'something' travelled to Rome from Florence, and may have upset someone's plans, is found in a 'secret' letter by Querini to his brother Zorzi (George) in Venice, of 23rd July 1514, a month later. Querini writes to his brother, in secret, not through official channels, in order to ask him to report '*secretamente al serenissimo principe* – secretly to the most serene prince' the Doge Loredan[40] of certain difficulties of communication with the pope he has being having recently.

Among the various complications of foreign policy, Querini admits to his brother that he is not finding it so easy to be received by pope Leo X any more.

Querini, who used to see the pontiff every day, also several times, who used to go with him to the Magliana for hunts and entertainments, who was "*apud hos nosotros maxime auctoritatis*", now writes to his brother in Venice: 'you must know that since the return of these most Reverend cardinals from Florence, I find many more obstacles, and it is much harder for me than before, to conduct the business that from time to time our Most Illustrious Signore (the Doge Loredan) desires...they try in indirect ways to interrupt my meetings, they order the servants not to let His Holiness know when I want to talk to him...

sapiate che da poi il ritorno di questi Reverendissimi cardinali da Firenze molti piú contrasti e molte piú fatiche io prendo che prima non faceva a condur a fine quanto da quella Ill. Ma S.ria è di tempo in tempo desiderato ... cercano per vie indirecte di rompermi talhora le audientie, muovere li camerieri a non far moto a S.S. quando gli vogli favellare. [41]

Querini, the Venetian nobleman now Camaldolese 'hermit' known to be even expecting to become the recipient of a cardinals hat, connects the new considerable difficulties experienced in trying to conduct his business for Venice (which was about the chartering of or ships) to the return of the cardinals from Florence, as if he saw the new obstacles as a consequence of something that had happened in Florence.

Something indeed changed in Rome after the return of those cardinals from Florence. The wind is taken out from Querini's sails[42]. Something has come to restrain the Venetian sympathies of Leo X. Perhaps a shadow. A ship of shadows. Charon's boat, the *Fusta piena di matti*, a damned Venetian ship. Perhaps.

The Crusade which seemed to inspire such enthusiasm in the pope as to see himself leading it in person and achieve immediate victory [43], although not yet forgotten, will not happen, as we know.

Was any conclusion reached by the not-concluded open-ended boat? The *Fusta piena di matti* of that 22nd June 1514? That ship of fools at the opening of a civic celebratory festival of San Giovanni. It has represented hidden feelings, projects, fears, and dissent that troubled people of consequence during the months leading to the San Giovanni and yet could not be told . The *Fusta* managed to stage all that, in a fleeting event lasting a few hours, a whirlwind of folly, yet meaningful and very real. And with method in its folly.

Made of wood *'una fusta di legname in sun carro'* is recorded by historians and diarists. It will be remembered, with Carafulla, by Aretino many years later. So it is real enough. But it is also a symbolical system.

What it reveals is a historical background of rumours, moods, family bickering, harebrained ideas, preposterous plans. These are ephemeral. The crusade, the catholic reform, the shifting favours and alliances. It is an ephemeral historical level this, that is the historical background of the *Fusta piena di matti* and it, nevertheless, validates the symbolical system of the *Fusta* with its fools and devils, festive characteristics, supernatural connotations, transgressive extensions that have been examined and reconstructed in the first part of this book.

1 SANUDO, *Diarii*, the letter from Florence cit., Vol. XVIII, p.313

2 The *festa* is in fact on the point of being suffocated by power. It is becoming now more and more a spectacle to watch, not to participate in There is a striking and sad metaphore in one of these festivals, indeed the first after the restoration, when in the Carnival of 1513 the *Signoria* organized the *Trionfo del Secol d'Oro*, to celebrate the return of the Medici and recall the Golden Age of Lorenzo *il Magnifico* VASARI tells the story in his *Vita di Pontormo* (*Vite*, edizione Milanesi, vol.VI, p.255) A young child son of a baker had been hired to represent the new Golden Age He was covered all in gold paint from which he died A very sad story, which, however, by coincidence makes me think also of the death of of a popular festival, as it is taken up by 'the system', the *règime*, and makes it an instrument of power The system can cover it in gold, make it more 'beautiful' and yet, just by this intervention, kills it Of course we know of organized festivals and pageants in the previous centuries, and Carnivals and popular festivals may have continued, but what is becoming more established is as '*la festa del Cinquecento*' is a the sort of civic or court spectacle which has not much left in it of the model *festa*, that we knew from the Middle Ages, spontaneous although within the ritual and cyclical occasions The *cinquecento* will derive its theatre from the festival.

3 Asserted also by TREXLER, *Public life in Renaissance Florence,* cit., pp.507-509

4 Anton Francesco GRAZZINI, *detto il Lasca* published an edition of *Canti Carnascialeschi* by various authors, as well as anonymous, in 1559, and his *Canto di Zanni e Magnifici* is considered the first mention in a literary composition of the beginning of the *Commedia dell Arte* I think it is very interesting to find that exactly in a *Canto Carnascialesco*, a composition that belongs specifically to the 'Carnival' there should be the first appearance of the *Commedia*, as if we could recognise in it a hinge between popular festival and popular theatre. It is also true that the *Commedia erudita*, had its origin, not only in the city squares, but also in the palaces and rich homes, still on the occasion of Carnival.however.

5. Goro or Gregorio DATI, *L'istoria di Firenze*, a cura di L. Pratesi, illustrata e pubblicata secondo il codice inedito stradiniano collazionato con altri manoscritti e con la stampa del 1735 Norcia 1902

The San Giovanni is from p.91 to p.96, ...

6 Goro DATI cit., *Libro nono nel quale faremo menzione degli ordini a costumi e governo della città di Firenze:* ARALDO: '*E più hanno uno cavalier araldo, giovane di grande eccellenzia e virtù , dotato di gentile ingegno e fantasia sopra il trovar ogni dí cose nuove e piacevoli per dare sollazzo alla detta Signoria, e ha per suo salario per ciascuno mese fior. 3, e dal Capitano e podestà ha l'anno la somma di fior. 60, sí che gli viene in tutto l'anno fior. 120*" – p.147

7 '*Kavaliere di palagio over buffone*' This is Antonio di Matteo di Meglio, who thus defines himself in 1430 I quote from R.C. TREXLER, Introduction to *The Libro cerimoniale of the Florentine Republic by Francesco Filarete and Angelo Manfidi,* Geneva, *1978*, p. 40 As someone who received a salary, the '*buffone*' was conferred also the title of *Cavaliere* so that he could officially be part of the court (TREXLER quoted above, pp.13 ff.)

8 Author of *Canti Carnascialeschi* and also Comedies He was appointed *Araldo* by the *Signoria* on 23rd February 1517.

9 For this particular San Giovanni, see Bartolomeo MASI, *Ricordanze*, cit., p.141, where the regulations about the closing of shops and the exceptional permits to enter the city are reported (In Antonio PUCCI, *Centiloquio* cit., we can also deduce information about the customary banns, as well as no doubt in the history of Villani that he puts into verse).

10 Beside political considerations, and perhaps real hardship, there must have been a feeling of disillusionment if pope Leo X , and Giuliano, who were also rulers of Florence, went after

differnt interests, and yesterday's political rivals, find favour in Rome nowThe Fool can say it aloud, while the 'powers that be' cannotThe fool, like the heretic dressed as a fool, is allowed to say uncomfortable things, so long as he is dressed a s a Fool (see III.4.ii, and notes 58 and 59)

11 SANUDO *Diarii* cit., vol. XVIII, p. 313

12 Jacopo NARDI, *Trionfo della fama e della gloria*, in SINGLETON, *Canti carnascialeschi del Rinascimento,* cit., p.252 (See also the text in Appendix I, below)

13 See R De ROOVER, *Il Banco dei Medici*, trad it Di Gino Corti, Firenze 1970, p.533 *The Rise and Decline of the Medici Bank, 1397-1494.*

14 SANUDO cit, see note 13 above.

15 Jacopo Nardi, *Trionfo della fama e della gloria* cit. The full text is quoted and translated in the Appendix –Texts See also the *Canzona di Firenzuola,* of 1515, object of my study *Un'occasione in cui la storia*....cit., in which the stanza referring to the unjust Medici exile from 1494 to 1513, and the violence of the Savonarolian interlude are represented in very similar terms. II.2., note 11,

16 Venice had signed a treaty with the King of France on 23rd March 1513 See V.CIAN, *A proposito di un'ambasceria di M. Pietro Bemebo*, in 'Archivio Veneto' 1885, Vol .XXX, p. 359.

17 Andrea SANSOVINO's payment notes '*per una nave di marmo per la navicella*' are published by G.GIOVANNONI, in *Palladium,* anno V, n.1, pp.157-150 See also Appendix .... See also the present writer's article *Simbologia pagana e cristiana nella navicella di Santa Maria in Domnica,* in 'Studi Romani' XXXI, n.1, Gennaio-marzo 1983.

18 See IV.4. and the letter quoted.

19 As well as the grade of Master in the trades, Maestro could also be a honorific title, for instance Giovanni de' Medici, now the pope, had in the past been granted the title of Maestro d' ostello, by Charles VII, that is master of the household of the French king (Nardi, *Istorie*, vol .I, p.32 And in 'Archivio storico italiano' (1853, tomo IV, vol.II, p. cxxii): Maestro, titolo di dignità, principalissimo presso i francesi, di cui vedasi anche il Machiavelli nei suoi *Ritratti delle cose di Francia*.

20 Cara – face in Spanish, and we notice Spanish fashion in language (perhaps ironical, or perhaps just a habitual whim) of *'apud hos nosotros',* and , following below, in the Cardinals 'in disguise'

21 See IV.6.i, and note 89, : *La Compagnia del mantellaccio*, the '*Compagnia* of the Tattered Cloak' Burlesque *Capitolo*, printed in Florence in 1489, with a frontispice representing Lorenzo de' Medici, il Magnifico, with a '*compagnia*' or '*brigata*', a festive 'gang', all wearing tattered cloaks (and repair patches on their hoses) From M. SANDER, *Le livre à figures italien depuis 1467 jusq'à 1530*, Milano 1942, number 578. It does not seem to be known whether the *Compagnia del Mantellaccio* was a real fixture for the festivities (like the *Compagnia del Broncone* at present), or whether it was a literary invention, representative, nevertheless, of the festive spirit The *Capitolo,* in verse, which presents it, was reprinted several times in the early XVI century It is cited by the Accademia della Crusca and was edited, with a facsimile reproduction of the first edition, in Florence, by Antonio Cecchi, 1861 The characters in the poem which is in part a dialogue, go under pseudonims or nicknames (the *Compagnie* were formed also with a clause of secrecy as to the participants), and whether with a real life contingent or not, the *Compagnia del Mantellccio* is an ideal entity of the Florentine festive society, and certainly also in this year 1514, as, like other examples, it is a document to be revived and used in the spirit of *le temps revient,* the return of the time, the Golden Age of Lorenzo *il Magnifico* See also Roberto RIDOLFI, in ' La Bibliofilia', n. 42, 1940, p 282, for the copy in his library In any case, the frontispice is representing Lorenzo, in a similar way and pose as the forntispice of *Canzone per*

andare in maschera per carnesciale, printed not before 1515, but without date,and definitely in a format (the old typographical types, for instance, lack of mention of date or printer) suggesting an earlier time, the time of Lorenzo the Magnificent, what is now, in 1514, the Golden Age to be revived For the dating of *Canzone per andare in maschera per carnesciale* to 1515 see the article by the present writer, *Un' occasione in cui la storia...*, cit (Chapter II, note 11, above, and Chapter III, note 18.

21 It seems very likely to me that Cambi must have been handed a sort of 'press release' by the organizers, about this character, so comprehensive is his description.

22 Although the Golden Age recalled refers to Lorenzo il Magnifico – and also the embezzlement accusation – it was actually our, young Lorenzo's father, Piero, who had been rejected and exiled by the 'Savonarolians' aided by the French invasion So it was Piero's fall too that is vindicated with the *Trionfo di Camillo*.

Piero had died by drowning, in a battle, near Naples, in 1503.

23 LANDUCCI, Luca, *Diario*, cit, p. 346;

24 CAMBI, *Istoria*, cit., p. 48 He sees 6 cardinals, lists four he has recognized, plus Giuliano '*fuori d'abito*', not in ecclesiastical habit, all dressed in black, armed, and with faces covered But he knew who they were.

25 SANUDO (says the cardinals are 7) ; CAMBI report them as 'turati' which means with covered faces, but they know who they are; SANUDO says that although covered *tutti si conoscievano* – they were all recognized While MASI, *Ricordanze*, cit., p. 144 sees them '*coperti el viso* – with their faces covered – *di modo che non si conoscievano* – so that they would not be recognized MASI , without naming them, mentions 8 cardinals (including Giuliano, I expect).

26 Also L. LANDUCCI, *Diario*, cit., p. 346.

27 'Beche' in the relevant footnote in Corazzini's edition (Firenze 1906) of MASI's *Ricordanze* are said to signify 'garters' which would fit with the Spanish dress. However, BATTAGLIA in his Dictionary gives for 'beche': *fasce o bande di seta che si portavano a tracolla nell'abbigliamento veneziano* – silken bands worn diagonally across the chest (silken sashes) used in Venetian dress.

28 ASF, MAP, filza CVII, n. 36 (11 giugno 1514) The cardinal is Ippolito (I) d'Este, the dedicatee of Ariosto's *Orlando furioso*.

29 ASF, MAP, filza CVII, n. 38 (16 giugno 1514)

30 *Ibidem*.

31 This is also why it was so significant that they were *tutti turati*, with their faces covered It was a very serious challenge.

32 *Statuta Populi et Communis Florentiae, Collecta ... 1415* Friburgo 1778, Vol. I, p. 288 Rubrica LXIX.

33 Quoted from the description of the 1515 *entrata* edited by John SHEARMAN in his: *The Florentine Entrata of Leo X, 1515*, in 'Journal of the Warburg Courtaud Institutes', XXVIII, 1975, pp. 148-153.

Descriptione de la Entrata de la S.ta di N.S. papa Leone X in la città di Fiorenza significata per lo Rev.do Francesco Chierigato alla Ill.ma et Ex.ma madonna nostra: la quale fu a di XXX novembre MDXV.

Relevant is also the note about the preparatory talks when the Signoria had been trying to obtain to '*non solum equales ituri Cardinalibus, sed non nisi scutiferi eorum, idest pedites* – to go as equals to the Cardinals, and not like their servants (equerries) i.e. on foot, but the negotiations were not successful and they had to go on foot.. The 'Princes of the Church' have to this day precedence in certain cases of protocol...like their place at the Ambassador's table...

34 Lorenzo was *informed*, and he was also asked to organize their lodgings. (Letters ASF, MAP,

filza CVII, n. 36 and 37) So it is clear that he had to accept them He may have been pleased that they would see his splendid celebrationYet, it cannot be denied that the public aspect of the black cardinals and their cavalcade of nearly one hundred cavalry should be menacing, notable and noted.

35 Sanudo, *Diarii* cit., vol XVIII, p. 313 The cardinals were: **Ragona** – Cardinal Luigi d'Aragona Cardinal, Bishop of Leon & Aversa, Marchese di Gerace, *1474, +1519; m. Vatican 1492 (annulled 1494) Battistina Usodimari, niece of Pope Innocent VIII

Bandinello **Sauli**,(Genoese) bishop of Gerace Alfonso Petrucci, bishop of Massa Marittima. (**Siena**) also in his twenties Marco **Cornaro** Cardinal Patriarch,(1482-1524) (S.ta Maria in Portico a little problem about this title – him or Bibiena, see IV.4, note 45, p. 106) made a Cardinal 28th Sept. 1500. Bernardo Dovizi da **Bibbiena** (author of the comedy *La Calandria*, friend of Fra Mariano, a jester) made a Cardinal in 1513 **Ferrara** – Ippolito d'Este (1482-1524) (the dedicatee of Ariosto's *Orlando furioso*) Cibo (**il nipote del Papa**) Innocenzo Cibo (21 year old in 1513).

36 CAMBI, *Istorie* cit. , p. 48.

37 The danger of plots during the state of confusion and excitement of the *festa* was ever present (see for instance at I.2. above) In times of recent restoration perhaps the instability was even more to be feared Sanudo, as often the better informed of the historians, records that the Florentine 'expedition' of the cardinals had been financed by the banker Agostino Chigi, and with good reason 'Siena' the cardinal had to take time off to go to Siena and quell an attempt of a *coup* by some re-entered exiles. (*Diarii* cit., XVIII, p. 114) In Florence there was no imminent danger, perhaps, and it was also to hold this at bay that Leo X was forgiving and friendly with the former *piagnoni* and *cappucci*.

From another point of view (not the Florentine), the cardinals and their cavalcade may have had the task of keeping an eye on Florence, insteadThe following year ther will be an incident, in fact, on the occasion of the solemn *Entrata*, of Leo X, when the pope's guard had to deal with '*molti fiorentini incappucciati* – many hooded Florentines' (we find here the *cappucci*)who had tried to mix with the pope's followers on a visit to the convent of the *Murate* They had to be beaten back by the pope's guards (M. ZORZI, *Relazione al Senato,* in *Rlelazioni degli Ambasciatori Veneti* cit., series II, vol. III, pp. 52-53.

38 SANUDO, *Diarii*, loc. cit.

39 I quote from V. CIAN, *A proposito di un'ambasceria di M. Pietro Bembo,* cit., where the letter is transcribed at p. 376The Doge is Leonardo Loredan (1501-1521)

40 In what follows in the letter, Querini tries to say and not say who it may be that is making his access to the pope difficult; it transpires, however, that his relationship with the Venetian Bembo, close friend of the Medici, particularly of Giuliano, and papal secretary – much later, 1539, cardinal Bembo – was taking a turn for the worse Nevertheless he says clearly that his new uncharacteristic difficulties arose '*da poi il ritorno di questi Reverendissimi Cardinali da Firenze* – since the return of these Most Reverend Cardinals from Florence', a more causal that casual coincidence, it seems.

41 It is worth remembering that Querini's task was to charter the Venetian ships, and also that there had been bitter words from Florence about money obtained for Venice when there did not seem to be any for Lorenzo. See IV.4, and notes 29, 37;

42 as in IV, note 33, I must say that a purpose or promise relating to conversion of infidels is one of the principles of faith to which a new pope is asked to adhere to, as I read in Landucci's *Diary*, where a list of a promises, including this one, is submitted to Leo X on his accession, is reported And indeed, all the Crusades that were undertaken in the early centuries had that ideal as a basisTerritorial gains, profits from wars, plunder and so forth came with it as well Like for all the following colonizations and missions However, matters of Crusade were by

now a distant matter, nor were they entertained by the secular, albeit Catholic, powers. Offshoots of Crusading times, like the orders of the Knights, like the Templars, for instance, had already been outlawed and eliminated by the Church and some states like France. So a Crusade now was an outlandish thought, out of place and out of time And in particular in very recent years, and precisely in Florence it had been given a very bad name by inflamed preaching from an altogether disreputable source – the recently direly disgraced Dominican Friar Savonarola.

EPILOGUE

Symbols and validations.

Thanks to the information collected second factual part of this study, I can now revise the historical background left unmentioned by the official celebrations as it comes through by way of the theatrical performance of the *Fusta piena di Matti* in its function of burlesque Herald, officer of the *Signoria*, collective court jester of the *festa,* and how, at the same time, this background gives the *fusta* its *raison d'être* and its validation.

The *Fusta* says, like the ideal Court Fool or Jester, a number of 'truths' that the representatives of authority, in their day of legitimization, with the official 'Triumph of Fame and Glory' have not the power to say. They cannot say them because they imply criticism of those very structures of power on which they themselves, the restored Mèdici *Signoria*, rely. This San Giovanni of the restoration is meant to be the celebration of Lorenzo de' Mèdici in Florence, but Lorenzo's vital support are the Pope, Leo X, and Giuliano, his uncles. He must accept and bow to the higher power. He owes deference to 'His Holiness Most Reverend'.

Yet he has found an indirect way, through burlesque, through the *Fusta.* The Fusta's choreography and the characters in it, hidden and revealed through their masks and disguises speaks for Lorenzo. Names, attributes, allusive gestures, with an intelligent and intelligible construction of visual riddles which hide and reveal their sense and their aim will be made to speak for him, and his Florentine allies.

All that needed to be said, was said by the elusive fleeting *Fusta* going through the street of Florence for just two hours at the start of the festival.. They needed to say that there were situations and problems in the papal court about which one could only exclaim that they were foolish crazy things, ill advised follies. These were stories ofVenetian ships, devilish counsellors, money flowing where it shouldn't, a fool for a captain of a ship, a megalomaniac fool playing with heresy, and a foolishness more foolish than any other, something that had to do with a Giovanni Crusader, a Tancredi summing up all the stories of ships and all that Turkish nonsense.

A special friendship, and the business of chartering ships, with the Venetians was pursued by the emissaries of the Most Serene Republic of Venice (The *Serenissima*) at the Roman Curia. But Venice had recently signed a new alliance with France, and Florence could not but feel hostility and fear for such a prospect, after the invasion of 1494 when Piero de Medici was forced into exile. This was one important aspect in the metaphor of the official festival, the liberation from the French. The Roman Camillo, had founded his city anew, having come back and liberated it from the Gauls. And so had the Medici, after a painful French invasion.

While the pope in Rome now loved the Venetian emissary Querini, and Bembo, too much. Querini's influence, was waylaying money for Venetian ships for various expensive and senseless enterprises – '*navicelle*' were flowing from the Pope's pockets to pay for Venetian ships, little ships on a senseless course. But these friendships touched also questions of faith, brought winds of reform and touched heresy. The very *Navicula Sancti Petri*, the Ship of Salvation, was on a dangerous course. The *Fusta* with her foolish captain, the Giovanni Tancredi di Santa Croce taunted in a basket by the fools, were in fact driven by devils incarnate.

The general picture is fairly clear by now, but further details come of use in order to weave an even more solid tapestry.

The black cloak, ensign of the poor and the fool, confirms, on the one hand, the statute of madness according to which Carafulla, jester and Governor of the *Fusta* acts – he acts as a double of the titular of the Church of the *Navicella*, the prodigal captain of the ship of Saint Peter, and aspiring admiral of a Crusade Fleet.

On the other hand it recalls the 'Company of the Tattered Cloak' – *La Compagnia del Mantellaccio* (1489) – which maintains how a black cloak cannot but mean madness (see IV.6.i.) – but also indicates a happy time, the age of Lorenzo the Magnificent, as well as the motif – his dream now in a double-take – of the return of the Golden Age (*il Secol d'Oro* celebrated on the previous S. Giovanni, 1513).

Besides, on the burlesque-festive plane this black threadbare, and tattered, cloak gives us the means of remembering *Carnasciale* exiled from Florence by the *piagnoni* of Savonarola with his cloak all in tatters (see II.1.), now returning from his Roman exile. So, let the festivities begin.

Furthermore, on the dark side, in the tearing of the black cloak from the very body of Carafulla by the devils with their hooks, we spy dark memories of those condemned as heretics as being conveyed on the hangman's cart on the way to the scaffold: on the way to the scaffold they had their very flesh torn by hooks, as a preparation to the stake, as we saw in the case of Fra Dolcino. Allusions to heresy and execution are not altogether strange if we remember the fate of Savonarola, certainly fresh in the minds of the Florentine people, and the fact that his follower Francesco da Meleto (see IV.3.) is now in Rome actually convened there recently, staying as a guest of the Venetian Bembo and obviously connected with the Venetian would-be reformers. They are all in great favour in the Curia, all possibly fomenting ideas of 'reform'. Thus also this idea of a dreamt of Crusade, expensive, mad and foolish devilry.

The fool's hood, and (extraordinary coincidence) Carafulla's art as Master hood-maker (and mad as a hatter), spins multiple threads to link a constellation of references: there are Florentine *cappucci* in exile in Rome being – although of the anti-Medicean faction – favoured by the Pope, first of all Pier Soderini, ex head of government of the terminated Florentine republic. Soderini is a *cappuccio* as to his political side, and has been represented hooded, in *cappuccio*, also as humbled penitent, at the bottom of a wheel of fortune (see IV.6.i.). The Wheel of Fortune, also one of the emblems dear to Lorenzo the Magnificent went on a carnival pageant in Rome for the carnival 1513, precisely to signify the restoration of the Medici to the rule of Florence, only the previous year. A Medici was represented at the top, a lion of Florence, the Marzocco, climbing up, and Soderini, a hooded figure at the bottom. The Mèdici's rise is contextual with Soderini's fall. Yet now this *cappuccio*, Piero Soderini is praised by the Medici Pope – in contrast to the Florentines that he blames – side by side with Carafulla. Each a sort of shadowy double of the other, one wise, one fool, (a wise-fool pair, an oxymoron), worthy of praise together, in the words of the Pope in Rome. Therefore they are plausibly together in the *Fusta*, as Carafulla in his hood carries both sides (the wise-fool, the praised and the blamed, the winner and the loser).

The one, the manifest double, is Carafulla, master of ceremonies, mock-king and governor of this accomplished *Fusta*, the other, included under the hood, is the republican *cappuccio*, held close to the heart by that same Pope Medici who should instead have at heart the fortunes of his own family and of those governing Florence now. In Florence they would be likely to make such remarks. Turning the very words of the Pope on to himself, through Carafulla.

Cappuccio is the habit of the Friar. It is in part because of Savonarola that the anti-medicean faction of the *popolani* came to become merged as *cappucci*; and there are other Friars, one is Piero-Vincenzo Querini (a Camaldolese hermit, no less) who, with his friend Giustiniani, should be more modest and penitent. They are all *cappucci*, recycled *cappucci, cappucci* on the make, and it is the Pope who is making them, making their fortune, raising them up. And Carafulla, hood maker, in a hood himself, is a multiple double and mirror of all these, Friars, republicans, Medici Pope. He takes them for a ride on the *Fusta*, all of them, as he opens the *festa* as Captain of the *Fusta piena di matti*, gentleman herald, collective fool, and court jester.

And then there is another. Another (another multifarious and polyvalent) mirror, a double of the double of those others in Rome, the miniaturized double of the captain and his *fusta*, a fool more foolish even than The Fool – and he gets taken up in a basket. This is the bearer , in his firs name, 'Gio.', of the Christian name of Pope Leo X, Giovanni, while his second name that of a famous Crusader, Tancredi, of the first Crusade, and he is of Santa Croce, as Cross bearer. But Santa Croce is also the Franciscan Church and Convent in whose theological school the future Pope Leo got his early education, and where the Friar Inquisitor would stay in Florence.

Persons, known names, but also hints, threats… dangers … memories … warnings …

Giovanni Tancredi di S.ta Croce represents the Pope Medici by means of this play of names sufficiently clear, and he does it also in his position of one caught by devils and taken for a ride in a basket, the miniaturized ship, another '*navicella*' – we have met them before (see IV.4) – a little ship of which he is passenger and captain together. The basket being a 'gulliverizing' mirror, the *mise en abîme* of the whole system of *Fusta*, fools and Carafulla the jester, all of which was already a mirror of crazy situations in contemporary reality.

Like Carafulla, Gio. Tancredi also spins several threads which are woven with and into the *fusta*'s tapestry. In fact we can read in Gio. Tancredi who carries and wears the wool also a satirized Fra Mariano (IV.5.) – the 'careerist' who had arrived, in the Roman world of careers, but as a buffoon and a jester also a representative of counter-power, and furthermore, as a rival of Carafulla, a counter-counter-power. And perhaps he represents also a caricature of the ever present and central Venetian Friar Piero-Vincenzo Querini, Cardinal *in pectore*, perhaps nearer to the cardinal's hat than to the hood, and much nearer to a scarlet robe than to the humble dark wool of the hermit friar. It is a game of mirrors turning over and over

Giovanni Tancredi in his basket **is to** Carafulla on his *fusta* what the bauble, the *marotte* – that is to say a portrait, fixed, charged and mocking – **is to** the Fool.

It is a game of mirrors which bounces and multiplies images, in a process of *mise en abîme* which is a spiralling of meanings which catch up with, and amplify, one another. They come up in repetitions seen from different angles and on different planes. While crossing one another the images acquire depth and power At the same time the connections achieve reciprocal validation and weave a background on which the details that have been emerging acquire full relief.

And yet, it is only a ship full of fools. It is only a *festa*. A few hours on Midsummer night.

The ship goes by, sailing through the streets of Florence on her carriage of wheels, with her load of fools and crazies, at the mercy of devils (diabolical forces), unstable as 'folly that goes sailing on the sea that is perilous', with a fault, a break on its side. At the end, before disappearing, the ship finds her miniature, her caricature, her *marotte*, the quintessence, the conscience of her unconscious. This at the end has confirmed the evidence we only vaguely suspected at the beginning, and which had led to the search of the method in all this folly.

It is precisely Gio. Tancredi of S.ta Croce the most foolish of all, in his small basket-ship, who actually mentions the Pope Leo by his Christian name of Giovanni, his education and his crusader dream: no more doubts, no more perhaps.

There *was* method in their folly.

And now, with her unstable load, the *fusta* goes, having, in passing, opened the games of the three days of celebration of the new stability, one hopes, of the Medici *Signoria* on Florence.

Visions and symbols, between wisdom and folly. The reality behind the play. The justness of the jesters.

A further recapitulation and juxtaposition of the two parts of this essay, to see how each gathers lights form the other now follows. It may be useful.

Let's go the opposite way, through the events examined, from Gio. Tancredi in his miniaturized ship, the basket, to Maestro Carafulla, who holds him in his power, from Carafulla in his container, the ship, from the ship in her environment, the sea, the devils and the *festa* in the water, and find the whole symbolical system of the *Fusta piena di matti* in all its parts as well as in the whole with its roots, as we have seen, in the Florentine festive tradition.

The *Fusta piena di matti* is at the centre of *both* the ritual plane, or field, in which a relationship with the supernatural can be traced – the ferryman Charon's boat, the ship of the dead, the deaths by water of 1304 – *and* of the real topical festive 'place', contingent and temporal-topical, in its potentially de-stabilizing and subversive function. All this movement within, and in contrast with, the monolithic civic ritual solemnity of the rest this S. Giovanni festival of 1514, which was meant to be, on the other hand, celebratory of a new found stability.

This centrality, this capturing and expressing the essence of the *festa* – including the darker side of death and subversion – is achieved by means of the traditional thematic elements of devils, fools, foolishness, *currus navalis*, jests and games. These are used both in their playful (*ludic*) function of diversion and laughter, and in the function of actual cathartic ritual for those in authority. After all the *fusta* is of their devising. The official *Compagnie* put it together. So it speaks for them. Those in power are after all admitting their impotence to speak openly for themselves. They have to enlist those irresponsible characters, the fools. And give them scripts.

The *Fusta piena di matti* is a symbolical system which was borne of what we called the 'ephemeral' historical humus. It was made of rumours about projects eventually unfulfilled, Crusade, reform – so were there projects, or just rumours? It was made of feelings of emulation, moods – Lorenzo was 'angry' about money, about *piagnoni* and *cappucci* being too well loved in Rome – *navicelle* slipping away. Yet, where are all these moods and conflicts when, the following year, Pope Leo X will make his great '*Entrata*', his official visit to Florence, in November 1515? When Giuliano will also come with his new French bride. The French threat is averted, it just vanishes. The Crusade only a distant bell tolling. Only the impenitently arrogant Cardinals on their high horses persist.

But precisely by these 'ephemera' of history the symbolical system of ship, fools and devil, finds validation. Likewise those rumours and moods between Florence and Rome were given some substance by this symbolical system which brings them to light.. The reality of each is confirmed by the presence of the other. A mutual validation.

If the Fool, and he who is made a fool of by the Fool, represent the Medici Pope in Florence, they are not indifferent figures, not just a joke, not just characters happening by chance. If the ship of fools of the St John's festival represents the ship of St Peter, that is the Papacy in these months of 1514, then it is a symbolical system invested of real power. It has the potential to intervene on to present reality. It is not a trifle, nor is it a just a joke.

In the fist part of this essay we have searched for sources in tradition, for the fool, the devils and their respective attributes, for the ship, and the ship of fools. Their *rationale* and their symbolism.

Specifically we have attempted to establish the possibility of placing them in the Florentine festive tradition. From a simply practical point of view we could recall also the *Palio delle Navi*, which was held on the river Arno. Small ships and racing boats were not unfamiliar near the streets of Florence.

We seem to have been able to gather evidence both in local reality (Villani – Pucci), and in the literay-theoretical elaboration (Alberti). We have seen the *festa* as hinge or *fulcrum* around which a reversal of 'orders' can occur, a reversal from legality to lawlessness, from the natural to the supernatural, from political to symbolical, from celebratory to punitive, from subversive to cathartic, from destabilizing to restoration... and the *festa* sits, in *active equilibrium*, between these possibilities, or realities.

We have also looked for a specifically Florentine source for the *Fusta piena di matti,* a Mediterranean ship of fools, to be clear. We have found signs along the way, and gone searching for a deep structure, so to speak, that might have emerged as our *Fusta*. The way has led to, on the one end, to the early 1300, to Charon's and Flegiás' boats, ferrymen of the souls of the dead in Dante's *Inferno* (as drawn later by Botticelli), to the infernal boats and rafts in the river Arno with the souls of the dead described by Villani (1304). Later we meet the boat, at times upturned, of Charon (again) in *Momus* by Alberti (middle of XV century) At the nearer end then, we meet the almost contemporary boats of the drawings by Botticelli for the same ferrymen's boats of Dante's *Inferno*: always the same boat, a boat for the souls of the dead. All in Chapter One.

We have found the soul of the ship (of fools) in the ship of the (dead) souls.

This ship of souls, under the definition of *fusta,* that is a Venetian ship, contains and carries Leo X, on a background of historical pre-texts, humours, emulations and discontents, foolish plans unrealized rumours and gossip between Florence, Rome and Venice. This is the loose historical weave that has become text and fabric of the *festa*.

All this makes of this symbolical event, namely the appearing of a traditional ship of fools as the *Fusta piena di matti* in Florence for the Feast of St. John the

Baptist of 1514, an all round historical event, while the humours and rumours that were its pre-text will be revealed as ephemeral although based on aspects of historical reality.

The Pontiff who is so clearly alluded to comes therefore to qualify the fools and to support the apparition *Fusta piena di matti,* to legitimize its sense and meaning, to give it an undisputably central place in the historical, real, contemporary world. And exactly what we have called the 'ephemera of history' confer a validation to the *Fusta piena di matti* which makes of this symbolical system, by enriching its resonance, the real historical event.

This fact, this event, is not a sort of repetition, nor is it a more or less abstract reconstruction of known motifs with a fixed seasonal or otherwise ritual recurrence. This *Fusta* has had a necessary and all round reason of being such as it is in the present moment. She has come to carry through fully, in the historical reality, however ephemeral, her symbolical, ritual and cathartic functions. She has come to being in order to be a mirror, to say truths which could not otherwise have been said, in order to hold a dialogue, however oblique, with the highest representative of absolute power, political and divine as well.

I want to say that we have met, at last, in the *fusta*, in this episode that was real and reported in history, something that appears to me as the construction of the ideal court Fool, the counterpart of he, or those, who are in power. The Fool is he who sees what others do not, he who knows, and he who can say, what others, small or powerful, cannot say. I wanted to remember, and to find, Erasmus's Folly, and the spirit of the great theatrical Fools. The ideal court jester. I think I have found him, albeit in a collective apparition, here.

He does manifest himself here in a play of mirrors and multiple images. He is constructed as a composite, and collective, being in the whole *Fusta*, the herald announcing the *festa*. He appears as an individual in Carafulla. He is miniaturized in the basket *navicella* and as such he is the 'core of the question' as Gio. Tancredi. In Giovanni Tancredi he, the fool, reaches the essence of the ambivalence of the oxymoron. He, with <u>that</u> name that names him, is perhaps the figure the most <u>rooted</u> in reality Yet he is the most elusive. In the miniaturization of the whole *Fusta* he collects all the other figures, images, allusions. Gio. Tancredi is the *mise en abîme* of the whole lot, yet he is the most flighty and volatile of all. He has been named only by Cambi, just mentioned by Masi, and in the end we find that he is not even a professional fool or jester as was Carafulla, for instance, but he is only impersonating one. He is a made-up part, a theatrical role, a character played by an actor, <u>pure invention</u>.

The collective fool, the whole *Fusta piena di matti*, appears in a festive context which, he, the collective Fool, in his turn, validates and confirms as a field of *reality*. A reality which can be made to react. That this is a wide ranging reality, we see again and again.

That system of unstable equilibrium that was the historical ambience during the months of May and June 1514 as revealed by letters and comments which is reflected in the *Fusta piena di matti*, and the symbolical system of the *Fusta*, find mutual validation. Together they make of the festive environment that is their context an event that fully manifests the ideal, and yet real, festive tradition. A tradition that is in touch with the transcendent, from the cart of fools to the boat of the dead, seen in that series of points of interface between civic, natural and supernatural, or metaphysical, orders. As we see in Dante, Villani-Pucci, Poggio, Alberti, Botticelli.

The *Fusta piena di matti*, like the ships of fools, like the boats of the dead by Botticelli, is a boat 'not concluded', and such it remains, rightly so. Earthly paradise is the enclosed garden, *hortus conclusus*, while the boat of the fallen is not a finite body, it is not enclosed, not concluded, open ended. It has a fault.

The symbolical system has taken body, without however losing complexity, resonance, expressive power, depth of perspective and range of implications. It is a game of mirrors, of multifaceted repeated images. I may add that the comparison with the historical reality of the moment only pushes it further into the play of mirrors, causes the images to radiate, divide and re-combine, multiply and intersect, now real now imaginary. They are impersonations of real figures, in some case single ones, more often superimposed, at times in several functions – and they move in the fluidity of moods, gossip and rumours.

Both in the real and the symbolical realm, we deal with cloaked figures, veiled, enclosed in their hoods and their disguises, hidden but therefore, paradoxically, open to multiple functions and interpretations.

It is in the statute of the symbol to signify more than what is actually seen or said. The symbol is equipped to suggest and represent in its configuration, may it be a picture, a character or a story, more than can be clearly enunciated in the visible or linear dimension of pictures or words.

And it is thus, peopled as she is of elusive and composite figures, emanating allusive and fleeting images, that the *Fusta piena di matti* finds lasting life as a symbolic system. She is an un-enclosed ship as we have seen her in iconography and chronicle, and remains, after all, unwilling to be defined or concluded. She has nevertheless suggested and represented all that we have collected in this essay. The evidence is all there, acted out, as reported in three contemporary records by historians.

Unwilling to be defined or concluded and enclosed, the *Fusta piena di matti*, as a real ship of fools, is a subversive project, subversive and critical, as subversive as a ship of fools (or monks, like Brendan's) which sets sail, against conventional reason perhaps, but on a vision and perhaps a mission, on a search for knowledge and wisdom beyond reason, on a search for the Happy Isles and for the Golden Age. The passing of the *Fusta* must be read also in this sense, at this moment of restoration, when the Golden Age is the age of Lorenzo the Magnificent, as well as the ideal and literary motif by him so loved. This had been indeed recalled and celebrated recently, in the Carnival 1513, with the great allegory of the *Trionfo dell'etá del' oro* (cfr. Chapter Two, note 19) accompanied by a canto also by Jacopo Nardi.

We were saying, the justness of the jesters, 'between recklessness and knowledge'. Knowledge as self knowledge, and knowledge of the other world. Recklessness in launching oneself into a search of a better world, a sort of challenge to the established society, and the acting out of a longing for a better world, a world of wisdom and justice, happiness and equality, ideas, or ideals, of which the fool and his voyage over the seas is the carrier. Both wise and reckless. Reckless in the view conventional reason. But wise beyond that reason.

The *Fusta* is a subversive project also in the reality of the *festa* of which she announces the opening, this San Giovanni of 1514. With her unstable load, and her rebellious course, the *Fusta* is a dark focal point in contrast with the splendid stability of the *Trionfo di Camillo*, the allegory of the Medicean rule restored, rehabilitated, recognized as rightful and worthy.

The sadow. It is a shadow, an elusive but pervasive shadow. Behind, or rather before, the fixed certainty of the official statement, of the civic ritual, behind the celebration of the restored *status quo ante* constructed by means of a monument of the past, the swift vessel goes by like an elusive shadow, it goes through the streets of Florence amid a turbulence of devils and festive crowds, it only lasts a few hours of the four days of celebration. This brief apparition, the *Fusta*, this ship of shadows is the herald of the *festa*, indeed it is its very spirit. The soul of the *festa,* this ship of souls.

After the festival in Florence, changes will occur in Rome, Venetian ships will lose favour.

A shift of attitudes registers regarding matters that were alluded to by the *Fusta* Perhaps its fleeting apparition had touched a fragile equilibrium, even imperceptibly?

The celebration of this San Giovanni was an important event for the Roman court. We have seen the Cardinals, with Giuliano, make a trial of strength by descending on Florence, not officially invited, their attitude ambiguous, flaunting their presence and their power *in disguise* but not exactly unnoticed. The Cardinals too have their part in the series of games where the various forces have their play, the power games.

In their presence we can take a reading of the grades of power, the hierarchies. We see how the cardinals can assert themselves and give a display of power on to the contiguous, lesser power. Rome, generally speaking, with Giuliano as *Gonfaloniere di Santa Chiesa*, the major lay authority in Rome, and the Cardinals, override the Florentine *Signoria*. The Roman contingent, by being masked and armed flaunts unpunished the laws of Florence.

The *Signoria*, uses the civic *festa*, for its controlled celebration, its official statement. The civic festival, towers in matters of time and importance, on the burlesque *Fusta* that is only a Fool after all, and gets only a few hours for its act..

The *Fusta* in its turn towers over the basket-*navicella* which it will draw up. Carafulla towers over Fra Mariano (who we know had asked to come to Florence as the official fool). Finally Carafulla, with the fools of the *Fusta* towers over the crowd from which they capture this fool the most foolish of all, Gio. Tancredi of S.ta Croce, not even a person but a *dramatis persona*, pure mask.

This last, nevertheless, this mask, this scripted character, Gio. Tancredi, the very last and least in the grades of power in the festive theatricals, closes, in a way, the circle. He is the conclusive turn of the spiral, since he is the one who indicates and represents specifically pope Leo X, Giovanni de' Medici, the apex and the maximum authority on the contemporary historical stage, who is impersonated by this mere mask in the festive *mise en scène*. The pure mask, the very last and very least in line, is indeed the key to the whole.

Each power asserts and validates itself against the next and lesser in line, in a game of interdependent assertions and validations. But in the end it is the very least and last in line who has the last word and holds the key by naming Giovanni, Leo X. The opposites coincide. The cycle is completed. The overturning of values characteristic of the *festa* is attained.

And yet, precisely this subversive and rebellious project escapes also this sort of abstract circle. Probably as a good spiral, never exactly concluded.

The ship of fools is a ship not concluded, it is an open-ended ship. We have seen the breach in the side of the ship. And as a symbolical system, it is open to exchange, to some commerce with reality. It repeats itself while, at the same time, it also transforms itself. Each of its manifestations is an altogether new discourse and a new design in which the collective structures from the deep emerge on to the space opened by the license of the game of the new *festa*. In this, the deep structures find a new way of expressing themselves, of helping understanding, of acting out whatever needs to be acted out.

In times of change, the ship appears. The days of the feast of Saint John the Baptist, the Summer Solstice, Midsummer, a key point in the yearly cycle, the beginning of the end, are the moment of the highest peak of splendour which contains a premonition of the descent, a premonition of the end. San Giovanni, Midsummer, contains the shadow. The peak is over, the descent commences. So at the moment of the celebration of the glory of the restoration, at San Giovanni, a shadow goes by, the ship of shadows, the ship of the dead. In the guise of the *Fusta piena di matti*, between knowledge and recklessness, the ship goes by, full of prancing fools, here, in Florence on 22nd June 1514, accompanied by ghosts from hell, yes the devils, who remain, however, on the hard dry land. It is guided by folly and like folly herself she can say:'*io son la follia che vo cercando il mar ch'è periglioso* – I am folly who goes scouring the sea that is full of danger', the sea where there are no marked roads.

The *fusta,* above the ocean of the crowd, outside the boundaries of power, goes by on its own way, a handsome ship on a cart drawn by two pairs of oxen.

In a wider geographical, temporal and seasonal, perspective, I would like to say that it is a notable coincidence. It is not by chance that a ship of fools, in the shape of the punitive one of Brant's, and in the shape of the *Fusta piena di matti,* the festive one, as well as in the new iconographic blossoming of the symbol in the North and South of Europe, up to Bosch at the end of the century, should appear on the foreground at the beginning of the age of the great seafaring achievements in the West, the geographical discoveries of the modern age, new nations, new wars. The shadow appears.

It re-appears accompanied by the first turbulence of Reformation. and Counter-Reformation.

Perhaps spied by the first dreams of the telescope.

At that moment when the safety of a flat earth at the centre of the universe as designed by the cartographers begins to fade, to shift, to turn on itself.

So then, as the old roads are changing, it is becoming clear that we may as well, we must, indeed, take to the sea where there are no known roads, in a ship governed by the wise, reckless and most praiseworthy Folly.

Curtain.

Appendices

Appendices

Trionfo della Fama e della Gloria

Canto per il Trionfo di Camillo – di Jacopo Nardi

Contempla in quanta altezza se' salita.
Felice alma Fiorenza,
poichè dal ciel discesa è in tua presenza
la gloria, e cogli esempi a sè t'invita:
la quale ha tal potenza
ch'a morti rende la vita,
ond'ella il morto già Camillo mostra
viver ancor per fama all'età nostra.

Admire (see, reflect) what heights you have reached
Happy beloved Florence
because from the heavens has come to your presence
Glory, and with examples invites you to her:
because she has such power
as to give life to the dead,
as she shows that the dead Camillo
lives still thanks to fame in our age.

Quell'è Furio Camillo il gran romano
per cui Roma esaltata
fu tanto, che l'invidia scellerata
usó 'ver lui la rabbia, benchè invano:
perchè la patria ingrata
il consiglio non sano
conobbe poi che gli levò la soma,
e fu costretta a dir: per te son Roma.

That one is the Roman Furio Camillo
for whom Rome excited
was so, that hateful envy
used against him, and rage, but invane:
because the ungrateful homeland
recognized the ill advice
when they relieved him of office
and was obliged to say, because of you I am Rome.

Le pompe trionfal nel tuo cospetto,
le barbariche spoglie,
le tempie ornate delle sacre foglie
mostron le laude sue: ma tal concetto
una parola accoglie,
poiché lui solo è detto
della patria, per l'opre alte e leggiadre,
primo liberatore, secondo padre.

Trimphal pomp now in front of you
the spoils of war
his temples adorned by the sacred leaves
show praise for him: and such concept
a word contains
because only he is said
of the homeland, thanks to his high and good deeds,
first liberator and second father.

Manca la vita in un tanto superba,
mancan le sue sante ale,
la nostra dea contr' al ordine fatale
trae 'l buon fuor dal sepolcro e 'n vita il serba:
la virtù sola vale
contr'alla morte acerba,
e senza lei cercar gloria non giova:
ma seguendo virtù costei si trova.

There is no life in one so great
life with its holy wings
but our goddess against the fateful order
takes the good out of his tomb and keeps him alive
only valour is worthy
against bitter death
and without it it is not possible to find glory
but following valour one achieves it.

Come vedete seco insieme vanno
la dea Minerva e Marte
che colla spada, con scienza e arte
all'uom mortale immortal vita danno;
e le vergate carte
lo ristoron del danno,

poiché come l'allor foglia non perde,
la storia e poesia sempre sta verde.

As you see the goddess Minerva and Mars
together go by, who with the sword and science and art
give immortal life to mortal man
and the writings
make up for the waste (death)
as like the laurel which does not shed its leaves [1]

1 The Italic Minerva Medica (afterwards conjoined with Pallas Athena) in ancient times had her feast on March 19th, the same day as the day of Mars, the *Quinquatrus*. Both the feast days were then shifted, at the time of Augustus, to 19th June, Midsummer.

Mars was the ancient patron god of Florence (see Dante, *Inferno*, 143-145), a position later and thereafter occupied by St. John the Baptist, at the same time, in Midsummer.

Minerva Mèdica, with the obvious analogy of name with the family name of the Mèdici, become also Pallas Athena, entertains close emblematic as well as euphonic ties with the family Medici by way of their coat of arms (the balls- *palle*) and the victory cry '*palle, palle*', much used in Florence – as well as in Rome at the time of this restoration, and then of the election of cardinal Giovanni de' Mèdici to Pope Leo X.

So this pair of warrior gods were well suited to being mentioned for the celebration of this S.Giovanni of the restoration in 1514.

Minerva Medica, the Pallas Athena of the 'just and rightful war', the goddess who tamed the horse (she had invented the bridle), who had fought the giants and the centaurs, who had invented the flute (later passed on to Dionysus), later adopting her brother Apollo's lyra, is frequently taken up in these years for the classical allegories (Lorenzo the Magnificent had done so in his jousts of the years 1460-1470). We find her in great evidence in the buildings and mottoes displayed for the great *Ingresso* to the Lateran of pope Leo X at his election in April 1513: es. '*nunc sua tempora Pallas habet* – now it is the time of Pallas'. Minerva Pallas indicates, like Mars, Strength, but in a further progress through and from strength to reason, with a constellation of resonances with the ideals of the Mèdici, statesmen, diplomats (notably Lorenzo the Magnificent), educated poets and musicians, patrons of the arts.

I must remember the painting '*Pallade e il Centauro* – Pallas and the Centaurus', by Botticelli where Minerva-Pallas, dressed in fabric decorated by the *Diamante* emblem (three joined rings) of the Mèdici, enveloped by the olive branches of Athena, her head crowned by laurel holds the head of a Centaurus whose face looks suspiciously like Lorenzo the Magnificent's (see for instance the characteristic nose) that she has tamed..

So in this stanza is Lorenzo, who has acquired immortality with sword, science and art, and his writings, so that the laurel, like his history and poetry, remains ever green.

Source texts

Istorie di Giovanni Cambi fiorentino pubblicate da Fr. Ildefonso di S.Luigi. In "Delizie degli eruditi toscani", Tomo XXII, vol.III, pp.43-45 and p.48.

"l'anno 1514...addi 22 sera andorno a Hoferta i Magistrat di Firenze, cho Sei...Andó di nuovo in detta sera, mentre andava detta hoferta per detta via, una fusta piena di pazzi, cioè buffoni, e chon molti diavoli appiè di detta fusta, faciendo molte buffonerie, e missonvi su uno, chera un pocho isciemo, ma era verboso, e piacevole, che si chiamava per sopranome Maestro Antonio di Pierrozzo da Vespignano, che faceva chapucci, che lo presono il dì dinanzi appetizione de' festaioli, e missollo nel Palazzo del Podestà, poi lo missono detto dì insù detta fusta in mantello, e in chapuccio nero, chom usava vestire, cherassai consumato, perch' era povero, e que' diavoli con oncini glielo straciorno di dosso. Chredo lo rivestirno dipoi di nuovo. Mentre chandavano per detta processione trovorono Gio. Tancredi ciptadino per arteficie, del Quart. di S. Croce, che portava la lana, ed era piú sciocho assai di Maestro Antonio sopradetto, perchè non sapeva far' altro, che portare la lana, e dessere mai maestro non pensava, che in 50. anni non mutò mai arte; in un tratto que' diavoli, ch'eran appiè della fusta lo presono, ella fusta mandò giú un chorbello, e in un tratto lo tirorono insulla fusta, e messono a remo; e chon un bastone di chuoio pien di vento gli dettono parechi bastonate, acciò remassi bene lui, e degli altri». (pp. 43-45)

'The year 1514, on the evening of the 22nd day [of June] (went) the Magistrates of Florence, with the Six [*della Mercatura*, of the Guilds] went in procession with the Offerings (in the procession of the Offerings). And also, while the said procession was going on the said street, a *fusta* full of fools, that is jesters, buffoons, also went, with many devils at the foot of the said fusta, and they played many pranks and buffooneries, and having put in her a certain character, who was a little silly but smart of tongue and pleasant, and was called with the surname of Maestro Antonio di Pierrozzo da Vespignano, who was a maker of hoods-*cappucci* (*faceva chappucci*), and whom they had taken the day before on demand of the organizers (*i festaioli* – the masters of the revels), and they had put him in the Palace of the *Podestà*, and then the said day they put him on the *fusta*, wearing, as he was normally clothed, his black cloak and hood, which was rather worn, because he was poor, and those devils with their hooks tore it off his back. I believe they clothed him again later.

While they were going on the said procession they came across Gio. Tancredi citizen and (worker) craftsman, of the Quart. of S. Croce, who wore and/or carried the wool and was much more foolish than Maestro Antonio mentioned above, because he was not able to do anything else than carry (and wear) the wool, and he never thought he could become 'maestro', and in 50 years had never changed his trade; all at once those devils, who were at the foot of the *fusta*, caught him, the *fusta* sent down a basket, and suddenly pulled him up into the *fusta*, and put him to the oar and with a club (cudgel, bludgeon) made of leather filled with wind they hit him several times so as to make him row well, him and the others'.

"*Venneci da Roma a vedere la festa Giuliano de' Medici fratello del Papa con 6. Chardinali, che vera il nipote del Papa, figiuolo del Signor Franceschetto da Genova, el Chardinale sanese, e un Viniziano, el nostro da Bibiena, e tutti andavano fuori d'abito vestiti di nero alla Spagnuola, colla spada allato, e turati, el simile Giuliano, sicché ci davano buono axempro e a questo modo si riforma la Chiexa. Iddio lo perdoni loro, effacili ravedere de' loro erori, e alsì noi altri Christiani*" [Cibo, Alfonso Petrucci, Cornaro, Bibiena](p.48)

"Giuliano de' Medici came here from Rome to see the festival with 6 Cardinals, and there was the Pope's nephew (Giulio), The Senese Cardinal, a Venetian one, our Da Bibiena, and they all walked about not in their (Cardinal's) habits but all dressed in black in the Spanish fashion, with swords at their sides, and their faces covered (turati), the same as Giuliano, so that they were giving us a good example and in this way one reforms the church. May God forgive them, and may he make them repent of their errors, like all of us Christians.".

Ricordanze di Bartolomeo Masi calderaio fiorentino a cura di G.O. Corazzini, Firenze, 1906.

«El giorno di poi, che fu a dí XXII di detto, si fece una solenne e bella procissione.. E di poi, dopo desinare, andó per tutta Firenze una fusta di legniame in su un carro, tirata da due paia di buoi, la quale era fatta e di grandezza e con tutti gli ordini che si conviene a uno simile legnio; et avevonvi messo su cierti pazzi, o vogliam dire mezzi pazzi, per dare piacere al popolo. E drieto a detta fusta erano vestiti circa di trenta a uso di diavoli con cierti oncini e campanelle in mano; i quali pigliavano qualcuno e mettevollo in su detta fusta; e se voleva uscire, gli facevano pagare la taglia» (p.142)

'Venne a vedere la sopraddetta festa dimolti signori e gran maestri, e quali vennano col mognifico Giuliano de' Medici; et ancora venne con esso lui da sette a otto Cardinali; andavano per la città turati, a cavallo, con cappe, cappegli e beche, coperti el viso di modo che non si conoscievano' (p.144)

'The following day, that was the XXII day of said [June] a solemn and beautiful procession was organized ... And after, after dinner, through the whole of Florence went 'A fusta, well built of wood (and carried) on a wagon pulled by two pairs of oxen, which was made, both in size and with full complement (furnishing) as it is suitable to such a ship, and they had put in her certain (fools) madmen, or we should say half-mad, to entertain the people. And behind the said fusta about thirty were dressed as devils, with some hooks and bells in their hands; these caught someone here and there [i.e. Gio. Tancredi that Masi, not being 'into things' could not identify] and put him on to the fusta; if he wanted to get out, they made him pay a fine (forfeit) (*taglia*) (p. 142)

Many Gentlemen and Very Important People came to see the said festival, and those come with the Magnifico Giuliano de' Medici; and with him came seven or eight Cardinals; they were going through the city masked, on horseback, with capes, hats and silken scarves of office (*beche*), their faces covered so that they would not be recognized'. (p. 144)

SANUDO, *Diari*
XVIII, 313. Il 22 giugno 1514 – Procession.

' e il giorno, dopo disnare, sopra un longo carro andó fuora una fusta ornata con tutti soi coriedi, come se in proprio mare avessa a navicare, e fornita di huomeni piazevoli e bufoni, e tutti a una livrea marinaresca, fra quali el Barlachii, dove avevano su racolti i pochi pazi che si trovavano in questa nostra città, uno el Carafulla in capuzo. e andando per tutta la terra come in destare el populo a festa fu solazosa piacevolezza, dove concoreva tutto el populo e quanti forestieri vi si trovava, che da Roma ce n'è assai, fra quelli sette cardinali, zoè Cornaro, Sauli, Bibiena, Ferara, Cibo, Siena et Ragona e il nostro Magnifico confaloniere di Santa Chiesa, tutti turati, ma tutti si conoscevano'.

'...and the following day, after dinner, on top of a long wagon, a *fusta* was carried out, furnished with all her structures (full complement-*coriedi*)... complete as if really ready to go to sea, and it was crewed by amusing men, jesters and buffoons, and all in a mariner livery, among whom was Barlacchii [the actor], having collected the few madmen (fools)that could be found in this city of ours, one of them Carafulla in his hood (*in capuzo*). And as she went through all the land as if to awaken the people for the festival, it was an amusing pleasantry, where all the population concurred as well as what foreigners there were, as from Rome there were many, among whom seven cardinals, that is Cornaro, Sauli, Bibiena, Ferrara, Cibo, Siena e Ragona, e our *Magnifico confaloniere* of the Holy Church [Giuliano], all with their faces covered, but one knew them all'.

CARDINALS. as named by SANUDO:

Ragona – Cardinal Luigi d'Aragona. **Luigi** d'Aragona, Cardinal, Bishop of Leon & Aversa, Marchese di Gerace, *1474, +1519; m. Vatican 1492 (annulled 1494) Battistina Usodimari, niece of Pope Innocent VIII

Bandinello **Sauli**, (Genoese) bishop of Gerace.

Alfonso Petrucci, bishop of Massa Marittima mentioned as **Siena**, also in his twenties

Marco **Cornaro,** Cardinal Patriarch, (1482-1524) (S.ta Maria in Portico) made a Cardinal 28th Sept. 1500

Bernardo Dovizi da **Bibbiena,** author of the comedy *La Calandria*, friend of Fra Mariano, the jester.

Ferrara – Ippolito d'Este (1482-1524) (the dedicatee of Ariosto's *Orlando furioso*)

Cibo (***il nipote del Papa***) Innocenzo Cibo (21 year old in 1513)

Glossary

Capitano generale Head of the militia

Cappucci. Cappucci (hoods, cowls) – pronouced 'capp-oo-chi' like cappuchins or, indeed like the now well known 'cappuccino' the coffe with milk and froth, of the colour of the habit of the Cappuchin monks.

Some Florentines may have written (Cambi does) the word as 'chappucci' using the initial **ch** to indicate the peculiarity of the vernacular Florentine pronunciation of a '**voiced h**' for the initial '**c**'. This is not found elsewhere in Italian.

As for the '**cappucci**' as political-social definition for the friars and the 'popolani' (see Chapter Four, IV.6.ii.) it seems strange to hear of the contemporary 'hoodies' nowadays.

Festa : see III.3. plus notes and cross references, **carnival tradition**, **reversal of roles** are all explained and defined as the **"*festa*"** pattern.

Gonfaloniere. The highest Authority of a city or state (descending from the 'Comuni') as he was the protector, the holder, the defender of the *Gonfalone*, the flag or banner representing the City.

La Magliana

- Magliana – the group **gl**i is pronounced like the double **ll** in the English 'millions'.
- Magliana was the villa and estate near Rome which was the pope's hunting lodge, and was much frequented by Leo X and his court, for hunting, hawking and ferretting. Leo X himself was not fit enough for riding the hunt, but he kept teams of dogs and watched the hunters from some suitable seat of observation,
- The hunting lodge, was initially built by Sixtus IV. Innocentius VIII, Julius II and Leo X enlarged it with the advice of Giuliano da Sangallo and Bramante. Later on Pius IV added a large fountain at the center of the courtyard. Because of its unprotected location the lodge was also fortified and from the outside it has the appearance of a castle.
- While during the Renaissance no one objected to the fact that a pope spent his time hunting, in the following centuries this pastime was no

longer regarded as appropriate for a pope and the lodge was abandoned. Today it is part of a hospital run by the Knights of Malta.

- In John Osborne's play a scene (act II , scene v) is set in the Hunting Lodge at the Magliana, in 1519

Lana – Portare – in portare la lana – either to carry the wool, or to wear the wool. In Italian it can mean either – or both. And in the circumstances, I see an intentional ambiguity, and the ambivalece of meaning to indicate both.

Maestro. Master of the trades. But also title due to some honorary office, attributed to an 'Important Person'. And obviously eventually a master in his art.

Magnifico

Il Magnifico – the **gn**i group is pronounced as a nasal, like the Spanish **ñ** for which the nearest English pronunciation can be found in the words 'op**ini**on' and 'm**ini**on', or 'mi**ni**ature'.

Mèdici, or de' Mèdici (de': abbreviation of 'dei' 'of the') carries the stress on the first syllable, a position not at all unusual in Italian (parole sdrúcciole, to be technical, with the accent of the third last syllable)

As for Magnifico as a title, it was applied to people in high office, we see it applied (before the name) to Giuliano, as il Magnifico Gonfaloniere di Santa Chiesa, to our young il Magnifico Lorenzo as the *Signore* in Florence.

Magnifico has been used also generically some sort of would be grandiose individual, like 'the Magnifico' in the *Commedia dell'Arte,* who is just an old man, perhaps a 'has been' person of note, and probably still very rich.

As for 'Lorenzo Il Magnifico', that had become his appellation carrying probably the ambiguity of the word – of Authority in the state, and for the magnificence of his life and times. In this particular use 'il Magnifico' comes always after the name.

Signoria, Government, Authority, the complement of the people in power, in a government not necessarily elected. Those surrounding and supporting 'Il Signore', in this case the head of the Mèdici family.

Illustrations

Illustration n.1 From Sebastian Brant, *Das Narrenshiff*, Basel, 1494. Title page

Periculū non vitare.

Qui amat piculū in illo pibit. Iusticia simplicis diriget viā ei⁹: & i impietate sua corruet impius: ppter peccata labiorū ruina pximat malo: effugiet autē iust⁹ de angustia via stulti recta in oculis ei⁹. Iter āt impiorū decipiet eos in semita iusticię vita. Iter āt deuium ducit ad mortem.

in psāl. de non alie. aut p. ec. col. ii. puer. xi Sapien. iiii.

Rebus in humanis ꝙ sit constantia nulla:
Nec sit certa fides: perstabilis ve gradus:
Hoc monstrant hominū casus & fata caduca.
Hoc te fortunę mobilitasq; docet.

De via felicitatis

Sapiētia callidi ē intelligere viā suā & prudētia stultorū errans. Est via q̄ videt hōi iusta nouissima aūt ei⁹ deducūt ad mortem. vir insipiens nō cognoscet. & stultus nō intelliget hęc. Nescierunt neq; intellexerūt in tenebris ambulant

Non sinit ipse deus fatuū quemcunq; prophanū
Scire sup terram quę nam miracula fecit:
Quotidieq; facit: quapropter pars perit ingens
Stultorū: morit terreno in corpore semper.

pe. r. xiiii. Ps 3t. & .91. Sa ien. xiii.

Illustration n.2. Examples of ship and cart. From S. Brant, *Stultifera Navis*, Basel 1497

I

Stultifera Navis.

Narragonice profectionis nunquam satis laudata Navis: per Sebastianum Brant: vernaculo vulgarique sermone & rhythmo / pro cunctorum mortalium fatuitatis semitas effugere cupientium directione / speculo, commodoque & salute: proque inertis ignavaeque stultitiae perpetua infamia / execratione / & confutatione / nuper fabricata: Atque iampridem per Iacobum Locher / cognomento Philomusum: Suevum: in latinum traducta eloquium: & per Sebastianum Brant: denuo seduloque revisa / & nova quadam exactaque emendatione elimata: atque superadditis quibusdam novis / admirandisque fatuorum generibus suppleta: foelici exorditur principio.

·1497·

Nihil sine causa.

Io. de. Olpe.

Latina navis seu barca socialis.

Innumeros classes / fatuos sine fine furentes
Hactenus in nostra ducere classe iuvat:
Si quis forte locum potuit minus accomodatum
Nanciscithuc veniat cum sociisque vehat.

societas fatuorum.

Gaudium est miseris socios habere penarum. Sed non minus ardebunt: qui cum multis ardent Quiiter huiusce modi letantur: & esse sub sentibus delicias computant: filii sunt stultorum & ignobilium oppressi quasi fluctibus semitis suis: fratres sunt draconum & socii strutionum. Sic fuit / est & erit. similis similem sibi querit.

Currite sulcamus festinis aequora remis:
Et premit immensum carbasa nostra fretum.
En socialis adest classis: properate sodales:
Et fatui pariter nunc properate mei:

ii. q. i. multi
Eccle. xx. & .7
Iob. xxx.
i. Esdre. v.
Sapien. iiii

Illustration n.3. More Ships of Fools. From S. Brant, *Stulitifera Navis*, Basel, 1497

Illustration n.4, from Josse Bade, *Stultiferae Naves,* Lion, 1502

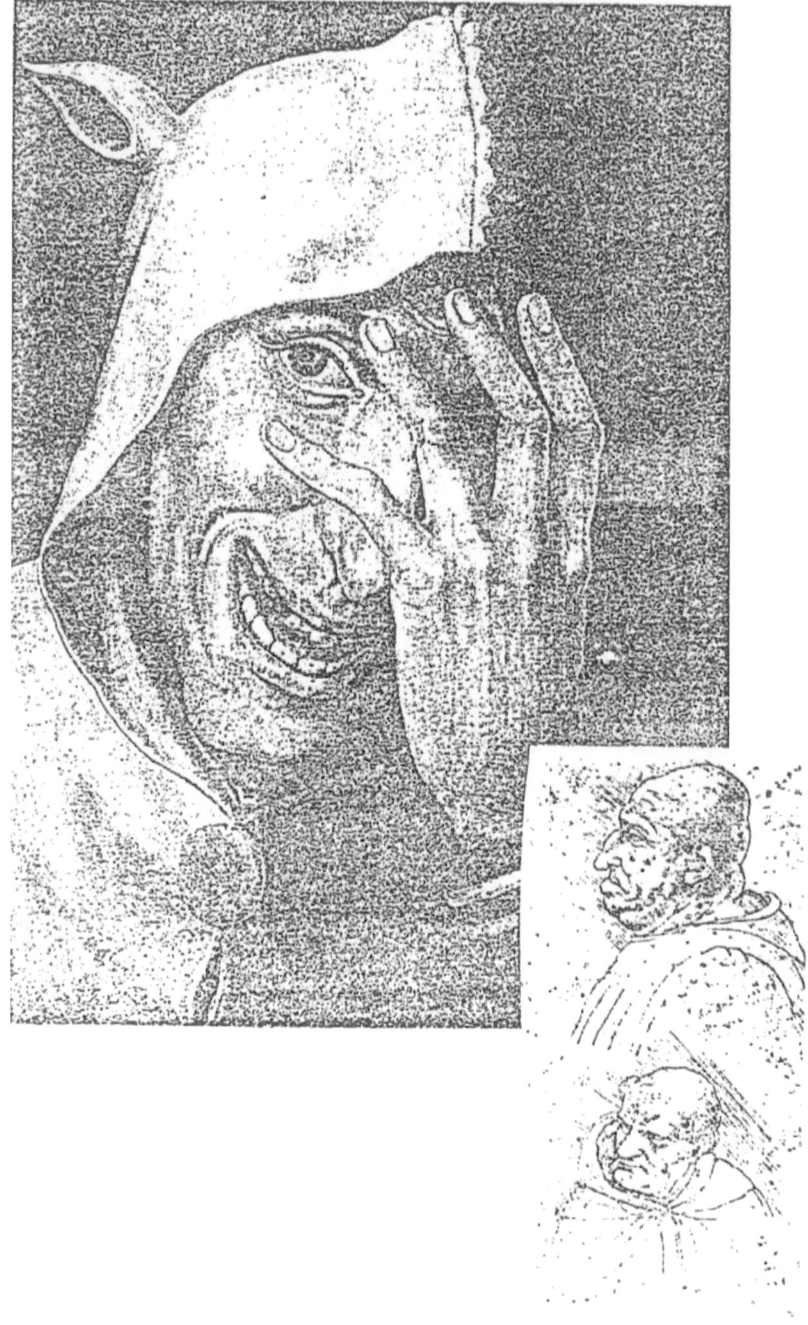

Illustration n.5. *Cappucci*, hoods. Portrait of a Fool.
Two drawings by Leonardo

PLATE 10. Jesters' baubles. Figures 7 and 9 represent a late development of the bauble from the more primitive club; in them the human image is reduced to the fool's head and the exaggerated phallus. The ass's ears (of 7 and 8) and the cockscomb (of 9) link the figures to animals famous for their sexuality as well as their silliness. The figures represent the intelligence of the phallus—a counterpart, on the level of instinct, to the reason of the head; or they represent reason drawn into the sphere of the instinctual element and overwhelmed by it. The figures are sticking their tongues out insultingly, like the image in the mirror in Holbein's drawing (Plate 8). Thus these baubles may be seen as a symbolic form of the power behind or within the encounter between fool and nonfool in which the customary lines between folly and nonfolly are blurred or broken.

Illustration n.6. Examples of the fool's bauble, or *marotte*, with one club (4) and examples of the phallic bladder

Illustration n. 7. Fools and their *Marottes*

Illustration n 8. Giotto, *Stultitia*, Chapel of the Scrovegni, Padua, Italy.

Illustration n.9. Examples of Devils with masks and clubs. Agnolo Gaddi. (XV cent.) *Tentazioni di S. Antonio* Santa Croce, Florence, Italy.

Illustration n.10. Example of transitional cratures, between Devils and Fools. From Josse Bade, *Stultiferae Naves*, Lion, 1502

Illustration n.11. Drawing by Hieronymous Bosch. The boat on the dwarf's shoulders is similar to Bosch's painting of a ship of fools in the Louvre.

Illustration n. 12. Boats (extracted) from Botticelli's drawings for Dante, *Inferno*, Canto VIII

Illustration n.13. Devils from Botticelli's drawing for Dante, *Inferno*, canto XXIII

Bibliography

This is just an 'essential' bibliography, that is the list of books immediately connected with the present work. They are the sources of my quotations and of the published information I used. They can be used, of course, as further reading in areas of the background to my work.

The unpublished letters of the Medici family are quoted and referred to only in the notes.

But I must mention again Erasmus and his *Praise of Folly* as being not only an 'immediate' source, but as having accompanied my studies, and my life, for very many years and also in other occasions in my research.

ALBERTI, Leon Battista, *Momus, o del principe,* traduzione, testo critico, introduzione e note, S.G. MARTINI, Bologna, Zanichelli, 1942

ALBERTI, L.B., *Momus*, English translation by Sarah Knight University of Warwick The "I Tatti Renaissance Library", 2003. 448 pp. ISBN O-674-OO753-9

ALBERTI, L. B., *Momus*, a cura di Virginia Brown, Sarah Knight Cambridge (Mass.), Ed. Harvard University Press – 2003

ARETINO, Pietro, *Ragionamento delle Corti*, Lanciano , 1914

ARLIA, C., (ed) *I sonetti rusticani di Biagio del Capperone,* (Bernardo Giambullari), Città di Castello , 1902.

BAKHTIN, M. *Rabelais and His World*, Cambrdge, (Massachusetts) M.I.T., 1963.

BARTOLINI SALIMBENI, Gherardo, *Cronichetta sopra le ultime azioni di Lorenzo de' Medici Duca d'Urbino,* a cura di Isidoro del Luigi, Firenze 1786, in *Delizie degli eruditi toscani*, appendice, vol, 23.

BATTAGLIA, S., *Grande Dizionario della Lingua Italiana,* 1961 .... – Battaglia up to vol. L. (now completed under other editor) Torino U.T.E.T.

—— *Mitografia del personaggio,* Milano, Rizzoli, 1968.

BERTELLI, Sergio, *Firenze, Venezia, politica estera* in X.802.5075

BONICATTI, M., *La tematica della Follia in chiave moralistica, Sebastian Brant e Hieronymus Bosch,* in *L'Umanesimo e" la follia"*, a cura di E. Castelli, Roma, Abete, 1971.

BOSCH, Hieronymus, *Opera completa,* a cura di Dino Buzzati e Mia Cinotti, Milano, Rizzoli, 1966.

BOWD Stephen_*Reform before the Reformation: Vincenzo Querini and the Religious Renaissanc in Italy,* (Brill Studies in Medieval and Reformation Thought, vol 87; Leiden, Boston, Cologne, 2002

BRANT, Sebastian, 1458-1521. *Das Narrenschiff* : Faksimile der Erstausgabe Basel 1494 mit dem Nachwort von Franz Schultz (Strassburg 1912) / herausgegeben von Dieter Wuttke. Baden-Baden : Valentin Koerner, 1994. (facsimile with all the illustrations)

BRANT, Sebastian, 1458-1521. Title *Das Narrenschiff.* English *The Ship of Fools /* by Sebastian Brant ; translated into rhyming couplets, with introduction and commentary, by Edwin H. Zeydel ; with reproductions of the original woodcuts. Imprint New York : Columbia University Press, 1944.

BUTTERS, H.C., *Governors and Government in Early XVI century Florence_(1502-1519)* Oxford 1985 Oxford : Clarendon, 1985. Descript. xviii, 350p ; 22cm

CAMBI, Giovanni, *Istorie di Giovanni Cambi cittadino fiorentino,* a cura di Ildefonso di San Luigi, in *Delizie degli eruditi toscani,* Tomo XXII, vol.3 (pp.43-45 – *fusta*)

CAIRNS, Christopher (ed), *The Commedia dell'arte from the Renaissance to Dario Fo / edited by Christopher Cairns.* (Conference 1988) Lewiston : Edwin Mellen Press, 1989.

CAMPORESI, Piero, *La maschera di Bertoldo,* Torino, Einaudi, 1976.

—, *Il paese della fame,* Bologna, il Mulino, 1978.

CANTIMORI, Delio, *Eretici italiani del cinquecento* : ricerche storiche. Imprint Firenze : G.C. Sansoni— editore, [1939]

CASTELLI, Enrico, *Il demoniaco nell'arte,* Milano–Firenze 1952

— *Simboli e immagini,* Roma, 1966.

— (ed.) *L'Umanesimo e "la follia",* Roma, Abete, 1971

CIAN, Vittorio, *A proposito di un'ambasceria di M. Pietro Bembo,* in Archivio Veneto, XXX, 1885.

D'ANCONA, Alessandro, *Origini del teatro italiano,* Torino, (2nd ed.) 1891.

Libri tre con due appendici sulla rappresentazione drammatica del contado toscano e sul teatro mantovano nel sec. XVI. Imprint Torino : E. Loescher, 1891.

— *La poesia popolare italiana* : Studj di Alessandro d'Ancona. Imprint Livorno : R. Giusti, 1906, viii, 571 p ; 19 cm.

DATI, Goro (Gregorio), *L'istoria di Firenze di Gregorio Dati dal 1380 al 1405,* a cura di Luigi Pratesi. Illustrata e pubblicata second il codice inedito stradiniano collazionatocon altri manoscritti e con la stampa del 1725. Norcia 1902. (San Giovanni from p. 91 to p.96 and pp. 140-170 – dialogo "Degli ordini e governo")

DAVANZATI, Chiaro, *Rime*, edizione critica con note e glossario a cura di Aldo Menichetti, Bologna, 1965 ("…e io son la follia…": dal Sonetto n.305 "A guisa di temente" ll.13-14)

D'AYALA (P.G.) et BOITEUX (M.), *Carnavals et mascarades.*, Paris, Bordas, 1988

DE BARTHOLOMAEIS, V., *Le origini della poesia drammatica italiana*, Bologna, 1924.

DE ROOVER, Raymond Adrien, *The Medici Bank : its organization, management, operations and decline*. New York : New York Univ. Press, 1948.

DE ROOVER, Raymond Adrien, *The Rise and Decline of the Medici Bank, 1397-1494*. Cambridge : Harvard University Press, 1963.

DE ROOVER, Raymond Adrien, *Il Banco Medici dalle origini al declino (1397-1494)*. Firenze : La nuova Italia, 1970.

DIZIONARIO della marina – Medievale e moderno, Roma 1937

DIZIONARIO Etimologico, C. Battisti e G. Alessio, Firenze 1950

DUCHARTRE, Pierre-Louis, *La comédie italienne : l'improvisation, les canevas, vies, caractères, portraits, masques des illustres personnages de la commedia dell'arte*. Paris : Librairie de France, [c1924]

DUCHARTRE, *The Italian Comedy*, New York, 1966

DURAND Gilbert, 1960, *Les structures anthropologiques de l'imaginaire*, Paris, Dunod, 1992, p. 535.

ERASMUS OF ROTTERDAM, *The Praise of Folly*, and letter to Maritn Dorp, 1515, Translated by Betty Radice, With an Introduction and notes by A.H.Y. Levi. Penguin Books, 1971.

Folie et déraison à ala Renaissance, (Colloque International -1973) Editions de l' Université libre de Bruxelles, 1976

FABRE, *Carnaval ou la fête à l' envers.*, Paris, Gallimard, Evreux, 1992

FRAZER, J. C., *The Golden Bough*, London 1967

Frazer, James George, Sir, 1854-1941.

The golden bough : a study in magic and religion / by J.G. Frazer. London : Macmillan and Co., limited ; New York : The Macmillan Company, 1900.

The golden bough : a study in magic and religion / by Sir James George Frazer. London : Macmillan, 1990.

GAIGNEBET, C., et FLORENTIN, M.C., *Le carnaval. Essai de mythologie populaire*, Paris, Peyot, 1974

GELLI, J., *Divise, motti, imprese di famiglie e personaggi italiani*, Milano, Hoepli, 1916. (*Ruota della fortuna*, p112)

GENTILI, Vanna, *La recita della follia*, Torino, P.B.E., 1978.

GIORGETTI, A., *Il dialogo di Bartolomeo Cerretani, fonte delle 'Storie fiorentine di Jacopo Pitti'*, in 'Miscellanea fiorentina di erudizione e storia', I, 1886.

GIOVANNONI, G., (documents by J. Sansovino about the reconstruction of the Navicella for Leo X) in 'Palladium', anno V, n.1, (1943, pp.157-158)

GNOLI, Domenico, *La Roma di Leone X,* Quadri e studi pubblicati a cura di Aldo Gnoli, Milano, 1938.

GORI, P.ietro, Feste fiorentine attraverso i secoli, vol.I, Le feste per San Giovanni, Firenze, Bemporad, 1926.

GUASTI, C.esare, *Le feste di San Giovanni Batista in Firenze descritte in prosa e in rima da contemporanei,* Firenze, 1884.

GRAF, Arturo., *Attraverso il Cinquecento,* Torino, 1926 (for Fra Mariano)

HAMMERSTEIN, R., *Diabolus in Musica*, Studien zur ikonographie der Musik in Mettelhalter, Bern und München, 1974.

HERRICK, Marvin Theodore, *Italian comedy in the Renaissance.* Urbana : University of Illinois Press, 1960.

KAISER Walter Jacob, *Praisers of Folly: Erasmus, Rabelais, Shakespeare.* Cambridge, Harvard University Press, 1963.

KLEIN, R., *Un aspect de l'hermeneutique à l'age de l'humanisme classique – Le theme du fou et l'ironie humaniste*: in *Umanesimo e ermeneutica,* Padova, Cedam, 1963.

JACQUOT, Jean, *Les Fêtes de la Renaissance* (Paris: CNRS, 3 vols, 1956, 1960 and 1975)

LANDUCCI, Luca, *Diario,* a cura di Jodco del Badía, Firenze, 1889.

— *A Florentine Diary from 1450 to 1516 by Luca Landucci,* continued by an anonymous writer till 1542, with notes by Jodoco del Badia. Translated from the italian by Alice de Rosen Jervis, and published in London in 1927, J.M. Dent & sons – New York E.P. Dutton & Co.

LEFEBVRE, Joël, *Les fols et la folie,* Paris, Librèrie Klinksiek, 1968.

LEVER, Maurice, *Le sceptre et la marotte.* Histoire de fous de cour. Paris, Fayard, 1983.

LEHMAN, Karl,. *The Ship Fountain from Victory of Samothrace to the Galera,* in P. William Lehman and K.Lehman *Samoracian Reflections*, Princeton University Press, 1973.

MARCHETTI, , J., *Rime inedite o rare di Bernardo Giambullari*, Firenze, Sansoni Antiquariato, 1955.

MASI, B., *Ricordanze di Bartolomeo Masi calderaio fiorentino,* a cura di G.O. Corazzini, Firenze, 1906.

MEDICI, Lorenzo.de', *Scritti d'amore,* Milano, Rizzoli, 1958.

MINIO-PALUELLO, M.-L., *Un'occasione in cui la storia detta il canto alla festa,* in: Il teatro dei Medici, numero monografico di 'Quaderni di Teatro', Firenze, Marzo 1980, pp.114-134.

— *Oro e Argento,* in 'Quaderni Medievali', 11, giugno 1981.

— *Simbologia pagana e cristiana nella navicella di Santa Maria in Domnica*, in 'Studi romani', gennaio-marzo 1986.

MITCHELL, Bonner, *The Majesty of the State: Triumphal Progresses of Foreign Sovereigns in Renaissance Italy (1494-1600)*, Florence: Leo S. Olschki Editore, 1986.

MUNTONI, F., *Le monete di papi e degli stati pontifici*, Roma. 1972.

NARDI, Jacopo, *Istorie della città fi Firenze*, a cura di A.Gelli, Firenze 1858.

Navigatio Sancti Brenctani, a cura di M.A. Grignani, Milano, Bompiani, 1973.

NICOLL, Allardyce, *Masks, mimes and miracles : studies in the popular theatre / by Allardyce Nicoll ...With two hundred and twenty-six illustrations*. London : G. C. Harrap, [1931]

NICOLL, Allardyce, *The world of Harlequin : a critical study of the commedia dell'arte*. Cambridge [Eng] : University Press, 1963.

ORVIETO, E., *Un poemetto inedito di Bernardo Giambullari*, in 'Biblioteque d'Humanisme et Renaissance', Genève, 1977.

OTTO, Beatrice K. *Fools are everywhere : the court jester around the world* Imprint Chicago; London : University of Chicago Press, 2001.

PASTOR, L. *The History of the Popes*, Vol VII, edited by Ralph Francis Kerr, London, Kegan Paul, Trench, Trubner & Co. Ltd, 1908.

PICCINELLI, PH., *Mundus Symbolicus*, Enciclopedia del simbolismo rinascimentale, Sec XVI, Ristampa Anastatica, Garland Publishing Co. , New York, 1976.

PITTI, Jacopo, *Apologia dei Cappucci*, in Archivio storico Italiano, Tomo IV, vol. II, (1853)

PRAMPOLINI, Giovanni, *La mitologia nella vita dei popoli*, Milano, 1942.

PUCCI, Antonio, *Centiloquio*, in Delizie degli Eruditi Toscani, vol. 4, Firenze 1773.

Relazioni degli Ambasciatori Veneti, editore Albèri, Bari, Laterza, 1846.

RIDOLFI, Roberto., *La Compagnia del Mantellaccio*, in 'La Bibliofilia', n.42 (1940), pp.282-288.

ROSCOE, William, *The Life and Pontificate of Leo X*, 2 vols, London, Henry G. Bohn, 1846.

ROSSI, A., De SMONE, R., *Carnevale si chiamava Vincenzo*, Roma, 1077.

ROTELLI, Elena, *Fra Dolcino*, Torino, 1979.

SALZA, A., *Domenico Barlacchi araldo attore scapigliato fiorentino del secolo XVI*, in "Rassegna bibliografica della letteratura italiana", n.IX, 1901, pp.27-33.

SANUDO, Marino, *Diari*, Venezia, 1887, Vol. XVIII.

SAVELLI, Marcantonio, *Summa Sententiarum*, Venezia, 1748.

SHEARMAN, John, *The Florentine Entrata of Leo X – 1515*. in "Journal of the Warburg and Courtauld Institutes", XXVIII, (1975), pp.136-154.

— *Pontormo and Andrea del Sarto – 1513*, in "Burtlington Magazine", CIV, 1962.
SODERINI, P. e RIDOLFI, G., *Commissioni di P.A.S. E G.B.R. Oratori della Repubblica Fiorentina a Venezia negli anni 1494-1498*, Venezia, 1901.
STABILE, Giorgio, (Istituto di filosofia, Universitá di Roma) *La ruota della fortuna. Tempo ciclico e ricorso storico.* Communication.
Statuta Populi et Comunis Florentiae, Collecta..... 1415, Friburgo, 1778.
THOMSON, Etta, *Lorenzo de' Medici's Puzzling Present for a Papal Buffoon, in* "Biblioteque d'Humanisme et Renaissance" n. 41, (1980), pp.157-165.
TOSCHI, Paolo, *Le origini del teatro italiano*, Torino, Einaudi, 1955.
TREXLER, R.C., *Lorenzo de' Medici and Savonarola, Martyrs for Florence*, in "Renaissance Quarterly", XXXI (1978), n.3, pp. 293-308.
— *Florence by the Grace of the Lord Pope*, in "Studies in Medieval and Renaissance History", IX, (1972), pp. 115-215.
— *The Libro Cerimoniale della Repubblica*, 1978.
— *The Magi Enter Florence*, "Studies in Medieval and Renaissance History", n. Xi (1978), pp. 127-218.
— *Public Life in Renaissance Florence*, New York and London, 1980. Ithaca, 1981.
VANZAN MARCHINI, Elena, *Venezia, una nave,una città.*, Mira (VE), 1981.
VARCHI, Benedetto, *Ercolano*, Firenze, 1730.
VASOLI, Cesare, *La profezia di Francesco da Meleto*, in *Umanesimo e ermeneutica*, Padova, Cedam, 1963
Venezia e le sue lagune, Venezia, 1864
VETTORI, F., *Sommario della Storia d'Italia*, in *Scritti storici e politici* a cura di E. Nicolini, Bari, Laterza, 1972.
VASARI, G., *Le opere*, a cura di Gaetano Milanesi, Firenze, Sansoni, 1906.
VILLANI, G., *Cronaca*, Vol.I, Trieste, 1857.
WILLEFORD, W., *The Fool and his Sceptre*, London, E. Arnold, 1967

AFTERWORD

The life and adventures of this manuscript.

I did this research many years ago, in Florence where I was studying for a Ph.D. on the Renaissance Carnival songs. I was blocked and stuck. This Ship of Fools came as an illumination in the middle of that dark time, in which other enterprises – in work and in my life – were difficult, painful, or unsuccessful. Someone had suggested, casually, why don't you try to find out what comes of Carafulla and his *Fusta piena di matti*, his ship full of fools? Well I did, I had a photocopy of the page from the *Istorie fiorentine* by Cambi, where the episode is recorded. I had stuck it among the books, in the little bookshelf in the small dark flat where I was living, in Florence.

There is clatter, and clutter, here as I am writing this, other things on my mind, noises outside. And there was clatter, and clutter, there too. It was a small studio flat in the historical centre, in Via Dante Alighieri, no less, by the casa Buonarroti, no less, near the Casa di Dante, no less, in front of the Torre della Castagna, a tower house already extant in the XI century, no more. It had become seat of government in 1282 until the Palazzo Vecchio was built to house it. It was a glorious historical spot with hundreds of years of wear and tear and crowding in. The flat was a cooped up noisy flat, as well as dark. It was dark because it had only one window which gave onto a small court closed in by high buildings and took in hardly any light, *and* it had a brown felt carpet. It was noisy during the day, because there was a shirt-making laboratory adjacent to it, where sewing machines rumbled like monsters on and off, backward and forward from morning to evening. They sounded like monsters growling, and they shook the floor with their mechanical vibrations. At night, later, a nightclub, with a window onto the same court, blasted out Neapolitan songs until late. At least those did not shake the floor. I typed away with earplugs in my ears. That subdued the noise until my concentration on to the writing allowed me to forget the singers belting out their songs. I typed up my notes, from the day work in the library, but I was stuck.

Someone had suggested, if you are stuck now, why do you not try out this other thing, this Ship of Fools? Well, I did. Taking that photocopied page down from my bookshelf started a process that was like having found a ball of wool, and finding the thread, it all unwound slowly but surely along the Midsummer voyage of these Fools. Everything seemed to come out right, then. The right books came into my hands. A casual remark by someone met on the stairs of a library took me to a gold mine of information just as I needed it. A moment of *impasse,* and as I turned on my chair, gazing vacantly about, my eye fell, just behind me, on another shelf where I would not have looked otherwise, and another book, just right, came into my hands.

An important fact is also that the Fool had been a passion of mine for a long time before too. It was a river catching up with me. Reminding me that *that* was my stream. And Erasmus with his *Praise of Folly* came into focus again, because he was at my side as always.

However, I did work on it for some time, just a few months. Typing everything up at night, when the sewing machines had finished roaring, but with earplugs, nevertheless. I had a manuscript ready in about three months, some cutting and pasting, not as we do now on computers, but with real scissors and sticky glue. Literally pages were cut, they were pasted somewhere else, or over other pages, as necessary.

I gave a copy to someone I had met, who was teaching Social Anthropology, I think, at the University of Perugia. She happened to show it to a Professor who was also a Professor in Florence, a historian of the Crusades. Professor Franco Cardini. He was interested, he liked it. He called me up, invited me out for lunch, a choice restaurant in Florence.

"The book is good" he said "I like it, I would like to have it published for you. I would give it to the house of Sansoni, if you agree". Agree? Of course I would agree. Sansoni was, is, a long established prestigious publishing house in Florence. I was elated. He liked the book, he was giving it to Sansoni. My life of a somewhat freelance graduate student in the margins of Academia had taken a turn, had found unexpected and considerable confirmation. The wind had caught my sails after all!

The manuscript went to the editors. Not long after I received a phone call by one of the editors telling me how much she enjoyed reading it, going through it, as she had started the editing process. At Christmas, though came the shock. The publishing house had changed hands, their editorial policy had changed, they were going to concentrate on books for schools. Any other books they had in their offices which did not have a legal contract already signed (and I did not have yet, these things happen) were going to be dropped. Apologies from the Professor, some of his work had fallen through in the same way. Perhaps.

So I started searching again. There was another Professor at the University of Florence, he was in Medieval History, Domenico Maselli. I knew him very well, he was a friend, I went to his lectures occasionally, once he gave a lecture specifically on heretics and fools, for me, he said, for my work. However, he came up with a brother-in-law who intended to start a publishing business, he was glad to have my book ready, would I agree? Of course I would agree! The publishing house was going to be called Delta, the Greek letter. I am not sure why, I did not know his brother in law. But my car was a Beta, a Lancia Beta, I took it for a good omen. So, up and going again, I thought. But then this enterprise did not even start, the brother-in-law had gone bankrupt! Goodbye Delta. So much for the good omen of progress.

I went from Florence, my time of leave for research finished, I went back to Venice, to my school teaching. I was teaching while waiting to take my exams at the Ministry of Foreign Affairs, to go abroad again, with the Cultural Office of some Italian Embassy, as I later did.

But I had another friend in Florence, he was a writer. Now the late Mauro Senesi. Then at some point he had organised a literary club, he collected readers. He was in touch with a publisher. He would publish books for the expense of 200 copies bought in advance, and would I do my book with him? My book got done with him. The first Professor gave me an important and learned formal introduction, although unfortunately it did not help much selling any books. The publisher did not do any distribution – he had got his money from the 200 books that, in the end, or rather in advance, I had bought. I did not even get all of them, as by the time they were published I was off to the Cultural Office of the Italian Embassy in Mogadishu. I got a few books when I went on leave, a few packs of twenty books, and very heavy they were. The rest went into remainders shops, or just eliminated, I suppose.

I was in Somalia for three years. During one of my leaves we had a presentation at my friend the writer's club in Florence, '*Anzichè*' it was called, which I could translate with 'Or Rather'. Perhaps the club bought a few copies, I am not sure. Then at the end of 1990 I went to Washington with the Italian Embassy there, for another three years, and I could not do anything about my book. I was even farther away from the margins of the Universities I had brushed by before, Aberdeen and Florence. I was by now doing other things, thinking of other things, writing other things. Every so often I gave one of my books to some University library, when I had the opportunity, to the British Library, to the Warburg, in London, here and there. But from the publisher, no ISBN number, no news of sales, no royalties, no word or anything. A charming but slippery individual.

When I retired form the Ministry of Foreign affairs and the Italian Government, I went to live in London. At some point I decided to take up the Ship of Fools, again, Carafulla on his Midsummer voyage, the Mèdici and Leo X at that San Giovanni of 1514. I did, for one or two years go through the excitement and the fun of this story by updating it and translating it into English. Then I started to go through the publishers again. Completely out of Academic circles, now, retired, writing away dozen of letters with presentations, sample chapters, target audience, the lot. I received many kind and considerate letters of regret and refusal. For academic publishers being too short and too narrative, or not fitting in their lists, for ordinary publishers being too academic, or not suitable anyway. Market forces not in a direction suitable to me, or I not suitable to the market forces. Well, I tried.

But even though publishers could not see profit in it, people, intelliget, open minded readers, may want to see it anyway. I am sure regular lay readers may enjoy it. After all a young friend of mine, a physicist, read it recently, and he said he read it like a mystery story. Another, a musician, enjoyed it because he said he likes to learn new things and Renaissance Florence was fascinating to him. There may be things to be enjoyed, things to satisfy curiosities, for anyone, I think, I hope.

And in any case I do wish very much to publish it and make it available to 'the world'. I really would not have wanted it as a slim severe hardback volume buried in university libraries for specialists only. I wanted a paperback, easy to handle and easy to read which could find its way into the hands of students, be carried in the pockets of interested lay readers, of open minded people who may be or may be not specialists of the XVI century, or of Italian history, or of the origins of the theatre, (just to think of a few slots this book of mine may be put into) may well enjoy the meaningful theatricals of these fools in the streets of Florence for the St John the Baptist festival of 1514.

And may a good wind fill the sails of Carafulla's Ship full of fools now. And may it carry good news to whoever has the curiosity of looking into the wise folly of it.

It has been a long journey, for this manuscript, and for me. Since we started in Florence, I have been over African deserts and over the Atlantic Ocean, in good planes, of course. I have lived in Mogadishu where I corrected the Italian proofs. I lived in Washington D.C. where I planted a few of the books in libraries and with friends. And later in London where I scoured those wonderful libraries to update the text, and burned the midnight oil doing the translation into English for its further journey.

Now, living near Aberdeen, in the North East of Scotland, I am occupied in giving my work the finishing touches for the new launch.

May the Jesters sail on, playing away, happy and safe – and perhaps, having left the devils behind, even find the Happy Isles.

Index

www.ingramcontent.com/pod-product-compliance
Ingram Content Group UK Ltd.
Pitfield, Milton Keynes, MK11 3LW, UK
UKHW040602210726
13854UKWH00008B/1829